"Samuel Beckett's experiments at the intersection of music and literature are among the most unique and interesting of their kind. McGrath's study contributes new elements to our understanding of Beckett's work in this area, particularly in its potential to enrich the thinking of musicians and composers. Not 'just' a book on Beckett, it makes Beckett the starting point for a number of fruitful meditations on repetition, representation, improvisation, and structural experimentation in the arts. The chapters on Morton Feldman and Scott Fields are especially welcome in this regard."

Eric Prieto, *University of California, Santa Barbara, USA*

Samuel Beckett, Repetition and Modern Music

Music abounds in twentieth-century Irish literature. Whether it be the "thought-tormented" music of Joyce's "The Dead", the folk tunes and opera that resound throughout *Ulysses*, or the four-part threnody in Beckett's *Watt*, it is clear that the influence of music on the written word in Ireland is deeply significant. Samuel Beckett arguably went further than any other writer in the incorporation of musical ideas into his work. Musical quotations inhabit his texts, and structural devices such as the *da capo* are metaphorically employed. Perhaps most striking is the erosion of explicit meaning in Beckett's later prose brought about through an extensive use of repetition, influenced by his reading of Schopenhauer's philosophy of music.

Exploring this notion of "semantic fluidity", John McGrath discusses the ways in which Beckett utilised extreme repetition to create texts that operate and are received more like music. Beckett's writing has attracted the attention of numerous contemporary composers and an investigation into how this Beckettian "musicalized fiction" has been retranslated into contemporary music forms the second half of the book. Close analyses of the Beckett-inspired music of experimental composer Morton Feldman and the structured improvisations of avantjazz guitarist Scott Fields illustrate the cross-genre appeal of Beckett to musicians, but also demonstrate how repetition operates in diverse ways. Through the examination of the pivotal role of repetition in both music and literature of the twentieth century and beyond, John McGrath's book is a significant contribution to the field of Word and Music Studies.

John McGrath is a guitarist and academic from Ireland. He works in many styles of music including improvisation, noise, blues, avantfolk, scratch, rockabilly and avantrock and has collaborated on various performance, TV and art projects. His solo fingerstyle compositions have been featured in *The Wire* magazine and on numerous international radio stations. John is a lecturer at ICMP, having previously taught at University of Liverpool and LIPA.

Samuel Beckett, Repetition and Modern Music

John McGrath

Taylor & Francis Group
LONDON AND NEW YORK

First published 2018 by Routledge

2 Park Square, Milton Park, Abingdon, Oxfordshire OX14 4RN
52 Vanderbilt Avenue, New York, NY 10017

Routledge is an imprint of the Taylor & Francis Group, an informa business

First issued in paperback 2019

Copyright © 2018 John McGrath

The right of John McGrath to be identified as author of this work has been asserted by him in accordance with sections 77 and 78 of the Copyright, Designs and Patents Act 1988.

All rights reserved. No part of this book may be reprinted or reproduced or utilised in any form or by any electronic, mechanical, or other means, now known or hereafter invented, including photocopying and recording, or in any information storage or retrieval system, without permission in writing from the publishers.

Notice:
Product or corporate names may be trademarks or registered trademarks, and are used only for identification and explanation without intent to infringe.

British Library Cataloguing-in-Publication Data
A catalogue record for this book is available from the British Library

Library of Congress Cataloging-in-Publication Data
Names: McGrath, John (Guitarist) author.
Title: Samuel Beckett, repetition and modern music / John McGrath.
Description: Abingdon, Oxon ; New York, NY : Routledge, 2018. |
Includes bibliographical references and index.
Identifiers: LCCN 2017028278 | ISBN 9781472475374 (hardback) |
ISBN 9781315607566 (ebook)
Subjects: LCSH: Music and literature. | Beckett, Samuel, 1906–1989–Criticism and interpretation. | Music–20th century–History and criticism. |
Repetition in literature. | Repetition in music.
Classification: LCC ML3849 .M38 2018 | DDC 780/.082–dc23
LC record available at https://lccn.loc.gov/2017028278

ISBN: 978-1-472-47537-4 (hbk)
ISBN: 978-0-367-88150-4 (pbk)

Typeset in Times New Roman
by Out of House Publishing

Bach musicological font developed by © Yo Tomita

For Holly and Daisy

Contents

	List of figures	x
	Acknowledgements	xii
	Introduction	1
1	Music and literature	6
2	Repetition in music and literature	33
3	Musico-literary interaction in modern Ireland and the musical aesthetic of Samuel Beckett	53
4	Beckett's semantic fluidity: repetition in the later work	66
5	Beckett and Feldman: time, repetition and the liminal space	86
6	Improvising Beckett: chance, silence and repetition	124
	Conclusions	148
	Bibliography	156
	Index	169

Figures

4.1	*The Human Condition* (1933) – René Magritte © ADAGP, Paris and DACS, London 2016	67
4.2a	Analysis of segment no. 1 from *Ill Seen Ill Said*	75
4.2b	Analysis of segment no. 1 from *Ill Seen Ill Said*	76
4.3	Analysis of segment no. 2 from *Ill Seen Ill Said*	80
4.4	Analysis of segment from *Worstward Ho*	82
5.1	Analysis of *neither* text	101
5.2	*Neither*, bars 1–12	103
5.3	*Neither*, excerpt from figure 14	103
5.4	*Neither*, excerpt from figure 15	104
5.5	*Neither*, excerpt from figure 18	104
5.6	*Neither*, excerpt from figure 59	104
5.7	*Neither*, excerpt from figure 41	105
5.8	*Neither*, excerpt from figure 91	106
5.9	*Neither*, excerpt from figure 92	106
5.10	*Neither*, excerpt from figures 25/26	106
5.11	*Neither*, excerpt from figure 49	107
5.12	*Neither*, excerpt from figure 95	107
5.13	*Neither*, excerpt from figure 128	108
5.14	*Neither*, excerpt from figures 129/130	108
5.15	*Neither*, figure 135	109
5.16	*Neither*, figure 46	110
5.17	*Neither*, excerpt from figures 49/50	112
5.18	*Neither*, excerpt from figures 59/60	113
5.19	*Neither*, excerpt from figure 50	114
5.20	*Neither*, excerpt from figure 69	115
5.21	*Neither*, excerpt from figure 88	116
5.22	Analysis of *Words and Music*	120
5.23	*Words and Music*, 2 bars	121
5.24	*Words and Music*, 7 bars	122
6.1	The Scott Fields Ensemble – photo credit: Stefan Strasser	133
6.2	Page 1 of *Not I* analysis	136

6.3	Billie Whitelaw in *Not I*	138
6.4	Julianne Moore in *Not I*	139
6.5	Fields' *Not I*, page 1	141
6.6	Fields' *Not I*, page 2	144

Acknowledgements

First, I'd like to thank both Annie Vaughan and Emma Gallon for their support with the book.

Special thanks to Michael Spitzer, Anahid Kassabian, Kenneth Smith, Helen Abbott and Catherine Laws. I'm obliged to ADAGP, Paris and DACS, London for the Magritte permissions.

The Arts and Humanities Research Council and the Society for Musicology in Ireland both provided much-appreciated support for the project.

As always, I'm grateful for the continued encouragement from Bríd, Joe, Cormac, Cian, Emmet, Polly, John and most of all, Holly.

Lastly, a huge thank you to Gustavo Alberto Garcia Vaca for kindly granting the use of *neither* for the cover image and to Scott Fields for his time, scores and music.

Introduction

Music and words have always relied on each other; in fact, they are mutually dependent. We need words to try and make sense of music, to describe it, to fulfil the human need to compartmentalise, and to box music into disparate genres and subgenres. On the other hand, words need music to express what they cannot. Music can be seen to have a syntax of its own, a repertoire of signifiers that connote certain affiliations for listeners.

If we consider music and words historically, this mutual dependence is tangible. Linguistic and sonic articulations were not always separated into distinct artforms but rather were disciplines collected under the same heading: in Ancient Greece, words and music were described by the single term, "mousike", while for the Celts the *file* was the poet/musician for the community. It was only during the Enlightenment that the two arts gradually began to separate into recognisable discrete forms. As rhetoric shifted emphasis away from performance, "literature" became more of a "silent" artform. Words and music would continue to work together of course, in song, opera and music theatre, but one was usually subordinate to the other. Often, the work was divided, with librettists contributing the words and composers the music. With the Romantics and Symbolists in the late nineteenth century, however, came new ideas concerning music's ineffable qualities. Influenced by the philosophy of Arthur Schopenhauer and literary Wagnerism, these artists and thinkers began to view music as the highest artform, believing it expressed what could not be articulated in words; that it enabled a higher, and purer, form of engagement with the intangible. Walter Pater, part of the Symbolist movement, famously proclaimed that "all art constantly aspires to the condition of music" ([1873] 1980, 86) at this time, and certainly throughout the arts many were turning to musical ideas and devices to structure, form and sound their own work in novels, poems, plays and paintings. The use of the term "musical" has been a persistent debate in Word and Music Studies, the scholarly field that explores the various interactions of both arts. Any direct attempt of one artform to imitate another will always be metaphorical, and one of the main problems in the academy has been the futile search for the appropriateness of said metaphors, or an idealised set of absolute or direct correspondences. I employ the term "musical" in a manner similar to the way

2 Introduction

in which Proust, the Symbolists and the Romantics used it and not as an analytical object.[1] For these writers the idea of musicality represented that which was inexpressible in words alone. "Music" is itself a fluid term, acting as a label that encapsulates vast variance and disparate meanings. Music means many things to many cultures – it has "multiple ontologies" (Bohlman, 1999). As such, it is impossible to pin music down to a definitive set of identity conditions. This is important to consider when we reflect on how artists have conceptualised musical ideas in other artforms.

The twentieth century saw musicians and writers pushing at the boundaries, as ideas that had developed and evolved into particular disciplines began to be applied to other artforms. Crucially, intermedial Modernist artforms could no longer be re-separated in any intact manner, as one could not, for instance, read a libretto on its own to fully engage with an opera. Both music and literature were so intertwined that to remove any one component would reduce the whole to an incomplete fragment.

Repetition was one of the salient devices that musicians and writers began to explore and concentrate on at this time in a wide array of disciplines. Although the repetition of notes, motives or modal areas has always been a formative structural device in music, it began to assume a considerable creative influence that is traceable during the twentieth century from rock to minimalism, and from rave to ambient music. Repetition in music moved beyond the pejorative towards apotheosis, as it became heralded as an end in itself, rather than being a maligned necessity. A similar trajectory can be found in literature. Although the textual refrain had been key for the Symbolists, the traditional rhetorical repetitive qualities of alliteration, assonance, anaphora and epistrophe were taken to whole new levels, as individual words began themselves to be reiterated *in extremis*. The poems of Gertrude Stein, the cutups of William Burroughs, the jazz-inspired syncopations of the Beats all stem from the Symbolist and Modernist focus on transformation *through* repetition. Repetition's ubiquity in many artforms makes it a transmedial device, one that is shared amongst them, rather than belonging to one in particular. The historical thresholds reveal some of the reasons why repetition becomes attached to the idea of "musicality", a notion we will explore in Chapter 2.

The formation of transmedial discourse through the art of repetition was an integral part of Samuel Beckett's creative aesthetics. Inspired by the same Schopenhauerian philosophy of music that provoked the Symbolists, the Irish writer created an unprecedented form of "musicalized fiction" (Aldous Huxley's term ([1928] 1978, 301), adopted by Werner Wolf (1999)). Frustrated by the inability of words to express depth and intangibility sufficiently, Beckett strove to interrogate the essence of meaning and created a form that enabled a certain liquidity of semiotics. Repetition allowed Beckett to create a literary language that, at the levels of both creation and reception, appeared to assume certain musical traits. I propose that Beckett's late fiction represented a peak in twentieth-century investigation into transmedial culture: more than any other, Beckett's musicality enabled what I theorise as a *semantic fluidity*,

Introduction 3

a flow of meaning afforded in part by a common form of repetition. Related to semantic satiation or sometimes saturation, a scientific term for the point at which repetition begins to erode rather than reinforce meaning, I theorise that Beckett utilised repetition as a device that could endow his texts with a music-like quality – more fluid in their meanings. My term semantic fluidity describes this less explicit feature of Beckett's late prose, a style influenced by his Romantic philosophy of music. Inherent ambiguity is infused within the distilled precision of Beckett's texts while a perpetual semiosis ensues at the reception level. Through extensive repetition, Beckett's semantic fluidity erodes meaning instead of emphasising comprehension. I relate this semantic fluidity to a positive and transformative Deleuzian concept of repetition during the course of the book, and develop an original taxonomy of repetition that can be applied transmedially to both music and literature.

Although Beckett was influenced by the Symbolists, lived in Paris and wrote in French for much of his life, his musicalised literature situates him within a long line of Irish musicians-turned-writers. His friend and mentor of sorts, James Joyce, for instance, infused both *Ulysses* ([1922] 2000) and *Finnegans Wake* ([1939] 1975) with leitmotifs, songs, operatic references and even an attempted fugue in words in the famous "Sirens" episode. Playwright J. M. Synge had initially intended to become a composer; Yeats' lyricism placed him within a "singing school" of Irish balladeers – Mangan, Davis, Ferguson and Thomas Moore's *Irish Melodies* (1808–1834). George Bernard Shaw used many operatic devices in his plays and wrote extensive music criticism. The fact that many others shared such an affinity with music has led Harry White to believe that Irish literature is particularly "musical" in this regard (White, 2008).

The musical qualities that abound in Beckett's work have proved intensely attractive to many contemporary composers, and his writing has been used as the libretto, text or the inspiration for a variety of musical responses in several different genres. Through an examination of repetition in music and literature, and an investigation into several musical responses to, or sonic translations of, Beckett's texts, I will analyse the author's employment of recurrence and reiteration and explore the possibility of translating this Beckettian semantic fluidity into other artforms.

The following chapters trace the development of Beckett's musical aesthetic from his metaphorical understanding of musico-textual transmediality in his early fiction, to the foregrounding of musical devices in his later prose, a subject which remains as yet largely unexplored in the scholarly literature. The first chapter will investigate Gotthold Lessing's temporal classification of music and literature, in order to explain the particular transmedial affinity that both arts share. I offer a historical survey of music and literature interaction that outlines various types of combination. Next, I provide an overview of the recently blossoming field of Word and Music Studies. The main trajectories and issues of the field are explored before a progressive methodology is suggested.

4 *Introduction*

Building on this contextual work, Chapter 2 opens out to laterally investigate repetition's place in music and literature. Here, I offer a survey of repetition theory and explore the differences between the forms and traditional tolerances of repetition in music and those of literature. Chapter 3 opens with a discussion of Beckett's place within Irish literature before outlining the author's developing aesthetic of music in his early fiction. Early texts like *Murphy* ([1938] 2003) frequently use musical metaphor and show nascent signs of the repetition device. It is important to contextualise this work in terms of Beckett's merging of literature and music, as this was not an isolated endeavour but instead fed into a rich arena of intermedial experimentation during the twentieth century. In Beckett's semantic fluidity, however, the author took this medial convergence to unparalleled heights. To compare and contrast his work with that of his contemporaries in Ireland, such as Joyce, and globally, such as Pound, highlights the particular innovations that form the foundation of Beckett's work.

Chapter 4 provides an exploration of repetition in Beckett's aesthetic in terms of the semantic fluidity that underpins much of his later prose. In this chapter, repetition is viewed as a salient feature of Beckett's later aesthetic, one influenced, in particular, by his Schopenhauerian philosophy of music. We will see that Beckett's employment of musical repetition would become much more complex in his later prose, no more so than in *Ill Seen Ill Said* ([1981] 1997). Whereas the music in *Murphy* is relatively "intelligible", the repetitive nature of Beckett's later prose employs the "inexplicable" (Beckett, [1931] 1999, 92, quoting Schopenhauer) nature of music by providing a method of writing a "non-specific" text, to use Alec Reid's term, without clear meaning (Reid, 1968, 34). In his later prose, in other words, exact meaning erodes through the use of repetition (Cohn, 1980, 96). The musical metaphors of *Murphy* are replaced by a more formalist approach, whereby, alongside the introduction of notation in the text, the author began to experiment with a more "musicalized fiction" that would permeate *The Trilogy* (1951–53) and later prose. The chapter culminates in a close analysis of four distinct types of repetition in three separate Beckett excerpts.

The next two chapters delve into the translation of literature into music, exploring the ideas of transmediality (shared properties) within a single text: the movement between a written text and a musical object. Using two different forms of composition, I focus on the translation of Beckett's work into music alone and consider the problems of translation between disciplines. Chapter 5 extends my theory of repetition and semantic fluidity by focusing on Beckett's collaborations with composer Morton Feldman. Extended time, waiting and stasis were concerns that Beckett and Feldman both shared – themes that played themselves out through literary and musical repetition.[2] Can the transmedial offer us new insights into the ways in which repetition itself enables music and literature to collide?

In contrast, Chapter 6 investigates the ways in which aleatoric procedure operates in Beckett's *Lessness* (1970). I explore how indeterminacy and improvisation might be compared. After outlining some of the connections between the aesthetics of John Cage and Beckett, I provide a close analysis of Scott Fields' avantjazz instrumental music. Fields has used Beckett's repetitive texts as a structural device for his improvisations, and an examination of these works in relation to Beckett's prose raises theoretical questions around how temporal repetition transgresses the boundary of silence to become performed music. As fiction becomes sounded as inspiration for new music beyond Beckett, Fields' two albums based on Beckett texts display how transmedial repetition can be translated in transformative ways.

Samuel Beckett, Repetition and Modern Music, then, offers several things. I explore how repetition in music and in literature can create a semantic fluidity that can pull together the creative use of words and the musical treatment of sound. Contextual investigation into the work of artists, musicians and theorists, who used repetition as a salient creative device during the twentieth century provides an important backdrop to the work of Samuel Beckett, a writer who used a "musical" form of repetition, or rather a "musical" rate of employment of repetition (as we'll explore in Chapter 4), in his literature to form an *oeuvre* that has been and continues to allure many writers, artists and musicians. By analysing two very different instances of such inspiration – the work of Feldman and Fields – my theory of semantic fluidity is taken beyond the single artwork and into its afterlife; moving from written text created through "musical" ideas, back into repetitive forms of instrumental music that reflect this perpetual semiosis.

Notes

1 Peter Dayan is a progressive thinker in this regard. See Dayan (2002).
2 Both showed disdain for opera. In *Proust*, for instance, Beckett issues contempt for the subordination of music in opera, a corruption of the purity of music's "Idea that he views as worse than vaudeville" (Beckett, [1931] 1999, 91). Beckett wrote the libretto for Feldman's *Neither* (1977), a self-proclaimed "anti-opera".

1 Music and literature

"It is good for thought, when it takes music as an object, to lend an ear to literature"

(Lyotard, 1997, 220).

The twentieth century heralded a new era of intermedial and transmedial possibility. Modernist writers in particular seized the opportunity to interrogate the notion of discrete artforms and to utilise the powers that other disciplines could bring to their work. Samuel Beckett's creative aesthetic was founded on the nucleus between two separate artistic disciplines: music and literature. Not only did the author continually refer to his musical influences and incorporate musical devices into his writing, he also engaged with the philosophical *idea* of music at a time when the two artforms were reaching towards each other at an accelerated rate. The tumultuous history of intermedial practice had reached a point, during the twentieth century, where Beckett spoke of a "rupture in the lines of communication" and a "breakdown of the object" ([1934] 1983b, 70); language was being interrogated to such an extent that, in Daniel Albright's words, it was beginning to "lose connection to the world of hard objects" and "become more and more like musical notes" (Albright, 2000, 6). This chapter traces the historical trajectory that the idea of music took following the Enlightenment: a journey from sound to metaphor.

Aesthetic debates concerning intermediality have raged since the Enlightenment. For the Greeks, as in ancient Irish culture, poetry and music were one. Whereas medieval artists and composers sought a consonance that brought artforms together in a manner that reflected theological harmony, Enlightenment figures, such as Gotthold Lessing, argued that individual artforms should be divided into distinct categories, an idea that has been instrumental in the evolution of the separate disciplines that we still recognise today. Wagner's *Gesamtkunstwerk* would reclaim the power of unification in the arts during the nineteenth century, while the French Symbolist movement, and literary Wagnerism, brought about a new age for interdisciplinarity that would have a significant influence on the Modernists.

A roaring start

A marble statue dating from between 160 to 20 BC (excavated in Rome in 1506), depicting the mythical Greek Laocoön, was the beginning of an aesthetic debate that has lasted for almost 250 years. Virgil's *Aeneid* is the best source for the myth of this Trojan priest of Apollo (some say Poseidon) who warned his fellow citizens of the dangers inherent in the acceptance of the equestrian offering: "Have no faith in the horse! / Whatever it is, even when Greeks bring gifts / I fear them, gifts and all." After throwing a spear at the horse's leg, somewhat worse than looking it in the mouth you might say, Laocoön angered the gods, and subsequently two sea serpents were dispatched to strangle him and his two sons. Virgil depicts the gruesome episode as a noisy, chaotic affair:

> At the same time he raised to the stars
> hair-raising shouts like the roars of a bull
> when it flees wounded from a sacrificial altar
> and shakes the ineffectual axe from its neck
> (Virgil quoted in Albright, 2000, 8).

The excavated statue depicted the gruesome end of Laocoön, but with a single crucial difference: his mouth was only half-open, there were no bull-like roars on show as in Virgil's story. The sculpture became known as *Laocoön and his Sons*, and few could have envisioned the debate that this physical depiction of the anguished protagonist would fuel. The central aesthetic issue of contention for Enlightenment thinkers here is that for a sculptor in this period to have created a dynamic artwork paralleling Virgil, portraying such pain through fully open-mouthed contortions, would have been a transgression of certain parameters of decorum, as we will now explore.

Albright's *Untwisting the Serpent: Modernism in Music, Literature and Other Arts* (2000) traces the various historical intermedial trends through the reception history of Laocoön, a case study that allows him to investigate how successive aestheticians have dealt with, and used, the Trojan myth.[1] The first work to consider the incongruities between Virgil and the anonymous sculptor was Lessing's *Laokoon: or On the Limits of Painting and Poetry* ([1766] 1984). For him, the half-shut mouth embodied the essential abilities and limitations of the visual arts alongside those of literature: poetry and sculpture, he believed, should each have a separate set of rules to follow. Whilst Virgil could describe a terrible gaping mouth, a sculptor must adhere to the aesthetics of beauty and visual decorum, according to which a screaming mouth was impermissible. For Lessing, "[t]he wide naked opening of the mouth – leaving aside how violently and disgustingly it distorts and shoves aside the rest of the face – becomes in a painting a spot and in a sculpture a hollow, making the most repulsive effect" (Lessing quoted in Albright, 2000, 9). Using the Laocoön statue as an example, Lessing introduced an influential aesthetic

8   *Music and literature*

theory that saw the arts divided into two distinct categories: *Nacheinander* and *Nebeneinander*. The arts of *Nacheinander* were teleological artforms, such as music and poetry, which required the passing of time for complete comprehension. The arts of *Nebeneinander*, such as painting and sculpture, on the other hand, were juxtapositive forms in which the full picture is presented at once (Albright, 2003, 6–7). Lessing explains further:

> this essential difference between [poetry and the visual arts] is found in that the former is a visible progressive act, the various parts of which take place little by little [*nach und nach*] in the sequence of time; whereas the latter is a visible static act, the various parts of which develop next to one another [*neben einander*] in space.[2]

The idea that these discrete artforms inhabit separate worlds, a space–time divide, with painting and the visual arts bound by space, while poetry and music are bound by time, explains Lessing's disdain for the crossing of said borders. For him it was impossible and futile to combine these temporally and spatially distinct worlds in a sincere artistic fashion.

But such categories are, of course, highly problematic. Though poetry and music are categorised as *Nacheinander*, the clear distinction between temporal and visual arts (*Nebeneinander*) relies on a number of erroneous assumptions. Is time the defining factor that distinguishes one artform from another? Is the time it takes to look at a painting and glean some "understanding" from it less than the time it takes to "grasp" (Peter Kivy's term) that of a piece of music? It could be suggested, for instance, that in the first few seconds of a piece of music, a listener can gain a general sense of the music's trajectory. This is certainly the belief of many working in modern record companies, where often only the first 30 seconds of a demo is needed to make a judgement: this amount of time, it is believed, is adequate to form a good opinion of the work. This listening strategy is akin to the amount of information a reader is given in the first few paragraphs of a novel. While Susan McClary ([1998] 2004) reminds us of the historical importance of linear narratives in Western music, exactly how much time does it take a listener or a spectator to "comprehend" a work, if this is ever possible? Does it actually take less time for a painting than for a symphony? If so, then how long should one stand in front of a painting in a gallery before "understanding" it? Such specifics are of course neither attainable, nor should we yearn for them, having learned the lessons of postmodernism and poststructuralism – the fallacy of intention (Wimsatt and Beardsley, 1954), the creative powers of the reader and so on.

Laocoön has continued to ruffle feathers and he remains part of the modern aesthetic debate on intermediality. Irving Babbitt's *The New Laokoon* (1910), for instance, berates Wagner's *Gesamtkunstwerk* and Strauss' extramusical visual imitation in a Lessing-esque manner.[3] In Clement Greenberg's "Towards a Newer Laocoon" (1940), the Trojan priest appears again, this time in order to condemn intermedial practice as "artistic dishonesty", as the resort of an artist who fails to confront the problems and essence of his

Music and literature 9

chosen medium. In Greenberg's eyes, Shelley's description of poetry as the medium that comes closest to "being no medium at all" marks him as a coward (Greenberg quoted in Albright, 2000, 11). In contrast, Greenberg praises avant-garde art for its foregrounding of materials. The goal is for the "opacity" of a medium to be accentuated while the form itself remains undegraded by the artist seeking to explain herself/himself clearly through secondary media. Greenberg believes that if a work or idea is absolute, it will not require further clarification through attached music or text. He writes:

> The history of avant-garde painting is that of a progressive surrender to the resistance of its medium; which resistance consists chiefly in the flat picture plane's denial of efforts to "hole through" it for realistic perspectival space ... The motto of the Renaissance artist, *Ars est artem celare* [Art is the concealing of art], is exchanged for *Ars est artem demonstrare* [Art is the manifesting of art].
>
> (Greenberg quoted in Albright, 2000, 12).

Such foregrounding of materials occurs in Beckett's *All That Fall* ([1957] 2006), wherein the individual locational sounds are deliberately unsutured (like Laocoön's lips), instead occurring in a fragmentary stop-start fashion with intermediary pauses. This emphasises the artifice of the radio play, rather than seeking diegetic realism. Beckett was well aware of Lessing's aesthetics, as Franz Michael Maier points out in his study of the Trinity lectures and *German Diaries* (Till and Bailes, 2014, 9–25.) What Greenberg fails to notice, however, aside from the enormous issues regarding absolutism, is that in an intermedial work, the individual artforms can synthesise in a manner that foregrounds the individual materials. Sergei Eisenstein's call for cognitive dissonance in the employment of film music alongside image, for instance, ensures that the resulting ironic clash makes both media acutely manifest (Eisenstein, [1949] 1977).

The theoretical and practical implications of intermedial expansion in film, opera, art and technology has been the subject of productive scholarly debate. Dick Higgins first used the term "intermedia" in 1966 (Higgins modestly credits Samuel Taylor Coleridge with its actual coinage), in order "to define works which fall conceptually between media that are already known" (Higgins, 1998, 9). Since Higgins, the field has made strong progress. Yvonne Spielmann, a central figure in intermedial studies, describes the merging of artforms as "the exchange and transformation of elements that come from different media":

> Intermedia therefore is a formal category of exchange. It signifies an aesthetic encompassment of both form and content. In an intermedia work of art, content becomes a formal category that reveals the structure of combination and collision. The related meaning of content is to express such modes of transformation that are effected by the collision of painting and film, of film and electronic media, and so on. The contextual meaning of intermedia is to reveal the media forms themselves. The making visible of elements that are considered media specific can

10 *Music and literature*

be performed by ways of comparing and transforming elements such as the interval.

(Spielmann, 2001, 59)

Artforms have, since the Enlightenment, defined one another through difference, and will continue to do so, it seems. Irina O. Rajewsky provides a useful overview of the taxonomic difficulties relating to the scholarly field of intermediality studies (Rajewsky, 2005, 43–65). In her categorisation of the various, and often confused, forms of intermediality, she places the "musicalization of literature" type of intermediality within a group called "intermedial references" (Rajewsky, 2005, 52). The other two categories are "medial transposition" (such as adaptations in films and novels) and "media combination" (including opera, sound art installations and multimedia performances amongst others) (Rajewsky, 2005, 51). "Intermedial references", the category which contains the "musicalization of literature" within its remit, is what primarily concerns Rajewsky, however. She writes:

Intermedial references are thus to be understood as meaning-constitutional strategies that contribute the media product's overall signification: the media product uses its own media-specific means, either to refer to a specific, individual work produced in another medium (ie., what in the German tradition is called *Einselreferenz*, "individual reference"), or to refer to a specific medial subsystem (such as a certain film genre) or to another *qua* system (*Systemreferenz*, "system reference").

(Rajewsky, 2005, 52–53)

Yet the narrowing of the disciplinary gap between music and literature during the twentieth century has been left relatively untheorised until recently.

Music and literature interaction

The intermedial or transmedial (shared properties) possibilities of music and literature owe much to the philosophical journey that the idea of music has undergone in the last few centuries. As mentioned earlier, the artforms were considered to be one and the same in Greek culture: at a time of low literacy, for example, Homer's epics were sung, and the term "mousike" incorporated what we now call music, poetry and even dance (Prieto, 2002a, 2). It is believed that the rhythm and rhyme of these poems, or the alliterative poetry of Old English epics like *Beowulf*, helped the illiterate to remember and to find something familiar within the newness of a first telling. These "musical" qualities were also an aid towards the memorisation and promulgation of tales and narratives in oral traditions.

During the Enlightenment, artforms began to move into increasingly discrete entities, following Lessing's strict categorisations of the arts. While this was happening, music and literature continually gauged one another through

Music and literature 11

identification with their respective antithesis, in what Eric Prieto refers to as the "fundamental heterogeneity" of the two media (Prieto, 2002a, xi). While the desire of musicians to include certain qualities from literature led to programme music, symphonic poems and such, poets and writers began to "invent" a Romantic idea of music. This "idea" of music owed a great deal to Plato's "Idea", later developed by Schopenhauer and Walter Pater. While Plato believed in the power of the music of the spheres, he also feared its power to corrupt (banning the Lydian and Ionian modes from his *Republic* for their "relaxed" properties for instance) (Plato, [*c*.380BC] 1968, 117). For Schopenhauer and Pater, the essential power of music, and its aesthetic prominence over the other arts, rested upon its very lack of worldly denotation. Music was both "intelligible" (we could understand its forms), but at the same time "inexplicable", its essence and meaning a mystery (Beckett, [1931] 1999, 92). This "idea" of music was the beginning of the separation of music from sound. What literary Wagnerism and the French Symbolist movement (Mallarmé and Dujardin in particular) thought of as music had nothing to do with sounded music whatsoever: instead music acted as a metaphor for the spirit, or an idealised existence. The English Romantics echoed these sentiments; Keats' "heard melodies are sweet, but those unheard are sweeter still" ("Ode on a Grecian Urn"), for instance, adopts this rise of silent music.

Music and literature have interacted in many ways, particularly in view of the supremacy that music held during nineteenth-century Romanticism. As music became larger and longer (literally with bigger orchestras and extended symphonies), Mahler and Bruckner stretched the Beethoven paradigm. In such a climate, it is fairly easy to see why Pater and the Aesthetes bestowed music with such unparalleled status. Influenced by the developments in music, some authors sought an escape from mimetic realism via techniques such as the interior monologue (Dujardin) and the theme and variation (Pinget).[4] These innovations were very influential for the Modernists, who would take the "musicalization of fiction", to borrow Huxley's term, into the most experimental and extensive terrains.[5] The dawn of photography and film also clearly played their part, as artists turned to more abstract forms. If a photograph could accurately represent the exterior, artists would explore the interior – the inner working of the mind and its dreams. There are clear links here between Freudian psychoanalysis, photographic technology and the development of devices such as stream of consciousness, literary leitmotifs, interior monologues and various other transmedial musical devices. One tenet of modernism was its presentation of a shift from nineteenth-century exterior realism to interior expression.

Eric Prieto puts forward in *Listening In* the concept that the modernists turned to music to express the inner consciousness rather than an objective exterior; a complex web of interior monologues, leitmotifs and streams of consciousness for the twentieth century instead of the Aristotelian mimesis of nineteenth-century realism (Prieto, 2002a). Binaries were always part of modernism too, however – exterior and interior, ancient and contemporary. Let us not forget that one of the main tenets of the modernist approach was the

12   *Music and literature*

juxtaposition of the old with the new: the ancient bull in Picasso's *Guernica* or Joyce's paralleling of Homer's epic.

This exterior/interior dichotomy somewhat mirrors another binary – that of realism/fiction – occurring cyclically in aesthetic history. Oscar Wilde famously called for a return to fiction in what he saw as the mundane boredom of social realism ("The Decay of Lying", [1891] 1997b). James Bond and Batman both provide brief illustrations. The gritty realistic fight scenes and flawed humanity of Daniel Craig's Bond reflect certain semiotic codes of authenticity, attributes and values of the documentary aesthetic perhaps first appropriated by Jason Bourne. This is in stark contrast to the fantastical escapades of Roger Moore, of course. Similarly, we see Batman's journey from comic character to television comedy, on to the gothic Tim Burton representation, through to the camp and playful portrayal by George Clooney, before a return to a surrealistic comedic character constituted of Lego via the Bourne-esque realism of Christian Bale. The discourse of art is often one of reaction. The binary of perceived rawness versus decadence is another such trajectory – consider punk versus prog rock, grunge versus hair metal.

When Stephen Dedalus declares "the cracked looking glass of a servant" to be an apt symbol for Irish art, we must consider Joyce's dual role as a modernist with a laborious attention to factual detail – there is a famous expression that one could rebuild Dublin from its accurate depiction in *Ulysses* – but who at the same time created a highly complex, encyclopaedic novel teeming with interior monologues and streams of consciousness.[6] While working on the novel in exile he would often write back for specific cross-checking on specific geographic details – the verisimilitude of Bloom's walk across the city was one such concern. Joyce documented the interior as much as the exterior.

But what does the "cracked looking glass" say of Irish modernist art in terms of this dual position, and how might it relate to realism? How does a broken mirror symbolise modernist Irish literature and its employment of a musical aesthetic towards the creation of a "literature of the unword", to borrow Beckett's phrase? While Roy Foster reminds us that a cracked looking glass will depict multiple selves instead of the singular body of an intact mirror, we must also remember that a cracked looking glass may not represent the individual that peers into the shards at all; it may in fact merely appear as a glimmering mass (Foster, 2000, 16). What I mean here is this: the modernist use of music, a non-representational artform that could, in Schopenhauer's view, enable us to reach higher aesthetical states of purity, the philosophy that by music not saying anything it effectively says everything, enables the inner movements of modernist narratives to hold up a cracked looking glass to society and reflect, particularly in Joyce's Nighttown and Beckett's narrators, the schizophrenia of a consciousness that doesn't clearly recognise its face, or even looks "into the depths" of its character and doesn't particularly like what it finds.

Prieto's discussion of Beckett concentrates almost exclusively on the Parisian avant-garde, drawing many nuanced conclusions about French modernist literature. However, Beckett was also an Irish author who found freedom

Music and literature 13

in the French language at points in his life. Joyce and Beckett were trying to escape another nation's imposed language: English.[7] When in *A Portrait of the Artist*, Stephen Dedalus undergoes a revelation, recognising the gulf between himself and the dean upon a point of supposed Hiberno-English translation (tundish vs. funnel, Ch. 5), Joyce was highlighting such a point. Stephen sees his language as an "acquired speech" in a key moment in the *Bildungsroman*.

What does Beckett's musical syntax tell us about his relationship with Ireland, and his turn to the stylistic freedom of French? Might this "cracked looking glass of a servant" concern the Anglo-Irish use of an imposed language in a deconstructive way that set Beckett on his course of the "unword"? Can Beckett's breakdown of the semiotic signs, the relationship between signifier and signified be seen as part of this destruction of a borrowed language by an artist in exile?

Music and the literary diegesis

In Romantic novels of the nineteenth century, diegetic music (music created within the literary world and audible to the characters) became a useful narrative device. The occurrence of music performance within a story could fulfil many functions, whether to set a scene, enhance a location, adumbrate a plot twist or create a convincing backdrop for the unfolding drama. Most significant, however, are the listening strategies that such performances encourage within each character. Descriptions of listening, for instance, have played an important role in literary history.[8] By listening, I mean narrated instances of concentrated musical attention by certain characters within the diegetic world of the work.[9] In terms of contextualising a scene within a certain milieu, Austen's employment of diegetic music is abundant. Many of her characters perform music: Elizabeth Bennet sings, while Jane Fairfax plays piano. But more significant is the chronicling of musical taste and gendered practices within early nineteenth-century English high society, similar to the way in which Joyce, in "The Dead" ([1914] 1996), documents a bygone operatic culture in Dublin. In *Emma* ([1815] 2003), the Victorian vogue for the exoticism of Thomas Moore's *Irish Melodies* (1808–1834), in which he set old Irish tunes to original poetry, is suggested:

> He took some music from a chair near the piano-forte, and turning to Emma, said, – "Here is something quite new to me. Do you know it Cramer? And here are a new set of Irish melodies."
>
> (Austen, [1815] 2003, 207)

Music can also provide a dramatic backdrop, or afford an intense experience for a character, one that mirrors their personal journey. Dorian Gray's attendance at *Tannhäuser* leaves him "in rapt pleasure", for instance, as the young protagonist finds a kindred tortured soul in Wagner's hero:

14   *Music and literature*

He felt a curious delight in the thought that art, like Nature, has her monsters, things of bestial shape and with hideous voice. Yet, after some time, he wearied of them, and would sit in his box at the opera … listening in rapt pleasure to "Tannhäuser" and seeing in the prelude to that great work of art a presentation of the tragedy of his own soul.

(Wilde, [1891] 1997c, 94)

While diegetic narrative music presents for Gray the "tragedy of his own soul", such sound can also invoke strong emotional recollections, as does the "airy and perfumed phrase" of Vinteuil's sonata for Swann in Proust's *A La Recherche Du Temps Perdu* (*In Search of Lost Tim*e):

[s]carcely had the young pianist begun to play than suddenly, after a high note sustained through two whole bars, Swann sensed its approach, stealing forth, from beneath that long-drawn sonority … and recognized, secret, murmuring, detached, the airy and perfumed phrase that he had loved.

(Proust, [1913] 2001, 207)

The significance of music in Proust's *magnum opus* was of particular interest to Beckett, who described it as the "catalytic element" of the author's work in his monograph, *Proust* ([1931] 1999), further explored by Jean-Jacques Nattiez in *Proust as Musician* (1989). Other important studies are Peter Dayan's *Music Writing Literature* (2006) and Cormac Newark's *Opera in the Novel from Balzac to Proust* (2011).

Often, literary scenes of listening rely on the *aesthetic* interaction between music and text – on the emotional effects the heard melodies induce in the listening characters. The narrative impact of Bartell D'Arcy's rendition of "The Lass of Aughrim" in Joyce's "The Dead" is a good illustration of this: the song reminds Gretta of her lost love, Michael Fury, who "was going to study singing only for his health", a recollection that brings the story to its dramatic, melancholic conclusion (Joyce, [1914] 1996, 252). Here, music operates as a salient tool in the discourse, a means by which an author can reveal the underlying turmoil, hopes, despairs or joys experienced within his or her fiction. Like music in film, a particular melody or musical genre is placed in a scene in order to skew the reader towards a specific interpretation of events; the melodies, in other words, operate as a literary soundtrack, using cultural codes to counterpoint the fiction with a secondary narrative voice, one able to reinforce, or contradict, the principle discursive trajectory.

Music as structural device in literature

While scenes of listening embedded within the text help to flesh out the characters, allowing the reader to understand their state of mind better, some

Music and literature 15

authors also include musical reference at a more structural level. Texts can become music-like more formally in a number of ways through the employment of devices associated with musical form, such as the repetition of words or phrases, the interweaving of certain themes, subjects or voices (the structure of the three recorded voices, A, B and C, in Beckett's *That Time* ([1976] 2006)[10] for instance), motifs reappearing in different guises, and the use of silence. Of course, repetition is a transmedial link between music and literature; both artforms traditionally utilise it, but the proliferation of repetition in work like Beckett's prose is the result of the adoption of musical practice (music allows more repetition before seeming absurd) in literature as a means of achieving a music-like semantic fluidity, as will be explored later. As the written word is incapable of melody (apart from where a notated score is inserted on a specific page, as in Beckett's novel *Watt*, [1945] 1963), repetition and rhythm are the basic elements involved in creating a "musical" text. These devices are the fundamental building blocks of many musics throughout the world, and often hold a greater weight than melodic invention: the interlocking rhythmical patterns of Balinese gamelan music, for instance, or the complex polyrhythms of African drumming. While Western art music (at least until the twentieth century) has traditionally placed melody at the top of the list, it has always been underpinned and propelled by pulse and meter, an observation famously made by music analyst and theorist Heinrich Schenker, who claimed that "[o]ur understanding of musical technique would have advanced much further if only someone had asked: Where, when, and how did music first develop its most striking and distinctive characteristic – repetition?" (Schenker quoted in Kivy, 1993, 327). The Western focus on teleology is achieved largely through repetition in functional harmony. Repetition is fundamental to the form and pattern of a work. Sonata form, for instance, is predicated on the principle of repetition with growth: the recapitulation. Music must traditionally be heard in a sequence; to hear any movement out of place would sound nonsensical (Kivy, 1993, 353). Peter Kivy maintains that the practice of not including repeats in a performance is detrimental to the artform, as repeats not only allow the listener time to "grasp" (problematised earlier) the ideas given, but they also provide a fabric of sound that should not be altered:

> repetition is the means of grasping pattern; but, by definition, pattern is that very repetition, and to dispense with the remainder after it has been grasped would be to dispense with *it*, whereas *it*, the *pattern*, is the whole point of the exercise.
>
> (Kivy, 1993, 353)

Clearly modern music transgresses such boundaries as loops, cut-ups, DAWs (digital audio workstations) and new modes of listening enable sectional play,

16 *Music and literature*

but Kivy is here concerned with structural repeats in concert music, such as the cutting of a *da capo*. Such repeated material historically aided a new listener and quickened familiarisation, outlining significant moments; but such positions as Kivy's rely on the essentialist notion that form and content are one in music. If the receiver has an input into the creation of the meaning of a work, why and how could a singularly directed vehicle of form–content ever be communicated fully?

The lyricism of certain poetry has clear links with musical technique, through an emphasis on rhythm, metre and sound, such as that found in Yeats' employment of iambic tetrameter, trimeter and repeated refrains, reminiscent of the ballad tradition, in early poems like "The Stolen Child" (1889):

> Come away, O human child!
> To the waters and the wild
> With a faery, hand in hand,
> For the world's more full of weeping than you
> can understand
>
> (Yeats, [1889] 1990, 20)

Seamus Heaney recognised this quality in Yeats' work, and indeed carried on the lyrical tradition in his own poetry. His essay *The Makings of a Music: Reflections on the Poetry of Wordsworth and Yeats* (1992) links such technique with the more philosophical, Romantic idea of music in Yeats' work. Heaney praises Yeats' musicality, suggesting that the poet's contempt for poetry "that is effeminate in its continual insistence upon certain moments of strained lyricism" led him to create a music that, in Heaney's words, "came ringing back off the ear as barely and resonantly as a shout caught back off a pillar in an empty church. It is the music of energy reined down, of the mastered beast stirring" (Heaney, 1992, 12).

Keats' notion that "unheard" melodies could be sweeter than those sounded, extends easily to the format of fiction. Prose, being for the most part read in solitude to oneself, can, in this manner, develop an "unheard" music that enables fascinating fictions.

The sounding of text

The music/text relationship also operates contrarily, with poetry and dialogue providing the structure, theme and subject matter for many musical endeavours. In its incarnation, art music was predominantly a means for carrying a religious message or divine praise in an age before Romantic creative self-expression became normative. J. S. Bach saw himself as a deeply religious craftsman, in the service of his God – far from what the Romantics would refer to as the "genius" expressing his or her soul for all subsequent generations. The idea of infinite legacy superseded that of the infinite deity, as it were.

The relationship between text and music in art music was often tenuous, however; the frequent use of *contrafacta* (a vocal composition in which the original words are substituted for new ones), for instance, meant that certain melodies could be reused for a number of text settings with little regard for their suitability beyond that of metre and rhythm. Combined with the highly contrapuntal styles of Renaissance composers such as Palestrina (styles with a complexity that tends to obscure the clarity of words), such practice often favoured the beauty of the music over the didactic message. One might add that of course many of these texts would be well-known religious ones that were being repeatedly retransmitted. Indeed, the question of clarity of language when set to music, from early church music to the flamboyant fluidity of texture in the Baroque, to the obscured text of contemporary opera, Harrison Birtwistle's *The Minotaur* (2008) for instance, is a complicated issue.[11] The balance of power between words and music has continued to fluctuate over the centuries. Overall, perhaps it was music that reigned supreme in collaboration, while Monteverdi's early calls for unsubordinated operatic music still resonate with film composers.[12] Claudia Gorbman paradoxically suggests that a good film score is traditionally one that is not heard – that to notice the music would render a break from the diegesis and the immersion of the narrative (Gorbman, 1987). So, in this way the music is subservient to the narrative, although there are, of course, many composers and directors since the golden era of Hollywood who have put music first; consider John Williams' shark leitmotif from *Jaws* (1975) or Mark Mothersbaugh's scores for Wes Anderson's films. In opera, music's dominance restricted words to the limitations of metre and pitch and the conventions of musical form. The popularity of the *da capo* aria format, such as those in Mozart's *The Magic Flute* (1791) or in motets like Vivaldi's *Nulla in Mundo pax sincera* (RV 630), concretised the aesthetic position that it is perfectly fine to have words repeated over and over again in order for the music to play out the required structure. Certainly, the story is more likely to be followed after the second or third repeat, but the very fact that we must listen to these repeats is the result of hierarchical aesthetic choices.

The most literal form of music-text is word painting, a method by which music is used to sonically mirror the word content. Here, melody can enact the word or sentiment stated: the falling line for "descendit de caelis" ("He came down from Heaven") is a famous example (Carter, 2001, 563). That said, there is inevitable creative interpretation involved in how the word is painted; the degree of shade or colour chosen can yield various results no matter how literal the parallelism. Onomatopoeia, like Mahler's cuckoo, and scoring, such as the use of three voices to depict the Trinity, are forms of word painting. In 1624, Joachim Thuringus proposed three categories of words that could be expressed through music including "words of affection" ("weep", "laugh"), "words of motion and places" ("leap", "cast down") and "words

18 *Music and literature*

of time and number" ("quickly", "twice") (Carter, 2001, 564). This practice quickly became a staple of the madrigal and sixteenth-century chanson, and was popular with Renaissance Humanists, who, believing that the message of the words was paramount, held the view that music should help reinforce this through parallelism. In the words of Nicola Vicentino, music should be "written for words for no other purpose than to express the idea, the passions and the affections of these words by means of harmony" (Vicentino, quoted in Carter, 2001, 564). While some critics may have always considered the technique to be naive, such as Vincenzo Galilei, in his *Dialogo della Musica Antica et della Moderna* (1581), it has continued to be used (even in avantjazz, as we will see in Chapter 6). Examples of pictorialism can be found from Donizetti's birdsong to Berg's snoring and Hendrix's "Machine Gun" (1970). "Mickey-mousing" in film and of course animation works along similar lines – music sounding the movement in literal fashion.

A more symbolic example of music/text interaction is mood or tone-painting – the German *Tonmalerei* – where what starts out as a musical translation of words, such as Schubert's galloping horse in *Erlkönig* (1815), is taken into the accompaniment as the motivic basis for the entire song. In instrumental music, as in the tone poems of Liszt, for instance, a text or an image can be used as a springboard, a mood from which the music can grow. In these cases, the translation is even more subjective – the product of a composer's interpretation, rather than the more literal representations of word painting.

While Schenker might have seen the defining feature of music as its use of repetition, others have considered the non-referential nature of the artform to be the quality that truly sets it apart from the other arts. Schopenhauer believed that music was capable of enabling contact with a higher unknown sphere of consciousness, an intangible realm, inconceivable in perceived reality. Pater, as previously mentioned, saw music in a similar light, viewing it as a virtuous uncorrupted form to which all arts should aspire. "Absolute" music might not mean anything explicitly tangible, but when composers such as Berlioz began to incorporate narratives in what became known as programme music in the nineteenth century, an enormous rift opened up between the aesthetic purists and the textually influenced programmatic composers.

The debate between absolute and programme music continues even today, and is closely related to Lessing-esque media sectarianism: the belief that it benefits an artform to separate it from others permanently. Such segregation can indeed lead to a medium receiving unadulterated creative attention; and yet, this also relies on the purist aesthetic assumption that all arts exist outside of normal reality, somehow transgressing their respective mode of execution. Nevertheless, one is reminded of the simple truth of Goethe's dictum: "In der Beschränkung zeigt sich erst der Meister" (It is in working within limits that the master reveals himself) (Goethe quoted in Wilde, [1891] 1997b, 930). In the twentieth century, Theodor Adorno was perhaps the most significant advocate of the Lessing school, especially in regard to music's relationship to the other arts. In *Philosophie der neuen Musik* ([1949] 1973), Adorno declared

Music and literature   19

his contempt for what he termed *pseudomorphosis*, the mimesis of one art-form by another. Stravinsky was the arch-villain for Adorno in this regard, the trespasser of such an aesthetic border. Adorno argued that the Russian's work resembled that of a cubist painter instead of a true musician, writing that "the spatialisation of music is witness to a *pseudomorphosis* of music to painting, on the innermost level an abdication" (quoted in Albright, 2000, 17). Like Greenberg's view of Shelley, Stravinsky was a coward for not facing up to his own medium, instead running to another, in Adorno's eyes. The concept of *pseudomorphosis* reiterates Lessing's disdain for attempts of one artform to move into the realm of another, this time from the standpoint of a musicologist/sociologist. For a poet to write a lengthy poem depicting a flower would be wasteful, Lessing believed; we must know what our own medium can do and what it cannot. While the poet might take great effort to simulate the image, the painter could achieve this far better in the end (Albright, 2000, 17). The music of Stravinsky likewise embodied for Adorno such an "abdication" of the true abilities of "absolute" music. According to this belief, Stravinsky's music, instead of temporally expanding the discourse, stagnated in the spatial sphere of the visual arts. Lessing's categories were being breached and Adorno was fighting a losing battle to save a sinking ship. Of course, such judgements rest on the flawed assumption that the visual representation of a flower and the poetic description of it are "intended" to achieve the same result. Artists, no matter how realist, have always, whether it be deliberate or not, brought their own perspectives into their work, and no two artworks, whether they be poems or paintings, ever set out to express the same idea.

Despite the aesthetic purism of Adorno, the twentieth century witnessed a huge escalation in music–text interaction. Albright writes that:

> The twentieth century, perhaps more than any other age, demands a style of criticism in which the arts are considered as a whole. This is partly because the artists themselves insisted again and again upon the inextricability of the arts. Ezra Pound, for one, believed that in antiquity "music and poetry had been in alliance ... that the divorce of the two arts had been to the advantage of neither, and that melodic invention had declined simultaneously and progressively with their divergence. The rhythms of poetry grew stupider." He thought it was the duty of the poet to learn music, and the duty of the musician to study poetry.
>
> (Albright, 1999, vii)

Much of the interdisciplinary practice of the twentieth century is indebted to the radical experimentation of the Modernists. Modernism introduced a fresh outlook that brought the old and new together, revitalising the art world and abolishing many of the aesthetic taboos that had dominated it. Paul Klee began to explore the possibilities of creating static polyphony on canvas in imitation of the temporal flow of Bach's music, a mixture of *Nebeneinander* and *Nacheinander*, while Picasso's *Guernica* (1937), including a bull from the

20   *Music and literature*

ancient Spanish cave of Altamira, exemplified the Modernist sensibility for synthesising the prehistoric with the contemporary (Davenport, 1984, 16–28). The boundaries of Lessing's spatial and temporal realms were being interrogated and stretched as artists from all media, and new emerging media, experimented freely with the possibilities of intermedial art. The influence of musical technique and form in literature was obvious, but more significantly the non-referential, intangible qualities of music were also being utilised by the Modernists. George Steiner writes:

> Where poetry seeks to dissociate itself from the exactions of clear meaning and from the common usages of syntax, it will tend towards an ideal of musical form. This tendency plays a fascinating role in modern literature. The thought of giving to words and prosody values equivalent to music is an ancient one ... More recently, the submission of literary forms to musical examples and ideals has been carried even further. In Romain Rolland and Thomas Mann, we find the belief that the musician is the artist in essence (he is *more* an artist than, say, the painter or writer). This is because only music can achieve that total fusion of form and content, of means and meaning, which all art strives for. Two of the foremost poetic designs of our time, T. S. Eliot's *Four Quartets* and Hermann Broch's *Death of Virgil*, embody an idea that can be traced back to Mallarmé and *L'Après-midi d'un faune*: they attempt to suggest in language corresponding organizations of musical form.
>
> (Steiner, [1961] 1985, 47–48, original emphasis)

Language that attempts to "dissociate itself from the exactions of clear meaning" becomes essentially music-like, for Steiner. The non-referential qualities of music, those that Pater and Schopenhauer found so compelling, became for the Modernists a device whereby words could function in what Alec Reid calls a "non-specific" manner (Reid, 1968, 34). Wittgenstein wrote that "[u]nderstanding a sentence is much more akin to understanding a theme in music than one may think", and certainly the boundaries between the arts, and in particular those between music and literature, were becoming blurred in the minds of philosophers, linguists and artists (Wittgenstein quoted in Albright, 2000, 6). Albright further explains that "[t]he linguistics of Ferdinand de Saussure, the philosophies of Ludwig Wittgenstein and Jacques Derrida, tend to strip language of denotation, to make language a game of arbitrary signifiers; and as words lose connection to the world of hard objects, they become more and more like musical notes" (Albright, 2000, 6). Structuralism and post-structuralism (Barthes, Derrida, de Saussure) questioned the role of the listener/reader, how language is created in tandem with society, and how language itself is created in an arbitrary fashion; the reason that a word signifies and denotes any given concept or thing is essentially random. If we are denied any universals at the reception level, we are also denied them at the creation level.

If, where before the methods in which music and text were combined were for the most part weighted on the music side (in operatic arias, for example, the text being subordinate and subject to pitch, bar length and repetition – sometimes to the point of absurdity), in the twentieth century, there was a reversal of this: music became enveloped by literature. George Bernard Shaw observed that Wagner could repeat "Tristan" many times musically without any problems, whereas Shakespeare could not simply repeat the word "Romeo" ad infinitum; the audience required more variation in vocabulary in the absence of music (Shaw quoted in Meisel, 1963, 41). In the twentieth century, such a repetition of the word "Romeo" in place of new material would begin to appear in literature, as authors experimented with what had previously seemed absurd only in the pejorative sense.

Music began to receive a greater global literary attention, with many high-profile writers attempting to encompass it either formally, structurally or conceptually, from the scored violin music in Pound's *Pisan Cantos* (Canto 74 in particular), to the music notation in Zukofsky's *A* (1978), or the fiction of Hermann Hess, whose novel *The Glass Bead Game* emphasised the importance of music in culture. The "airy and perfumed phrase" that propelled Proust's world was not an isolated phenomenon.

The growth of Word and Music Studies

The increasing scholarly attention towards interdisciplinary practice has meant that an independent, international field of musico-literary exploration has begun to blossom in recent decades, with more musicologists in particular entering the foray in the last few years.[13] As a result, the field has come a long way since the pioneering work of Calvin S. Brown's *Music and Literature: A Comparison of the Arts*, first published in 1948. Brown's work was instrumental in setting the main aesthetic parameters of what would become the field of *musico-literary studies* (his term), later to be named *melopoetics* by Lawrence Kramer. Referred to as *Music and Literature Studies* or *Word and Music Studies* (the now established term) by many of Brown's later disciples, Brown's work introduced the long-standing issues and questions that were deemed most in need of scholarly attention, and which would remain so over the course of the next sixty or so years.

As a result of Brown's early work, the field began to expand, if somewhat sporadically, as did the worldwide academic predilection for interdisciplinary scrutiny. Word and Music Studies underwent its most vitalising burst of energy after a number of forging conferences in Dartmouth College (1988), Graz (1990) and Lund (1995). Perhaps the most beneficial result of these meetings was the joint decision to found the International Association for Word and Music Studies (WMA) in Graz in 1997. Since then the WMA has organised biennial conferences (the eleventh to be held in Stockholm in 2017) focusing on the salient problems and issues in the burgeoning field. The WMA also publishes collected volumes of scholars at the forefront of this

22 Music and literature

research. What had begun with Brown in 1948 is now a worldwide academic community. The WMA website boasts a membership of 129 scholars from 26 countries, representing a truly international field of scholarly attention.[14] In 2010 the inaugural conference of the Word and Music Association Forum (WMAF) was held in Dortmund, Germany. The WMAF is held on alternate years (most recently in Arizona 2016) between the WMA conferences, and is particularly geared towards younger scholars and current PhDs in the field with half of the conference being billed as a colloquium for works in progress.

The existence of these multi-institutional associations has had a positive impact on Word and Music Studies *within* universities: in the UK, for instance, the Open University began a Literature and Music Research Group with the aim of fostering a healthy research community within the OU; and a Words and Music Studies Graduate School was established in the University of Edinburgh where the world's first and, so far, only Professor of Words and Music Studies, Peter Dayan, was appointed. However, perhaps the call of the WMA was not as loud as it could have been; in 2009, for instance, one of the research strands that featured on the Royal Musical Association (RMA)'s annual call for papers was "music and literature", a call that seemed to suggest an institutional desire to encourage interdisciplinary work. But despite this public proclamation, in the end only one panel out of almost forty was allocated to the subject. Either there was a dearth of proposals, the submissions received were not very good, or perhaps the subject, although coming with a promise of innovation and intermedial conversion, is a tough one to engage with, not least as it requires a background in both musicology and literary studies.

More recently, the RMA 2010 conference, "Boundaries", hosted a single panel entitled "Literature at the Boundary of Music Research", and the RMA student conference 2011 featured a panel on "Music and Literature", in which I participated. There are signs that the field in the UK is beginning to flourish; in February 2011, I co-organised a study day at the Institute of Musical Research (IMR) in London on the topic of Music and Literature, alongside Peter Dayan, Helen Abbott and Delia da Sousa Correa, to an audience of researchers and scholars. The fact that the 2013 WMA conference was held in London did a great deal to strengthen the field in the UK.

The problems of cross-disciplinary work that focuses on music and literature are articulated by such scholars as Eric Prieto, Lawrence Kramer, Peter Dayan, Stephen Benson, Werner Wolf, Daniel Albright, Jean-Jacques Nattiez, Helen Abbott, Delia da Sousa Correa, Walter Bernhart, Catherine Laws, Robert Samuels, John Neubauer, Mary Breatnach, Steven Paul Scher, Mary Bryden, Timothy Martin and Harry White.[15] Many of these authors proclaim the particular difficulties inherent in holding together the disciplines of musicology and literary studies: at the same time, these difficulties are tackled with great excitement. Until the 2000s, the approach to the subject, beginning with Brown's book, was rather formalist. In *Music and Literature: A Comparison of the Arts*, for example, topics are arranged under

Music and literature 23

headings such as "Rhythm and Pitch", "The Literal Setting of Vocal Music" and "Repetition and Variation". Brown's study attempted to identify the underlying structures that both artforms shared and tried to find general points of convergence between them, rather than to cite specific similarities between individual works: by asking what music is and consequentially what literature is, Brown opened the Pandora's Box of interdisciplinary philosophical and aesthetic relations.

For Brown, music and literature shared certain characteristics: both, he argued, "are arts presented through the sense of hearing, having their development in time, and hence requiring a good memory for their comprehension" (Brown, 1948, 11). The use of the term "hearing", yet to be problematised at the time of Brown's study, is an issue here. Another point of conjecture might be that both arts can indeed be read visually. In his discussion of time, Brown could not account for process music (such as Minimalism) and does not consider Adorno's criticism of spatialisation in Stravinsky's work. As for the assumption that both arts require a "good memory for their comprehension", we must not only ask what defines "good" in this sense, but also, once accepted, whether this unquantified amount of memory is always necessary for "comprehension". Although some of Brown's assumptions may seem naive today, others were particularly astute, echoing the structuralism of de Saussure.

The key differentiating factor between the two artforms, in Brown's view, is that music is an "art of sound in and for itself, of sound qua sound" whereas literature is "an art employing *sounds to which external significance has been arbitrarily attached* " (Brown, 1948, 11, original emphasis). Another observation of Brown's that was to be theorised further by later writers was his recognition of the progressive abandonment of representation by authors during the twentieth century and the resultant move towards abstraction (Brown, 1948, 269). Like Schenker and Kivy, Brown recognised the transmedial nature of repetition and variation, and viewed them as the cornerstones of both artforms: "[r]epetition and variation can be seen in the smallest real structural units of both literature and music" (Brown, 1948, 103).

Steven Paul Scher was prolific in building on Brown's work, producing a wealth of scholarship in the field. Perhaps his most controversial move was to proclaim the uselessness of the term "musical" in reference to literature (Scher, 1972). This may seem rash, but it was the result of a highly frustrating canon of scholarship wherein the vague employment of a Romanticised adjective, "musical", was used in reference to anything that sounded pleasing to the ear. The traditional and uncritical use of the ambiguous word "musical" to denote subjective approval was a remnant of Romanticism that should, according to Scher, be scrapped by academics. In this rather uncritical sense, the academic employment of the term was of no use whatsoever, being simply an empty signifier. Perhaps Scher went too far in this regard: it does seem strange to outlaw a term simply because of its misuse, instead of trying to set clear and useful parameters for the word. However, this kind of intense interrogation

24 *Music and literature*

and circumnavigation – to the point of absurdity – would prove an ongoing tenet of meta-critical musico-literary investigation, one that scholars like Prieto began moving beyond in terms of methodology and focus. As previously discussed, Prieto and Dayan offer progressive licence in the use of the term "musical", but we are now far beyond the free-for-all that it had been pre-Scher. The term should be used metaphorically, in an informed manner, in relation to work that reflects the idea of music and its philosophical discourse, and not as an analytical classification.[16]

For Scher, the analogy of music with literature was only useful when it came to structure. He suggested a tripartite division, three distinct categories, into which he divided the myriad forms of musico-literary interaction. Simply put, these are: *music and literature* (the collaboration of literature and instrumental music, be it song or opera and so on); *music in literature* (the appropriation of musical devices in poetry or prose, such as Joyce's attempt at a fugue in the "Sirens" chapter of *Ulysses*); and *literature in music* (music influenced by or referring to literature, such as programme music). Scher's focus on subterranean embedded structural parallels would influence the work of Lawrence Kramer.

Kramer's contribution to the field marks a change in direction from these earlier theories. Whereas those before him had struggled to find general rules that applied to the interaction of music and literature, Kramer abandoned the notion of prescriptive practices, suggesting instead a "mobile" scholarship for a "mobile" artform:

> Any discourse that hopes to embrace both arts must, so to speak, be mobile. Its mobility would consist in the power to treat connotative and combinatory structures with equal exactness, agility, and sophistication. An interpretative language with this property would have access to both the tacit and explicit dimensions of music and poetry alike, its structural argument could incorporate materials as diverse as parallel chords and parallel metaphors.
>
> (Kramer, 1984, 7)

Kramer's *Music and Poetry: The Nineteenth Century and After* (1984) would prove a formative text for the new breed of scholars in the 1990s. Kramer saw time and process as major areas of similarity between the two artforms: music and literature, he argued, are "saturated with time" and the respective arts essentially go about the "transformation of time into form" (Kramer, 1984, 7). It is clear that we are never far from Lessing's temporal and spatial realms in musico-literary aesthetics. For Kramer, the "transformation of time into form" is the defining role of the composer and poet. This leads him to explore the structural similarities in the methods utilised by the respective artistic media: "[p]oetic structure or structural rhythm" is the deep subterranean level where the two artforms share an essential nature. Edward T. Cone's declaration (1968) that "musical form, as I conceive it, is basically rhythmic" is

Music and literature   25

used by Kramer to highlight what Barbara Herrnstein Smith calls the "temporal and dynamic qualities that poetry shares with music" (Smith, quoted in Kramer, 1984, 9–10).

For Kramer, what distinguishes the two artforms is not the nonrepresentational aspects of music; he finds a "richer fountain" of information in Liszt's "Les Jeux d'eaux à la Ville d'Este" than in Baudelaire's "Le Jet d'eau" for instance, but:

> A complementarity in the roles the two arts assign to their connotative and combinatory aspects: each art makes explicit the dimension that the other leaves tacit. Musical meaning, even when focused by a text or program, is always non-predictive and inexact. Its connotations are peripheral, always somewhat displaced – not so much vague as unlocalized, at a third remove, like a name on the tip of the tongue. Music achieves its unique suggestiveness, the power [first identified by Hegel] to embody complex states of mind as they might arise pre-verbally in consciousness, by resting its tacit connotations on an explicit combinatory structure that is highly charged with complexity, expectancy, and tension. In poetry, this expressive balance is reversed; poetic meaning, as it unfolds to an interpreter, is a virtually limitless play of explicit connotative relationships.
>
> (Kramer, 1984, 6)

He takes the terms "tacit" and "explicit" from Michael Polanyi's work, *The Tacit Dimension* ([1967] 2009), in order to address the great debate as to whether "music expresses feelings and states of mind or elicits them – the answer being: neither" (Kramer, 1984, 6). Kramer explains:

> When we listen, what we attend to is the music itself as it unfolds its combinatory sequence; this is the focus. The connotative element – which as Polanyi would predict seems to be internal to us – continually involves us in (and guides and shapes) the activity of listening. In a complementary way, the combinatory play of rhythm and sonority in poetry involves us in a reading of – a reading of ourselves into – the connotative play of the text.
>
> (Kramer, 1984, 6)

This key development in *Music and Poetry* is based on Kramer's faith in the existence of deep structural parallels between the two artforms, which he explores through a number of case studies. In Kramer's own words, "a poem and a composition may converge on a structural rhythm: that a shared pattern of unfolding can act as an interpretive framework for the explicit dimension of both works" (Kramer, 1984, 10). Like Brown, Kivy and Schenker, Kramer here emphasises the importance of rhythm and repetition in defining music and any further parallels with literature. Kramer recognises that the "possibility of convergence is a function of cultural history" (Kramer, 1984, 15).

26 *Music and literature*

In a similar way to what Peter Rabinowitz describes as "attributive screens", our socially constructed idea of what constitutes a specific artform, what distinguishes it from another, is, like all perception, influenced by our history of experience and affiliation. I will be returning to Rabinowitz's ideas shortly.

Music and Poetry is, as the title suggests, focused on music's relationship to poetry rather than to novels or drama. Kramer's coinage of the term "melopoetics" is also indicative of his preferred literary form. Narrative complicates the dialogue between the two arts for Kramer, as he explains: "[o]n the whole, narrative form is opposed to the heightened rhythm of connection and association that is typical of music and poetry" (Kramer, 1984, 10). He suggests that rhythmic continuity is disrupted by the presence of multiple narrators and personas (Kramer, 1984, 10). What then of Eliot's *The Wasteland*, with its series of narrators? Do such ideas offer us insights into the poetry of the Modernists, or do Kramer's ideas only remain relevant to the nineteenth century?

Kramer's method of studying two works in parallel, Beethoven's Piano Sonata in F minor, op. 57, "Apassionata" (1806), alongside Wordsworth's "The Thorn" (1800), for instance, exemplifies his belief in deep structural similarities, and cultural building blocks inherent in such designs. He discusses both pieces in terms of "reconciling the antithesis that shapes them", through a battle of style versus subject (Kramer, 1984, 15). His recognition of the futile search for "prescriptive" general criteria for music-literary synthesis, a key problem in the field, especially pre-Kramer, leads him to believe that only on an individual basis can real underlying useful links be made. Is there something more fundamental operating here than mere individual similarities? In Kramer's words, "the trouble is that convergence does not depend on overt formal similarities between works but on shared ways of organising change and provoking interpretation … [there is] no way to be prescriptive" (Kramer, 1984, 24). This very statement would seem to oppose the tenets of Brown and more recently that of Werner Wolf.

Wolf proclaims his dislike of the term "melopoetics" on the grounds that it can confuse perception of a field that includes the study of the "musicalization of fiction". Wolf adopts Huxley's term for the title of his book, *The Musicalization of Fiction: A Study in the History of Intermediality* (1999). Recognising the neglect shown to literary forms other than poetry within the field, Wolf is one of the first to dedicate an entire book to the study of musical ideas in the novel. He also believes in general principles of interaction that can and should even regulate what might and what might not constitute a musicalised literature. Under the chapter heading "[h]ow to recognize a musicalized fiction when reading one", and the subheading "[t]ypes of evidence and criteria for identifying musicalized fiction", Wolf enlists "circumstantial/contextual evidence" (including peripheral documents and facts like cultural and biographical evidence, parallel musicalised works by the author and direct commentaries by the author) as well as textual evidence (including use of notation, thematisation of music, evocation of vocal music, acoustic

Music and literature 27

foregrounding and unusual patterns) as the necessary factors in determining whether or not a text is truly "musicalized" (Wolf, 1999, 73–83). Wolf documents the evolution of musicalised fiction from early experimental works by De Quincey through to the Modernists and offers a contextual intermedial history that situates this emerging phenomenon. Wolf refutes the scholarship that heralds *Tristram Shandy* as an early precursor of an intermedial text:

> As far as textual evidence is concerned, *Tristram Shandy* does not contain overtly intermedial elements (musical notation) indicating a presence of, and perhaps also a concern with, music, nor are there paratextual thematizations of music which might betray a musicalized intention.
>
> (Wolf, 1999, 86)

While Wolf allows the fact that there are certain "musical" elements to *Tristram Shandy*, then, the novel does not meet his criteria for a "musicalized fiction", the experimentalism largely reflecting Sterne's concern for meta-fiction rather than music. Wolf, then, is particularly prescriptive when it comes to musico-literary interaction, a trait that scholars such as Prieto believe we should move beyond, as we'll return to shortly.

As mentioned earlier in relation to Kramer's ideas, Rabinowitz introduced some vital insights into the field. In Scher's edited collection, *Music and Text: Critical Enquiries* (1992), Rabinowitz's article, "Chord and Discourse: Listening Through the Written Word" investigates perception and reception in terms of interdisciplinary interaction (Rabinowitz, 1992, 38–56). Rabinowitz writes: "[m]y claim is that neither the score as written nor the sounds as performed offers sufficient grounds for interpretation or analysis … But I do believe that what you hear and experience is largely dependent upon the presuppositions with which you approach it, and that those presuppositions are to a generally unrecognised degree verbal in origin" (Rabinowitz, 1992, 39). He relates reception to a game of cards, in which a three of clubs means nothing without the prior knowledge of what it means within the context of the given game. The three of clubs represents the technical level of observation, but for it to make sense to others, an "attributive" level is required, wherein prior knowledge imbues the empty sign with a signifier of meaning. In this way, Rabinowitz explains the process by which we engage with music: according to him, a certain amount of prior knowledge is often necessary in order to make sense of it. What is significant here is that the individual reader/listener brings with him/her a matchless magnitude of "prior knowledge" or lack thereof. A person's history of experiences and tastes, his or her social context and listening history, all colour his or her initial experience of a new composition through what Rabinowitz calls "attributive screens" (Rabinowitz, 1992, 56). Slavoj Žižek suggests viewing ideology in a similar manner, that we must remove imaginary "ideological spectacles" in order to unpack the "real" mechanisms in operation (Fiennes *et al.*, 2012).

28   *Music and literature*

The presence of multiple "attributive screens" does not, however, make reception entirely subjective, but is, rather, an acknowledgement that we all live "and are partly formed by a culture (or cultures)" (Rabinowitz, 1992, 52). It follows that "attributive screens" are formed by social and cultural contexts. To take this idea further, in order for meaning to be created, it must be shared at some level and cannot be entirely subjective.[17] This is similar to how Wittgenstein pointed out the impossibility of a "private language"; the fundamental point of a language, communication, cannot exist without shared knowledge (Wittgenstein, [1953] 2009).

Peter Dayan's *Music Writing Literature: From Sand via Debussy to Derrida* (2006) echoes Kramer's ideas on the inseparable nature of the two artforms. Dayan concludes that:

> [m]usic and literature ... as defined by each other in an argument whose circularity is vicious to science but perhaps central to life, confound self-identity. They are never the same twice, they are never simply present; and they, too, in defiance of logic, and (often explicitly in the case of literature) also in defiance of the truth about our cultural and political life (which requires plurality to avoid imperialism and oppression).
>
> (Dayan, 2006, 132)

Dayan praises the "musical" writing of Barthes and Derrida, something for which they were often criticised. In a manner similar to Wilde's view expressed in "The Critic as Artist" ([1891] 1997a), Barthes and Derrida wrote their criticism as an artform, a poetic musical style that Dayan ties back to the French Symbolists. Dayan explores how George Sand understood there to be "sublime equivalents" between music and literature, rather than there being "servile repetition of external sounds" in the work of Chopin, for instance (Dayan, 2006, 5). In his discussion of Chopin's "raindrop" prelude (cited as 15D here, the legitimacy of which has been an ongoing area of scholarship), Dayan suggests that we have lost the post-Romantic unspoken uncertainty about representation in music. It seems to be suggested here that before the study of scores alongside contextual biographical anecdotes, scholars allowed a kind of Keatsian "negative capability" towards programme music.[18] It is Dayan's conviction that literature "depends" on:

> the presence of rain in Chopin's music ... The existence of literature, as distinct from any other kind of writing, can only be maintained through analogy with a non-verbal artform that is believed to be at once full of meaning, and irredeemably corrosive of reference.
>
> (Dayan, 2006, 10)

In other words, whether or not the composer intended a specific motif to sound like raindrops or not, whether or not it was composed during a torrential downpour or blazing sunshine, is trivial. What matters, for Dayan, is that

Music and literature 29

the relationship between a non-representational art (music) and a denotative one (literature) ensures their respective symbiotic evolution and mutual survival.

Though in line with Kramer and Dayan's understanding of the "mobility" of music and literature, Prieto's *Listening In: Music, Mind, and the Modernist Narrative* (2002a), calls for a further change of analytical direction. He reminds us that when an author applies musical techniques to his or her work (such as Joyce writing a fugue, or inserting an overture that introduces the material that is to be developed in the course of the chapter), this practice is always metaphorical in nature. It can be music-like, but it cannot be music. Nor does it claim to be absolute. While Dayan rightfully acknowledges this problem, Prieto pushes further that the fundamental flaw in the dominant methodology in musico-literary scholarship is, at its most basic level, the clichéd and vague use of music terminology in literary scholarship.

The field had begun to spiral out of control in a whirlpool of metacritical publications, with the "appropriateness" of a metaphor perhaps the most persistent quandary. Precursing and perhaps partly responsible for Scher's censorship of the term "musical", an early example of this was Northrop Frye's paradoxical declaration that "the literary meaning of musical *is* unmusical" (Frye, 1941–42, 178, emphasis added). Here, Frye suggests that, contrary to popular misuse, music-like poetry is more suited to the "grotesque and horrible" with its employment of "barking accents, crabbed and obscure language, mouthfuls of consonants, and long lumbering polysyllables" (Frye quoted in Prieto, 2002a, 22). Instead of pleasant poetry being termed "musical" (the clichéd and tired convention), Frye suggests the opposite, yet in doing so achieves very little other than replacing a vague usage with another equally ambiguous one. Brown entered equally troubled waters when he called for "more precise metaphors" (Brown, 1948, 20). How can a metaphor really be more precise? Prieto notes that, in the fifty years since Brown's pioneering study, "a viable methodology has not yet emerged" (Prieto, 2002a, 18). Instead, what dominates publications is, he argues, metacritical literature that attempts "to develop a methodology for the study of the relationship between literature and music", but that has hitherto been unsuccessful in 'defining' a field" (Prieto, 2002a, 18).

The first WMA publication, *Defining the Field* (Bernhart, Scher and Wolf, 1999), included an essay by Scher entitled "Melopoetics Revisited". In the final pages, Scher issued a mission statement in the form of a to-do list for the field, set out in eight bullet points, that included the planning of conferences, the launch of the new WMA book series, but also the formulation of a "definition of melopoetics that would reflect the field's disciplinary and institutional prospects" (Scher, 1999, 21). Scher called for scholars to "subject to renewed scrutiny the terminology employed in musico-literary studies"; "compile a dictionary/glossary of melopoetics terms"; "attempt a systematic overview of the different types of music-analogous structures in literature"; and "analyze

30 *Music and literature*

familiar music-related texts as well as newly emerging, more experimental ones" (Scher, 1999, 21). Eighteen years on, a viable definition of melopoetics remains elusive, as does a definitive methodology. Why is this?

Perhaps the wrong questions were being asked initially. Prieto questions the fifty-year delay it has taken for scholars to move beyond the pedantic in order to see the greater landscape. To rectify this delay, he proposes a model for moving beyond the metacritical minefield of musico-literary study: instead of seeking futile formal criteria, he asks what we can learn from metaphors. According to Prieto, the notion of setting out criteria by which to judge the appropriateness of a metaphor is a dead end – something, in other words, that no author will adhere to. Instead, we should attempt to understand the motives that drove writers to musical devices in the first place, and to assess the consequences that have resulted from such practices: we should look at how such phenomena affect the semiotic functioning of the "text".

J. P. Baricelli's critique ([1943] 1998) of Eliot's *Four Quartets* exemplifies such a problematic approach for Prieto, when he argues that: "Eliot does not seem to realize, nor do the critics who take his clues, that [the relationship between these two passages] is in no way contrapuntal" (Baricelli quoted in Prieto, 2002a, 21). The redundancy of a scholar deciding that an artist has "failed" in creating a metaphorical musical text, when the artist explicitly "intended" to – explaining this in documented interviews or notes, for example – misses the point completely. Should a critic or scholar have the right to tell an artist that he or she has failed in creating an adequate metaphor? When musicologists still have no complete set of identity conditions for "music" itself, how can we expect to have a clear set for metaphors for music within literature? If there are indeed "multiple ontologies" of the broad term "music" (Bohlman, 1999), music-like texts must then be even more difficult to define and categorise into prescribed units. Returning to Baricelli's critique of Eliot, how can a scholar expect an artist to adhere to a category invented by (and one not unanimously agreed upon) the scholar himself/herself after the artwork itself was created? The application of a category to an artist, to whom it doesn't apply, seems simply redundant (one is reminded of Groucho Marx's playful dictum regarding club membership (Marx, 1959, 321)). Aristotle viewed metaphors as didactic tools that could suggest new insights through the juxtaposition of two separate objects. Prieto recognises the potential of metaphors, after Aristotle, to "teach us something new" as the fundamental premise for scholarship "beyond musico-literary studies" (Prieto, 2002a, 23). He proposed a complete shake-up of the field and outlined his model in five distinct areas, which he set out in an article entitled "Metaphor and Methodology in Word and Music Studies" (Prieto, 2002b, 51) as follows:

1. **Metaphoricity.**
    Accept and embrace the inherently metaphorical status of all attempts to apply terms from one art to objects in another.

2. Cognitive dissonance.
Promote "surprise" and "cognitive dissonance", not "appropriateness" or "adequacy", as the primary criteria of value when studying word–music analogies.

3. Deep structures.
Emphasize the search for deep structures and underlying principles, not the description of direct one-to-one correspondences between the arts.

4. De-essentializing the arts.
Think of these analogies as tools helpful in reconfiguring and deepening our understanding of the arts and their various roles. Resist the temptation to force them to fit established definitions, however widely accepted.

5. Focus on significance and implications.
Analysis should always be guided by broader cultural questions of meaning and value. The central question for word and music studies is: why do these analogies matter?

These five points, a *quasi*-self-help list of aphorisms or mantras for the musico-literary scholar, summarise Prieto's general methodology. The second point introduces a new idea, however, as Prieto suggests that instead of seeking "appropriateness", we promote "surprise" and "cognitive dissonance". Unlike the other points, this point seems unnecessary and unqualified. It is reminiscent of Eisenstein's ideas promoting counterpoint in the employment of film music, bringing about an ironic effect in relation to the image, as mentioned earlier. It remains unclear in Prieto's work why an ironic effect might be deemed of more value than a text that operates in line with more predictable musical devices. Perhaps it is the fact that it would draw a clearer line between two narrative currents – the music and the words – beyond the obvious fact that it might be more innovative and experimental. The "opacity" of each medium is certainly foregrounded in such cases, the individual materials on full show, as Greenberg wanted. No matter how interesting the "surprise" might be, surely this should not be the sole or "primary criteria of value when studying word-music analogies"?

Aligned with Scher's aforementioned trinity of categories (*music and literature, music in literature,* and *literature in music*), the methodological toolkit for Word and Music Studies seems somewhat more substantial in recent years. The question remains: should we completely abandon, as Prieto suggests, the futile search for definitive terminologies that has consistently been called for in musico-literary inquiry? This quest would seem the basis of most scholarly fields, it might be posited, with the very intangibility of terms, the failures of language itself, accounting for much of the academic discourse. Despite the efforts of Scher and Wolf, such a satisfactory and conclusive taxonomy remains elusive, perhaps inevitably so. Is the fact that a clear methodology has not come to fruition a good enough reason to abandon the quest completely? Yes, the time has arrived to move on, as it were. When the right answers are unattainable, perhaps it is the question that needs interrogation. The original

32 *Music and literature*

questions – Scher's plea for definitions – were, I believe, the wrong ones to propose at the time. With Prieto, the right questions have begun to be explored. Perhaps what is really happening, a point touched on by Kramer and Dayan, is that each of the artforms, both music and literature, define one another in relation to the mirror, a kind of self-discovery through recognition, of the "other": morphing identification by antithesis.

Notes

1 Albright (2000, 7) calls this the "Laocoön problem".
2 The quote continues: "But if painting, by virtue of its signs or its means of imitation, which it can combine in space alone, must completely renounce time, then progressive acts, because progressive, do not belong among its subjects – painting must content itself with acts next to one another, or with mere bodies", (Lessing quoted in Albright (2000, 9)).
3 Babbitt refers to Wagner as an "eleutheromaniac" (freedom-crazed) (Albright, 2000, 10).
4 For a study of Pinget's theme and variation technique see Prieto, 2002a, 59–100.
5 Aldous Huxley coined the term in the novel *Point Counter Point* ([1928] 1978, 301).
6 Foster (2000, 323).
7 The postcolonial element in the author's aesthetic has been well discussed; see for instance Ann Banfield's article "Beckett's Tattered Syntax" (2003).
8 The Arts and Humanities Research Council-funded Listening Experience Database Project run by the the Royal College of Music and the Open University is one example of how listening has become a recent focus of scholarship.
9 Of course, there are problems with such terms as "listening", "diegetic", "concentrated", and indeed "attention", and these debates are outside of the scope of this book; but for the required purpose here, they will suffice. For problematised explorations of these terms, see the work of Anahid Kassabian and Janet Staiger.
10 I ACB ACB ACB CABII CBA CBA CBA BCAIII BAC BAC BAC BAC (Libera, 1980).
11 See Tristan Jakob-Hoff (2008).
12 Monteverdi called for music to be free from subservience to words in the preface to *Scherzi Musicali* (1607) (cited in Prieto, 2002a, 4).
13 The term "musico-literary studies" was coined by Brown (1948).
14 WMA website 2015 minutes – http://wordmusicstudies.net [accessed 22 August 2016].
15 This list is by no means exhaustive: for further information see the WMA website and publications – http://wordmusicstudies.net.
16 See Dayan (2002).
17 See Kassabian's theorisation of "distributive subjectivity" in *Ubiquitous Listening* (2013).
18 Keats defined his concept, in a letter dated 22 December 1817, as follows: "Negative Capability, that is when man is capable of being in uncertainties, Mysteries, doubts, without any irritable reaching after fact and reason", quoted in www.oxfordreference.com/view/10.1093/oi/authority.20110803100227203 [accessed 14 August 13].

2 Repetition in music and literature

Repetition as device spans all the arts; it is crucial to both music and literature, and is also integral to painting, film and even sculpture (we need only step onto Crosby Beach in Liverpool to witness the proliferation of Anthony Gormleys). For this reason, repetition has recently been theorised by Werner Wolf as a "transmedial" device.[1] Whereas the "intermedial" is achieved through synthesis, whereby two disciplines combine to achieve a new artform, as in video art-music, transmedial refers to devices or features that are not exclusive to a specific artform but are instead shared. The transmedial device is not founded on convergence, but rather employs a common technique among disciplines. For Wolf, repetition can therefore never be thought of as intermedial in itself. Within the interdisciplinary realm of Word and Music Studies such taxonomy has been the perennial goal, particularly for the Austro-German scholars, a practice that Chapter 1 explored to some degree.

Once alert to the idea of transmedial repetition, we begin to find it everywhere. How then are we to deal with such abundance theoretically? A lateral, wide-ranging approach is taken by Robert Fink, whose book on repetition in modern culture, *Repeating Ourselves: American Minimal Music as Cultural Practice* (2005) relates the abundance of repetition in American minimalism to the commercial material repetition and franchising of corporations such as McDonalds and Starbucks. While Fink makes eloquent observations concerning the high–low art convergence since Pop art, and the proliferation of repetitious material in society, his arguments follow the traditional concept of repetition as reproduction of the same, an idea that I would like to problematise.[2]

Focusing on repetition in words and music, the subject of this chapter, the idea of exact replication, as Fink envisions, becomes a difficult one to accept as it ignores the *reception* of the repeated fragment. When we hear something again, it is never the same. The very notion of "again" negates "sameness". How can something be the same at a different point in time and context? While the echo of a motif might sound the same, its repositioning, or recontextualisation, nevertheless achieves difference. Heraclitus' famous saying, as told by Plato, touches on this perpetual flux – we can indeed never step into the same river twice.[3] The second time we hear a motif, in other words, it is not

34   *Repetition in music and literature*

the same but changed utterly. There is no such thing as the "innocent eye"; we each approach what we experience with an individual history of experience, education, and taste (Stahn cited in Best, 1980, 10). The concept of an "innocent ear" is just as unfeasible. Philip Tagg's theorisation of "codal incompetence" and "codal interference" in the semiotics of music deals with the same issue (Tagg, 2012). A knowledge of the signifiers and the history of accumulated references adds a depth of appreciation for a listener and vice versa, while taste itself can often form a blockade against semiotic content reaching the more narrow-minded reader. Another layer is added upon hearing something for the third and each successive time thereafter, a rehearing that further engages our faculties of memory and both conscious, and unconscious, familiarisation. To return to Gormley's statues, – the repetition of the artist's own body in iron, an act that may seem narcissistic on the one hand but democratic on the other – difference results from the varying effects of erosion, but more fundamentally from where each figure is positioned. In broader terms, Gormley's repetition of a human body brings into question the complicated concept of identity, what concerned Freud with the *unheimlich*, or uncanny, effect of the Doppelganger. Collectively they face the sea, but individually their place in the sand provides difference. The shore provides a canvas of altered repetitions. Gormley has repeated this installation, albeit more temporarily than in Liverpool, at various locations, including across the skyscape of London's South Bank. Each time we encounter this iron man, his perspective transforms ours.

In *Difference and Repetition* ([1968] 1994, 18), Gilles Deleuze defines true repetition as "repetition of difference", contrary to a traditional opinion of sameness. For Deleuze, a repetition is never the same but both the same and other. Nietzsche's concept of "eternal return"[4] – a cyclical universe in which everything will at some stage repeat – is regarded by Deleuze to be pioneering in this regard; he writes: "The subject of the eternal return is not the same but the different, not the similar but the dissimilar, not the one but the many" (Deleuze, [1968] 1994, 126). For Nietzsche's universe to be infinite, repeated lives must be repeated differently. Each "Groundhog Day" must vary to some extent in order for all permutations to occur (Golan, 2007, 2–3). In Nietzsche, Deleuze finds a means whereby his ideas of repetition can be freed: "repetition cannot be understood as a repetition of the same, and becomes liberated from subjugation under the demands of traditional philosophy".[5] Kierkegaard's doubles, as portrayed in his seminal text *Repetition* ([1843] 2009), also somewhat foreshadow Deleuze's repetition as difference. He writes: "The dialectic of repetition is easy, for that which is repeated has been – otherwise it could not be repeated – but the very fact that it has been makes the repetition into something new" (Kierkegaard quoted in Gendron, 2008, 7).

Deleuze's concept of "passive synthesis" describes this perceptual difference in repetition (Deleuze, [1968] 1994, 70). Deleuze critiques Husserl's phenomenology a great deal as he does that of Kant and Hegel throughout

Repetition in music and literature   35

Difference and Repetition. If a melody is to be perceived in time, we must be able to retain some consciousness of previous notes and subsequently expect others, indicating consciousness of the not-present. Time and memory become the crucial factors of reception. If in the Berkeley sense ([1710] 2008), we must perceive in order to exist, does each perception bring about another existence? A motif might adumbrate another, prophesise the future, while with every repeat we travel "from the past to the future in the present" (Deleuze quoted in Latartara, 2011, 113). As John Latartara writes, when we listen to a piece of music, "the second statement, although physically identical, will be perceptually different from the first because the first statement is already retained in memory (past) and possible future statements of the same material generate anticipation (future)" (Latartara, 2011, 113).

In opposition to the negative forces of repetition found in Freudian concepts of regression and repression, Deleuze views repetition as "a creative activity of transformation", whereas "psychoanalysis limits repetition to representation" in attempting to cure and put an end to such re-enactments of trauma (Parr, 2005, 224). But who is right? As Adrian Parr writes: "Deleuze encourages us to repeat because he sees in it the possibility of reinvention, that is to say, repetition dissolves identities as it changes them, giving rise to something unrecognisable and productive. It is for this reason that he maintains that repetition is a positive power (*puissance*) of transformation" (Parr, 2005, 224–225). Further to this, Deleuze distinguishes between two distinct types of repetition, as Sarah Gendron explains:

> distinguishing between two types of repetition: "naked" or "mechanical" repetition that faithfully reproduces its original and "clothed" repetition – the Darwinian inspired variety … that distorts or adds to its original, creating difference from within. The difference between Deleuze's dual conceptualization of repetition and those who came before him is that the first form – "naked/mechanical" – is theorized as necessary for the sake of argument, in the sense that it sets up a relationship between an original or authentic element and a copy that seeks to duplicate it exactly. This form is nonetheless described as ultimately unattainable. The only possible repetition is therefore the "clothed" version which seeks to expose the difference that is inevitable (Gendron, 2008, 19).

Gendron describes how historical viewpoints on repetition have fluctuated from Plato's view that imitation was inherently "inferior", to Aristotle's positive spin on repetition, seeing it as an inbuilt part of human biology (Gendron, 2008, 16). Among repetition's more contemporary disparagers, following Freud, were both Jacques Attali and Frederic Jameson: Attali (1985) for what he saw as mass reproduction and standardisation (not unlike Adorno in some regards), while for Jameson "repetition effectively volatizes the original object" in commodification (quoted in Rose, 1994, 71). Tricia

36 *Repetition in music and literature*

Rose rightly argues that such a negative standpoint misses a great deal in the wide-ranging phenomenon that is repetition, that it "marginalizes and erases alternative uses" and identities (Rose, 1994, 72), such as negating the cultural capital of black music. She also puts forward African American music as the primary innovator of music that "identifies" positively with repetition. Yes, African developments utilise repetition extensively, but Rose's reliance on James A. Snead's declaration that Western music historically "secrets" repetition is flawed. While Snead (1981) and indeed Christopher Small (1987) successfully outline many of the cultural differences between Western and African traditions, an essentialist dichotomy between linear Western and a "deliberately" circular African music is tenuous. Gendron on the other hand recognises the fact that circularity goes far beyond one tradition, and in many ways the apotheosis that repetition underwent in the twentieth century was the result of a long cultural journey. She visualises various forms of repetition over time in terms of particular shapes, in fact: circles (The Eternal Return, the Egyptian Ouroboros, Neolithic burial mounds like Newgrange and solstice traditions, Buddhist beliefs in reincarnation, feasts, and farming practice, orbits, days and seasons); lines (Christian and Jewish teleology); and spirals (Hindustani philosophy). Gendron writes:

> As theorizations of repetition have evolved over time, so too has the shape one imagines them to embody. As previously stated, in Hindu philosophy, time is understood to be comprised of repetitive spirals. In Greco-roman thought, the dominant symbol of duration was that of the circle falling back upon itself in a self-seeking, self-absorbed way. Judeo-Christian belief systems flattened and straightened out the circle by theorizing linear interpretations of history. The 19th and 20th century thought of Kierkegaard, Nietzsche, and Deleuze, combined both ways of conceiving of duration, thereby bestowing on repetition the possibility of producing difference. Rather than closing back upon itself, the Eternal Return, by the addition of an "imperceptible difference", is thrown off center and propelled in another direction. While it may be propelled onward, upward, backward, even Beckett's preferred "worstward", what remains constant is that it is always propelled away from itself. The insistence on repetition with difference by Kierkegaard, Nietzsche, and Deleuze – again, despite the differences in how they choose to articulate the Eternal Return – represents, therefore, a departure from both Occidental cyclical and linear theorizations of duration and a return to ancient Oriental celebrations of cyclical growth, flow, movement, and deviation. The prevailing symbol is now – and again – that of the spiral.
>
> (Gendron, 2008, 12–13)

One might even compare such a visualisation of a straight line with the Adornian view of Modernism's need for a continually challenging new, and

Repetition in music and literature   37

the spiral perhaps as reflective of postmodern pastiche and the thought of Lyotard and Derrida, but such a course is outside of the scope of this chapter. Another avenue might include exploring the connections between Lacanian and Barthesian discussions of the loss inherent in *jouissance* and *signifiance* in relation to the transformative powers of repetition (see Middleton, 1983). As we shall see later, the spiralling world of Beckett's texts questions the very notion of the "original", as characters and themes consistently return inter-textually, from work to work.

Repetition in music

As a "*puissance* of transformation", repetition is fundamental to music. It enables structures, development, form, rhythm, tempo, pulse, metre, functional harmony and, at the most basic level, music itself.[6] Tonal music needs repetition in order to exist. With only twelve notes in a chromatic scale, repetition is an obvious necessity for melodic drive, serialist composition and many forms of music from other cultures. Operating both at a macro, formal or structural level and at the micro level of single repeats, there are many ways in which repetition is employed in music. Take for example the most widely known example of motivic development, the four-note motif that begins Beethoven's Fifth Symphony (1808). This raw material is transparently played out, composed through, for the remainder of the movement, being repeated in many guises until its original declamatory statement becomes a complex and multifaceted discourse. Repetitions of phrases or motifs can be transposed, inverted, appear in retrograde presented with different instrumentation, different attack, or dynamic, or even used to form new variant motifs, as in fugue. In the nineteenth century, sonata form became the ultimate paradigm of repetition with development: the original second subject returning in a triumphant tonic transposition during the recapitulation.

Antiphonal music, the call and response of liturgical music, in which a phrase sung solo or by a choir is repeated back by the congregation, shares a focus on repetition with binary and ternary forms, like the rondo, minuet, scherzo and trio (the third movement of Beethoven's Seventh Symphony (1812) is an extended trio – ABABA).[7] From the *tutti ritornello* in the Baroque concerto, interspersed with episodes of increasing virtuosity by the soloists making each return more emphatic than the last as familiarity builds a level of assurance and closure, to large-scale fugues (the first movement of Bartok's *Music for String Instruments, Percussion and Celeste* (1936), for instance) and canons (themselves repeated *ad nauseam* at countless weddings and graduations in the case of Pachelbel), it is clear that repetition is the prime catalyst of the tonal Western art music tradition. It is therefore obvious why Schenker would claim that repetition was the "most striking characteristic" of music. The "transformation" brought about by musical repetition is often transparent (for Steve Reich, a "process" especially deliberate).

38   *Repetition in music and literature*

Adam Ockelford goes further, proclaiming: "the source of perceived musical order lies ultimately in repetition" (Ockelford, 2005, 21). For Ockelford, it is deciding which repetition is "structurally salient" and determining the very "nature of that significance (in different listening contexts)" that amounts to "the principal challenge facing the analyst" (Ockelford, 2005, 34–35). Ockelford's formulation of zygonic theory, wherein the "interspective relationships through which imitative order is perceived", does much to explore how layers of repetitions interweave structurally.

Repetition, then, can be used to various ends: it can have a narrative role and can gain great importance – leitmotifs in Wagnerian opera, and film music, the *Jaws* motif for instance. The music can adumbrate the action – we know the shark is coming before the characters do – but it can also contradict the action – Eisenstein's cognitive dissonance. In Wagner's music, motifs are developed, juxtaposed, combined and transposed, all with narrative significance. Ruth Katz and Carl Dahlhaus suggest that the time-based nature of music is the very thing that brings repetition to life. Lessing's temporal categorisation of music holds in this regard:

> If repetition was "nothing but repetitions, nothing but 'the same thing over and over and over …' it would be incomprehensible how they could pre-empt so much space in statements intended to be meaningful. From the point of view of the tones, they are precisely this: the same thing again and again and again … But music is not only tone; it is tone and time. Tones may repeat themselves; time cannot repeat itself.
>
> (Katz, 1992, 726)

This concept of "tone and time" concerns the listening perceiver, the reception of the music. As Leonard Meyer wrote, musical repetition "never exists psychologically" – we never quite hear the same thing twice (Meyer cited in Ball, 2010, 125). Elizabeth Hellmuth Margulis does much to reveal the cognitive consequences of such listening practice from a scientific standpoint in her book *On Repeat: How Music Plays the Mind* (2013). Deleuzian repetition is also based on the limitations of time-based reality. For music to be new, it must engage with the past, converse with previous works, and participate in a vocabulary of signs and clichés that render it intelligible enough to adhere to the value criteria of what is perceived as "new". T. S. Eliot's "Tradition and the Individual Talent" ([1919] 2005) and Harold Bloom's *Anxiety of Influence* ([1973] 1997) interrogate the complex conversation between sameness and originality, the canon and the revolutionary work, repetition and difference. The threat of history always remains as composers and writers struggle to create something original while at the same time engaging with their context and place within a tradition of work – the ten years it took Brahms to write his first symphony under Beethoven's shadow, or Beckett's struggle to escape that of Joyce.

For Deleuze, repetitions are inextricably linked with difference, an interdependent relationship of past and present, old and new. Jeremy Begbie

Repetition in music and literature 39

posits that the "relations of sameness would appear to play a more crucial role than relations of difference" in music (Begbie, 2000, 156). Do the scales of Deleuze's symbiotic relationship seem a little heavy on the sameness side in music, though? Begbie writes: "This bias towards repetition need not, then, be seen as the enemy of newness (in the sense of the unprecedented, different from what has gone before); rather repetition serves to highlight the ever-new variegated material matrix which music 'rides'" (Begbie, 2000, 164). Peter Kivy, as mentioned previously, views repetition as a didactic tool, whereby the listener is given help in order to "grasp" the musical material, a guiding hand that itself becomes the very musical structure itself:

> Repeats not only allow the listener time to "grasp" the ideas given, they also provide a fabric of sound that should not be altered: "repetition is the means of grasping pattern; but, by definition, pattern is that very repetition, and to dispense with the remainder after it has been grasped would be to dispense with *it*, whereas *it*, the *pattern*, is the whole point of the exercise.
>
> (Kivy, 1993, 353, original emphasis)

We've already problematised this terminology, but the notion of repetitions allowing the listener to "grasp" the ideas or patterns within music is also part of a larger question that asks what the matter of "attention" really is. Surely listening is much more complicated than simply grasping and not grasping, understanding and misunderstanding; there exists instead a plane of comprehension. In any case, it is heavily debated as to whether there is indeed ever a single "right" way of understanding a work of art. Oscar Wilde, for instance, believed that the more interpretations a work enabled, the better the work, and certainly this is central to a work's longevity and survival; it is through each new audience's engagement with the text coming from their own context that brings about a new staging or interpretation of *Hamlet* (Wilde, [1891] 1997b, 965–1016).

Of course, it is not the case that simply anything goes in terms of interpretation – consider the famous Wittgensteinian duckrabbit. The image may clearly be interpreted as a duck or a rabbit, and either would be a justified intelligible and informed interpretation (Best, 1980, 126). It could not, however, be justifiably interpreted as a cello – as David Best writes, there is "an indefinite but not unlimited possibility of valid or intelligible interpretation" (Best, 1980, 126). If meaning itself is impossible to pin down, can repetition really be considered an important aspect of enabling the listener to "grasp" or comprehend the material?[8] If so, is this repeated, reinforced understanding the listener's own individual construct, somebody else's, or a combination of both? Programme notes, reviews, liner notes and critical views aside, when a listener hears a repeat, might we be certain that the fact that there is a repetition in the first place suggests that this note, or series of notes, requires more attention or focus?

40 *Repetition in music and literature*

As a means of differentiating between short motivic riff-based repeats and larger architectonic, structural ones, Richard Middleton formulated the terms *musematic* and *discursive* repetitions. He writes:

> Musematic repetition is the repetition of short units; the most immediately familiar examples – riffs – are found in Afro-American musics and in rock. Discursive repetition is the repetition of longer units, at the level of the phrase (defined as a unit roughly equivalent to a verbal clause or short sentence) ... The effects of the two types are usually very different, largely because the units differ widely in the amount of information and the amount of self-contained "sense" they contain, and in their degree of involvement with other syntactic processes. Moreover, musematic repetition is far more likely to be prolonged and unvaried, discursive repetition to be mixed in with contrasting units of various types (as in the AABA structure of the classic Tin Pan Alley ballad form). The former therefore tends towards a one-levelled structural effect, the latter to a hierarchically ordered discourse.
>
> (Middleton, 1983, 238).

Middleton's categorisations will be further extended as I employ my own taxonomy of repetition in relation to Beckett's later prose in Chapter 4.

Repetition in experimental music

Minimalist music brought with it the apotheosis of repetition: repetition for itself. Steve Reich wrote of "the gradual process" (Reich, [1968] 2002) in his music, while the structural units of repetition in Philip Glass' work take priority over melody.[9] Of course, the term minimalism brings with it certain pejorative connotations[10], Terry Riley and La Monte Young seemed most comfortable with the term, but the respective evolving compositional aesthetics of the so-called minimalist composers are so various and idiosyncratic that the term has a tenuous definition at times. Dan Warburton maintains that although the term "minimalism" is far from perfect, it is the best available, and there are certainly worse terms in use.[11] The minimalist canon rests, for Keith Potter, with the "four giants" of minimalism: Young, Riley, Glass and Reich (Potter, 2002), the same four that Michael Nyman's pioneering study focused upon (Nyman, [1974] 1999). Repetition is arguably the salient feature that connects and binds the approaches of these Americans together. What is striking in Nyman's study is his suggestion that, far from being the product of Americans hiding their heads in the sand, rather than face the European avant-garde, the "origins of this minimal process music lie in serialism" (Nyman, [1974] 1999, 139).[12] Webern's technique of "repeating pitches at the same register" would greatly influence Young, as did his method of stacking chords in static fashion (Potter, 2002, 44). Webern once wrote that "development is also a kind of repetition" (Webern quoted in Prieto, 2002a,

Repetition in music and literature   41

57), recognising its centrality to structural intelligibility. The antagonistic position towards repetition found in serialism, however, meant that no note could repeat until the other eleven had been played, the very notion of repetition or avoidance of it being paramount, an "anxiety of influence" in Modernist Europe (Bloom, [1973] 1997).

Potter has even suggested that Cage, another important influence on Young and Riley, was a "proto-minimalist" on account of his focus on rhythm and repetition rather than pitch as the organising principle of his early pre-indeterminate works, though Cage later positioned himself in vehement opposition to what he termed the "fascist" post-minimalism of Glenn Branca's guitar ensembles (Potter, 2002, 4).[13] Repetition in modern music was clearly a site for healthy debate.

In many ways, the high and low art dichotomy started to crumble in the downtown New York of the 1960s, as Andy Warhol, The Velvet Underground, Tony Conrad, Glass and Reich infused their work with repetition. Lou Reed wrote "The Ostrich" while a staff songwriter for Pickwick Records in 1964, an experimental popular song written with all the guitar strings tuned to a single note. John Cale, hired to perform this piece, noticed the similarities between what Reed was doing and the music he was performing with La Monte Young in the Theatre of Eternal Music – Cale soon joined Reed in the formation of The Velvet Underground.[14] For some, the repetitious qualities of minimalism evoked a corporeal sensuality – while other critics found Glass' music detached from emotion and "cool" (Greenaway, 1983), a result of the performers in the Philip Glass Ensemble's belief in the need to remove all expression – vibrato for instance – from their playing in order to let the music work (Greenaway, 1983). The removal of individual passionate expression enables the dense fabric of the music to operate clearly. With the bodily connotations affiliated to repetitive rhythms, the influence of African drumming and Balinese gamelan on Reich and Glass meant that they, like pop musicians from Muddy Waters to Elvis, could not escape being branded with the "devil's music" pitchfork of middle-class white America and beyond. In some ways blues, jazz, dance and rock – pop music – offer an interesting dichotomy with minimalism – the "accessible" high art music for the commercial public, as some labelled it.[15] Young and Riley were also particularly close to the jazz world; Riley's modal approach owed much to Coltrane's explorations. In "Poppy Nogood and the Phantom Band" (1969), Riley experimented with tapes and overdubs of his sax playing alongside influences from one of his other passions, Indian classical music.

While the tape technology that Riley employed on "Poppy Nogood and the Phantom Band" was primitive and expensive, with technological advancements, looping and sampling became available to the masses rather than just Institut de Recherche et Coordination Acoustique/Musique (IRCAM) alumni, and record studios. Riley's Phantom Band, the tape, was soon available in a cheap looper, sampler or digital delay pedal. The huge impact that loop pedals have had in modern music ranges from the innovations of

42 *Repetition in music and literature*

guitarists Bill Frisell and Nels Cline, the live manipulations of Colleen, the additive soundscapes of Dustin Wong and Noveller, to the avantpop of Low. But what should we make of the recent trend towards the use of loops in music? Technology plays a huge role in the development of new music: as the parameters are expanded, new technology inspires musical innovations; they may even be "imagined into existence", as Jason Toynbee writes:

> Technology and the social and cultural are always imbricated. Technology is never just selected, rather it is already a discursive formation ... technologies take off because they are congruent with an emerging aesthetic among musicians: they must literally be imagined into existence.
>
> (Toynbee, 2000, 99)

Keith Negus also recognises this fluidity when he writes: "[t]echnology has never been passive, neutral or natural. Music has for centuries been created through the interaction between 'art' and technology" (Negus, 1992, 31). Middleton sees it as a symbiotic relationship – "[t]echnology and music technique, content and meaning generally develop together, dialectically (Middleton, 1990, 90). Middleton equates such looping as the manifestation of the end of history: "The rise to prominence of digitalised sampling and looping techniques – 'borrowing' as a multi-faceted principle – can be regarded as a symptom of a new paradigm, marked by an increased blurring of the distinction between musical work and musical field" (Middleton, 1996). As Deleuzian repetition blurs the boundary between the new and old, the same and different, authorship too is called into question, especially when it comes to sampling and copyright.[16]

Noise music presents another relationship with repetition. Luigi Russolo recognised early on how the repetitive noises of the modern industrial world would inevitably infiltrate an art of that world (Russolo, [1913] 2001). Paul Hegarty suggests that at the heart of noise music is the quest for failure (Hegarty, 2009, 147). Is noise, then, a particularly Beckettian form of music? Hegarty's description of the form reminds us of Beckett's laments on the failures and inadequacies of language and of his famous statement in *Worstward Ho* to "fail better". This occurs at a much deeper level than simply trying to play things the "wrong" way, or at painful volumes. Japanese noise music in particular, Merzbow for instance, often sees performers either employing broken analogue equipment or breaking their equipment during performance. We have seen destruction on stage before of course – whether it was Hendrix setting his guitar alight or Pete Townshend smashing his; the destructive Romantic rock star seems very clichéd in the Spinal Tap sense nowadays, but beginning a performance with damaged equipment also brings to mind the lo-fi alternative music aesthetic of Pavement or Smog, or even Harry Partch's microtonal or "out-of-tune" instrument constructions. The construction of value through the fetishisation of fidelity has been a mainstay is popular music aesthetics from the "hiss" of vinyl to the

Repetition in music and literature 43

supposed "fakeness" of autotune. Technology often brings with it moral panic and stigma before initial "Judas" moments undergo a period of acclimatisation – the popularity of vocoders as a foreground instrument in current chart music is a case in point.

There is a balance between making the right mistakes in noise music and keeping the audience guessing. In a strange way the very striving for surprise, the avoidance of repetition and cliché, leads to much noise music being rather predictable – we usually get what we expect, a barrage of noise, an extremely loud, visceral wall of sound at some stage in the set or track. Like the drop in techno music, the climactic noise peak (also in some cases embodying a Romantic self-expressive catharsis) is appreciated or at least willingly tolerated by the audience. That is not to say that noise music is easy to create; it requires the ability to set up the *right* accidents, for the performer to be at one with the technology, which is, according to current aesthetic trends, generally analogue in nature. Through the negation of repetition, noise music increases its unsettling and difficult qualities. The listener is left without Kivy's didactic repeats.

Still, even in noise music we sometimes hear repeats or recurrence – as Hegarty shows in K2's *Molekular Terrorism* (1996) (Hegarty, 2009, 141). Certain repetitive blocks of sound start to be perceived by the audience. Are these moments, as with the serendipitous parallelism of such early mash-ups as *Dark Side of the Rainbow*, a result of the psychological need of humans to find patterns and conversely filter out data that does not fit the pattern – a process termed apophenia?[17] We might mistakenly recognise a face on Mars in a chance arrangement of shadows, yet such pattern recognition was an important part of human evolution – face recognition having obvious social benefits. Noise is certainly changed upon second hearing; the music mutates or morphs for the listener, like subatomic particles for the onlooker. John Latartara employs spectrographic analytical methods in order to highlight such repetitions in the later work of Merzbow, alongside Oval and Kid 606 (Latartara, 2011). Repetition is, however, as rare in noise music as it is in free improvisation. To repeat in an improvised performance might fit the moment, but the idea of repeating wholesale what was done in a previous performance goes entirely against the aesthetic. As Fred Frith (2006) explains, discussing repetition in improvised music, "it's usually the wrong path, and turns out badly" to return to what may have worked in previous performances: it generally proves more successful to start afresh. Derek Bailey, a key pioneer of free improvisation, shares this notion of avoiding repetition, viewing such a negation as paramount to successful improvisation (Bailey, 1980). John Cage believed that recorded music – records – amounted to an abomination, not "real music", and that they actually work against "real music" (Cage in Greenaway, 1983). When we hear a recording, we absorb a particular interpretation, a fully loaded text, with far more parameters concretised than on any notated score. The timbre, dynamics and playing style are set on the recorded text, and any subsequent relationship with the piece, whether from a performer's or listener's perspective, will be influenced, even where negated, by the record. The "anxiety of

44   *Repetition in music and literature*

influence" of the record holds a heavier threat than the notated score. Cage joked about this in an anecdote relaying a child's response to a Stravinsky concert, conducted by Stravinsky – the child familiar with the record exclaimed "they're not playing it right" (Cage in Greenaway, 1983). Equating "authenticity" with "liveness" is not wholly satisfactory, though; while Simon Frith links rock music's rawness with the live spectacle for instance, this does act to stigmatise somewhat the affordance that technology has awarded since the early twentieth century. We no longer need to be in a room with a musician, or perform ourselves, in order to engage with music. The cultural capital of a constructed badge like "authenticity" is often more problematic than useful.

Hegarty suggests that although noise music might be a non-commercial, underground music, the fact that so many new records are being released in small limited runs, in an attempt to work against commoditisation, actually achieves the opposite. The collector may become obsessed, but can never actually possess all Merzbow records, for example (Hegarty, 2009, 141). At least it would take a great deal of time and expense to do so. One Merzbow record, *Noisembyro* (1994), was initially available as a limited edition of one, sealed inside a Mercedes-Benz that was wired to play the album when the engine started. The car went unsold and subsequently broke down, the record ultimately becoming available through other means. Hegarty suggests that contrarily this music becomes "an ultra-commodity, an ultra-fetish" (Hegarty, 2009, 142). It follows, that to "know" all the work would seem impossible. So, it seems the lack of repetition, a deliberate aesthetic approach in noise music, is manifested in the production, industrial side too, in a manner that Cage might have approved. But what of the listener who listens attentively to one Merzbow record continuously? The product, the notes, the music remain the same in the real sense (the record was only pressed once), but the reception of the music for the listener changes. Likewise, even in a performance context, if we stand for 90 minutes listening to a Merzbow gig or even a continuous record, the effect or impact of noise changes; some may even be lulled to sleep – as a baby is comforted by womb-like white noise.. So, even in noise and improvised music, repetition's grip is tight; those who attempt to avoid it are made keenly aware of its ubiquity.

Cage's conch shells piece, *Inlets* (1977), formulated perhaps the truest method of free improvisation; there is literally no way of predictably controlling what sounds the shell would produce when the performer moves it back and forth with the water inside (Cage in Greenaway, 1983, 38 minutes). Is not being able to predict the outcome of an instrument, the sound produced, no matter how much practice and research is done, or conscious effort, the true goal of free improvisation? Free jazz as a genre became anything but free, sounding consistently exactly like itself: free jazz. When we hear Ornette Coleman, we know it is him; the style is constitutive, no matter what you label it, in a similar way to how much noise music is representative of the genre. With Cage's conch shells do we get any further? What does the fact that deliberate repetition is consciously or subconsciously impossible mean for the music? Or does this just sound like a conch shell making random sounds, what Cage would perhaps want most, a music devoid of extramusical content? Such an aesthetic is mirrored today in Brian Eno's computerised experiments with randomised sound.

Joe Pass once said that "if you hit a wrong note, then make [it] right by what you play afterwards" (Pass quoted in Sudo, [1997] 1998, 54). Any note can be made right (tonally resolved or not), but if we repeat a mistake, the audience might also consider it deliberate. In this way, particularly in jazz, to repeat is to emphasise intent. If we consider this idea of intent in terms of Deleuzian repetition, the fact that the repeated note is inherently "different" from the first sounding is significant. To intend to transform the reception of a note through repeating it is a manifestation of Deluzian positive repetition. In the words of Adrian Parr, "in terms of discovery and experimentation; it [Deleuzian repetition] allows new experiences, affects and expressions to emerge" (Parr, 2005, 223). As already mentioned, in the traditional jazz context any note can technically be resolved; one can always "step out" as long as a "step in" occurs soon enough afterwards. You can in a sense make that "wrong" note a "right" one. More than simply masking an error, the error itself becomes transformed or legitimised, accepted and absorbed, understood, contextualised or "grasped" even, to use Kivy's term, through repetition. This operates in a similar manner to how scatological terms become cutifyed by parents while teaching their children about the world through mimesis and repetitive learning.

That dissonant note when heard again seems to sound more consonant, as the player can "turn a wince into a smile" (Sudo, [1997] 1998, 54). Likewise, for Stephen Dedalus, accidents act as "the portals of discovery" (Joyce, [1922] 2000, Ch. 9).[18] In improvisation, of course, there are mistakes and then there are *real* mistakes. Errors that fit the bill, that adhere to the socially constructed codes or rules of practice, differ from blatant blunders. Sometimes the way to succeed is through "better" failure.[19]

Repetitions in literature

At the macro level, the word "car" only represents that particular danger to cyclists because it is repeated enough times in English to take on that meaning. The relationship of the signifier (medium) to the signified (concept) is arbitrary, as de Saussure taught us. Without repetition there can be no affiliations or connotations of meaning. At the micro level, the repetition of a word in a poem can reinforce meaning, emphasise weight and importance, or bring about a particular aural effect. As Derrida puts this, "there is no word, nor in general a sign, which is not constituted by the possibility of repeating itself. A sign which does not repeat itself, which is not already divided by repetition in its 'first time', is not a sign" (Derrida, 1978, 213). In literature, words, like music, need to be repeated in order for these signifiers to represent anything in the first place.

46 *Repetition in music and literature*

Repetitions may not be as frequent in literature but they have always been important. Let us consider briefly the importance of rhyme and alliteration. Rhyming involves the repetition of word endings with similar sounds; the eighteenth-century rhyming couplet, as those found in Pope's *Dunciad* for instance:

> Maggots half-form'd in rhyme exactly meet,
> And learn to crawl upon poetic feet.
> (Pope, [1743] 2004, 170)

Alliteration involves the repetition of the first letter in a series of successive words. In a line from Edgar Allen Poe's poem "The Raven" (1845), for instance, – "Startled at the stillness broken by reply so aptly spoken" – "startled", "stillness" and "spoken" all repeat the "s" sound. Alliteration has been crucial in the stylistic history of poetry, structurally important in Old English, in texts like *Beowulf*, written in the eighth century, through fourteenth-century Middle English, like *Sir Gawain and the Green Knight*, to contemporary lyrical poetry such as the work of Seamus Heaney.

In alliterative verse, the dominant form for Anglo-Saxon poets, alliteration is the crucial structural device rather than rhyme or metre. *Beowulf* exhibits this clearly as each line is composed around words that begin with the same letter, in this case "h" and "m":

> to bid his henchmen a hall uprear,
> ia master mead-house, mightier far
> (Gummere trans., [1910] 2008, 7)

Alliterative verse continued to be an important structural device in Middle English. Was this repetitive alliteration an aid to memory, in a society in which stories were transmitted orally? Did it help listeners to "grasp" the material?

Refrains employ the repetition of whole sentences or phrases in poetry. In Yeats' "September 1913" (Yeats, 1990) the famous refrain "Romantic Ireland's dead and gone / It's with O'Leary in the grave" repeats and ends every stanza. But single words can also be repeated as refrains. The raven from Poe's poem recites the word "nevermore" at the end of each stanza that follows his arrival. Here one word repeats while others rhyme with the bird's utterence:

> But the Raven, sitting lonely on the placid bust, spoke only
> That one word, as if his soul in that one word he did outpour.
> Nothing farther then he uttered – not a feather then he fluttered –
> Til I scarcely more than muttered "Other friends have flown before –
> On the Morow *he* will leave me, as my Hopes have flown before."
> Then the bird said "Nevermore".
> (Poe, 1845, in Ferguson, Salter and Stallworthy eds, 1996, 882)

Repetition in music and literature 47

The repetitions of the internal rhyme (lonely/only – uttered/fluttered/muttered) are also clear in this stanza, as is the rhyming scheme of ABCBBB. Rhythm and metre themselves are also, of course, repetitive in nature. The rhythm of the poem is trochaic, while the metre is, according to Poe himself, "octameter acatalectic, alternating with heptameter catalectic repeated in the *refrain* of the fifth verse, and terminating with tetrameter catalectic" (Poe, 1846, 166). Poe's repetitions would greatly influence Mallarmé. Helen Abbott discusses this mysterious quality that the Symbolists sought in the "variant refrain" (as opposed to the "fixed" exact refrain) through the process of "unexpected returns" (Abbott, 2009, 207–219). The altered rhyming of "fluttered" and "uttered" or of "feather" and "farther", for instance, from the same line above in "The Raven", resonate an echo of previous material but with subtle differences, as opposed to the fixed "nevermore". Mary Breatnach sees Mallarmé's interest in music as part of a turn towards the intangible, and works like "Un coup de dés" (1897) certainly show a poet less concerned with explicit meaning, and instead experimenting with the medium and form (Breatnach, 1996, 28).

Images and themes are also repeated in various ways in literature; Shakespeare repeats the idea of loss in various ways throughout Sonnet 30 for instance, while in Dylan Thomas' fine example of villanelle cyclical structure, "Do not go gentle into that good night" (1951), the first and third lines of the first stanza alternate as the closing lines of each successive stanza, while the last stanza ends with both:

> Good men, the last wave by, crying how bright
> Their frail deeds might have danced in a green bay,
> Rage, rage against the dying of the light.
> Wild men who caught and sang the sun in flight,
> And learn, too late, they grieved it on its way,
> Do not go gentle into that good night.
> (Thomas, 1951, in Ferguson, Salter
> and Stallworthy eds, 1996, 1465–1466)

The word "rage" forms a repeating couplet in the recurring line "Rage, rage against the dying of the light", also appearing earlier in the first stanza – here the anger of the poet in the face of inevitable death is torturously evoked with each repetitive plea. While in Ginsberg's "Howl" (1956), the word "who" repeatedly punctuates the beginning of each sentence (anaphora), giving an ostinato-like rhythm to the poem:

> who got busted in their public beards returning through Laredo with a
> belt of marijuana for New York
> who ate fire in paint hotels or drank turpentine in Paradise Alley, death
> or purgatoried their torsos night after night.
> (Ginsberg, 1956, in Ferguson, Salter and Stallworthy eds, 1996, 1599)

48 *Repetition in music and literature*

From sonnets, stanzas, couplets, triplets, ballads, to songs and alliterative verse, rhetorical devices like anaphora, epistrophe and anadiplosis, repetition, then, holds important large-scale structural and small-scale stylistic roles in literature.

In *Repetition and Semiotics: Interpreting Prose Poems* (1986), Stamos Metzidakis writes: "[t]he new is always seen in terms of the old, the unknown in terms of the known. Repetition is that process which allows the reader to grasp any meaning whatsoever" (Metzidakis, 1986, 2). Metzidakis believes that repetition brings with it understanding. Here again, like in Kivy, we have repetition being understood as a route to comprehension, a means of enabling the reader to "grasp" the material. But Metzidakis later concedes that with the developments of Deleuze and Derrida, alongside the now unconcretised "author" (Barthes, Lacan, Kristeva, Foucault), the reader's relationship towards the material has become far more complex (Metzidakis, 1986, 12). One can strive towards definitive interpretations of a poem, like music, but they are inevitably unachievable. There are simply too many variables involved to, as Metzidakis describes, "pinpoint such an imagined individual" (Metzidakis, 1986, 12).

Repetition in literature enables structural unity but it also allows Proustian memories, echoes, and in the Deleuzian sense what Bloom calls "recollecting forward", quoting Kierkegaard (Metzidakis, 1986, 14). Repetitions in literature, like music, can foreshadow future events. The "future present" is engaged in the time we take to read the temporal form of a poem or novel, or indeed sit to watch a play. We compare the specific differences in what we perceive in relation to what we have experienced before, while these new repetitions become the recollections of future experiences.

But what are the contrasting factors in the use of repetition in words and music? The difference in the conventions of employment of repetition between music and literature is of particular interest here. Put simply, the scale of tolerance is different. George Bernard Shaw made the observation that though repetition occurs in both music and literature, we the reader/listener accept separate thresholds of each (Shaw cited in Meisel, 1963, 41). Language requires more new material while music allows the use of more abundant repetitions and variations – transpositions, retrogrades, and so forth. Shaw suggests that in opera, the music can repeat the same phrase in multiple ways in a perfectly acceptable fashion; it is the sustenance of the intended feeling and its development through time that is important. Literature, on the other hand, must vary its language and ideas in order to hold interest: where Wagner can repeat "Tristan" twenty times, Shakespeare cannot have twenty lines consisting of the single word "Romeo" (Shaw cited in Meisel, 1963, 41).

Calvin Brown devoted a chapter (albeit a brief one) to the question of repetition and variation in both music and literature (Brown, 1948, 100–114). Like Shaw, Brown recognised the respective supposed rules governing the employment and acceptability of repetitions in both arts. He writes: "The general principles of repetition are much the same in music and in literature,

Repetition in music and literature 49

but there is a conspicuous difference in degree. In general, music demands far more repetition than poetry can tolerate" (Brown, 1948, 109). As Carolyn Abbate writes:

> Verbal repetition on a small scale is often read as a degradation of language, as a sign of a flattened self, as something to be feared, struggled against: as uncanny ... Repetition in *music* is as manifold as repetition in language, yet it tends to be accorded a higher value. In music, small- and large-scale recurrence is generally read as a fundamental means of coherence ... Music will bear far more repetition than any literary art – a thousand times more.
>
> (Abbate, 1996, 176, original emphasis)

But why this increased tolerance in music? For Brown, the abundance of repetition in music is first due to the relatively young age of music (Brown's understanding) as a discrete discipline compared to literature, and he believed such differences in the employment of repetition may become less apparent over time. He writes:

> [t]he repeat-marks often found in sonata-form ... are often ignored in present-day performance. Also, later composers seem not only to specify less of this formal repetition, but to repeat themselves in general somewhat less than did their predecessors. If this tendency continues, and if literature remains stable in this respect, five centuries from now the difference in the use of repetition in music and literature may be far less striking than it is now.
>
> (Brown, 1948, 113)

The claim that music is a younger discipline is somewhat tenuous, if we consider Steven Mithen's recent work *The Singing Neanderthals* ([2005] 2006), which offers persuasive conjecture on the primitive evolution of music and language from a possible Neanderthal hybrid medium. Writing in 1948, however, Brown could not have foreseen the huge importance that repetition would have in the new music that we have been documenting so far in this chapter. His theory does hold for the development from standards in jazz towards improvised music, however. Prior to the Historically Informed Performance (HIP) movement of the 1980s onwards, performers indeed often ignored the repeats in sonatas; in the same way that Shakespeare's songs were often omitted or swapped around between plays until recently, as directors became more informed and conscientious. Such instances generally resulted from an underestimation of their value to narrative function, mood-setting and formal coherence, something that recent developments in performance studies – Kivy, Dreyfus, Rifkin, McCreesh – have worked to rectify.

The second reason for such a tolerance of repetition in music, that Brown suggests, is the importance of repetition as a large-scale structural

50 *Repetition in music and literature*

compositional tool in music. He suggests that repetition has long been the basis for composition; a composer would begin with a motive, phrase or idea and then work through the music with repetitions, retrogrades, transpositions, recapitulations and so on, and that the literary author would proceed in a different manner (Brown, 1948, 111). Brown's idea of repetition seems particularly vague here, however. As we will explore later, repetition works differently at various structural levels, be they local or discursive. My analysis in Chapter 4 instead proposes a taxonomy of distinct forms of repetition.

But is there a more convincing reason for this scale of tolerance? The semantic content of words, the signification of specifics renders the insistent repetition of such materials boring or redundant in a relatively short period, it might be posited. Does the lack of clear representation in the content allow music more reworking of the materials? For Jeremy Begbie, the "relations of sameness would appear to play a more crucial role than relations of difference" in music (Begbie, 2000, 156). Similarly, Edward T. Cone believes there is no such thing as redundancy in music (Cone cited in Begbie, 2000, 162). Here we must clarify that redundancy in this respect refers to the idea of "boredom" rather than the Leonard B. Meyer use of the word "redundancy", which he describes as a pervasive and necessary repetition of musical material in order to achieve cohesion (Meyer, [1967] 1994, 277). It would seem that the pejorative qualities of the word "redundancy" being applied by Meyer to such an important feature of music is the issue here for Cone, and perhaps rightly so.

If sameness is important to music, it is because of the temporal nature of music described by Dahlhaus earlier. Theatre is traditionally closer to music than novels in this regard, being temporally directed. Peter Kivy differentiates between different types of time ("interrupted" and "continuous") in music, as does Max Paddison in his work on Adorno's Bergsonian division of time into "interpretative experience" (*Erfahrung*) and "lived experience" (*Erlebnis*).[20] Gérard Genette (1979), along similar lines, divided time into "discourse time" and "narrative time". To read a novel can take more or less time than the narrative itself takes to play out – *Ulysses*, for instance, takes place in the course of a single day, yet many never reach the end of the book, or if they do, it almost certainly takes more than twenty-four hours to complete (certain Bloomsday challenges notwithstanding): the "discourse time" in this case outweighs the "narrative time". We do not have to read a novel at a particular speed, with certain dynamics, or even in a specific order – much like how recording technology has changed the way listeners have developed new modes of listening. Literary modernism did much to deconstruct such restrictions of the realist novel, Cortázar's *Hopscotch* (1966), with its open form,[21] or the cyclical nature of Joyce's *Finnegans Wake*, in which the final sentence links back to the first in a continuous stream, a running river of endless reading, inspired by Vico's cyclical theory.

Musical repetition also allows a spatial depth that literature does not have. Contrapuntal textures cannot be represented on the page – Joyce's famous

Repetition in music and literature 51

attempt at a *fuga per canonem* during the "Sirens" episode of *Ulysses*, mentioned previously, is a fabulously ornate series of sounds, including an operatic overture at the start that contains all the materials to be worked through in the chapter. It is not, however, contrapuntal; each word follows another. We simply cannot read interwoven and layered worded text simultaneously. It would be wrong to say that Joyce failed in his attempt at textual counterpoint; it is a beautiful *metaphor* of fugue in a musicalised fiction, but a single line all the same.

There is a point at which repetition ceases to reinforce an idea or meaning, and instead begins to deconstruct it. This is sometimes called "semantic saturation" or "semantic satiation". As John Kuonios, Sonja A. Kotz and Philip J. Holcomb (2000, 1377) observe in their study of brain processes and semantic transformation, the destabilisation of word meaning through repetition is analogous to that of a retinal image as it starts to disappear.

It is at this later stage that Beckett's late work operates. As Ruby Cohn observed: "[i]n his verse and fiction of the 1930s he [Beckett] anchors an order in repetition, but from 1949 to 1976 he seems to erode order through the relentlessness of repetition, which is one of his ways 'to find a form that accommodates the mess'" (Cohn, 1980, 96). This "eroding" through repetition would continue after 1976, until Beckett's death in 1989 (Cohn's book was published in 1980). Indeed Beckett's arrangement of musical repetition would become much more complex in his later prose, no more so than *Ill Seen Ill Said* ([1981] 1997). Whereas in *Murphy*, as we'll see in the next chapter, the music is still relatively "intelligible", the repetitive nature of Beckett's later prose employs the "inexplicable" (Beckett, [1931] 1999, 92) nature of music towards providing a method of writing a "non-specific" text without clear meaning (Reid, 1968, 34). In his later prose exact meaning erodes, to use Cohn's term, through the use of repetition.

Notes

1 For more on transmedial theory see Wolf (2009).
2 Brian Hulse, "A Deleuzian Take on Repetition, Difference, and the 'Minimal' in Minimalism", available at www.operascore.com/files/Repetition_and_Minimalism. pdf [accessed 15 August 2013].
3 Graham, Daniel W., "Heraclitus", in *The Stanford Encyclopaedia of Philosophy* (Summer 2011 Edition), Edward N. Zalta ed., http://plato.stanford.edu/archives/ sum2011/entries/heraclitus [accessed 15 August 2013].
4 See Nietzsche, The *Gay Science* (1882) and *Thus Spake Zarathustra* (1891).
5 Anon (n.d.), "Gilles Deleuze (1925–1995)".
6 An exploration and contrasting study of metre, repetition and rhythm is outside of the scope of this book – my arguments keep to repetition as device, but for more problematisation see Christopher Hasty's *Meter as Rhythm* (1997).
7 The antiphonal nature of Caribbean and African musics and their ongoing influence on popular music is discussed by Tricia Rose in *Black Noise* (1994).
8 See Wimsatt and Beardsley (1954) and Roland Barthes ([1967] 1977b).
9 Philip Glass in Peter Greenaway's documentary *Four American Composers* (1983).

52 *Repetition in music and literature*

10 For more on the problems behind the taxonomy of minimalism, see Dan Warburton, "A Working Terminology for Minimal Music" at www.paristransatlantic.com/magazine/archives/minimalism.html [accessed 14 August 2013].
11 *Ibid.*
12 Of course there were many American serialists; Riley himself even studied and wrote some early twelve-tone pieces under the supervision of Leonard Stein at Los Angeles City College, where Stein was at one point an assistant to Schoenberg.
13 Ironically, some German critics would also call Reich's music fascist.
14 The term ostrich tuning has since described this practice of tuning many strings to a single note, enabling repetitive drones, and has been employed by post-minimalists such as New York composer Rhys Chatham, in compositions such as *Die Donnergotter*, (1987).
15 Middleton discusses the repetitive nature of chart pop songs and the verse–chorus format in "Play it Again Sam" (1983).
16 See Hesmondhalgh (2006).
17 For more on "apophany", see Conrad (1959).
18 The quote is: "A man of genius makes no mistakes. His errors are volitional and are the portals of discovery."
19 The famous Beckett quote – "Ever tried. Ever failed. No matter. Try Again. Fail again. Fail better" – occurs in *Worstward Ho* (1983c).
20 See the contributions by Paddison (2004) and Kivy (2004) in the special issue of *Musicae Scientiae* devoted to time.
21 Umberto Eco's (1989) concept of the "Open Work" is central here.

3 Musico-literary interaction in modern Ireland and the musical aesthetic of Samuel Beckett

Ireland in the early twentieth century was a hive of musico-literary invention. While Yeats was composing a verbal music that encompassed the song traditions of Ireland, many Irish authors working in the early twentieth century proclaimed a great interest in art music: Synge initially intended to be a composer but was financially thwarted; Shaw, who began his career as a London music critic, brought his extensive musical knowledge to his plays and viewed himself as a direct successor to Wagner – the "perfect Wagnerite" even, manifesting itself most clearly in his "play of ideas".[1] Joyce was an accomplished tenor, once appearing on the same bill as John McCormack. He was simultaneously documenting a bygone musical Dublin, most notably in "The Dead", while also developing texts that employed multiple musical devices, filling both *Ulysses* and *Finnegans Wake* with leitmotifs, operatic references, ballads and even an attempt at a fugue in prose (the structure of which has recently proven to have been taken from the second edition of Grove's *Dictionary of Music and Musicians*).[2] It is no coincidence that it is in the chapter entitled "Proteus" that we find Stephen Dedalus pondering upon Lessing's categories, *Nebeneinander* and *Nacheinander*. Ovid was a favourite of the Modernists and metamorphosis a liberating idea, a breath of fresh air from Lessing-esque aesthetic purism. Joyce's art was protean to its very core and encyclopaedic in its scope. The "Sirens" chapter of *Ulysses*, though historically the subject of intense debate and ranking up there amongst the most prevalent areas in the vast mountain of literature written on Joyce, displays categorically the writer's predilection for intermedial art.

But Beckett would go further than any of his precursors. He praised the music-like immediacy of expression in *Finnegans Wake* as "not to be read – or rather it is not only to be read. It is to be looked at and listened to" (Beckett, [1929] 1983a, 27). Joyce's musical text was, for Beckett, not "*about* something; it *is* that something itself" ([1929] 1983a, 27). In developing the non-representational musical text, Beckett would, as we will see, take Irish verbal music to a whole new realm. His music would, like Modernist music, be a difficult one to comprehend; it would provide his work with the mysterious "inexplicable" quality that he wanted to achieve but still maintain a certain intelligibility (Beckett [1931] 1999, 92). His reading of Schopenhauer's

54 *Musico-literary interaction in Ireland*

philosophy of music encouraged him to go beyond the employment of musical technique as superficial device; instead, his art of the "non-specific" could be enabled through invoking the non-referential qualities of music (Reid, 1968. 34).

Harry White's study of the phenomenon of Irish musicians-turned-writers suggests that the creative focus on literature, rather than on art music, in Ireland was the result of negative cultural-nationalism during the early twentieth century and a lack of educational infrastructure. The attitude of public figures like Richard Henebry, for instance, who maintained that "the more we foster modern music the more we help to silence our own" (quoted in White, 2008, 5) created a culture in which new music was shunned in favour of traditional folk music (or trad), which became increasingly audible in Irish culture. The reluctance to embrace the musical trends that were seizing Europe, however, had a significant impact on the Irish literary style. White theorises that a silent art music in Ireland, a country "entirely absent from the 'imaginary museum of musical works'", using Lydia Goehr's metaphor, found its voice within literature (White, 2008, 3). He suggests that the absence of a significant art music tradition resulted in the integration of musical ideas and concepts into Irish literature at a deep structural level. In fact, White claims that, during the 1890s, literature was utilising music to such an extent that "a verbal understanding of music (and of Irish music in particular) as the unheard melody of the literary imagination attained far more significance than music itself" (White, 2008, 6). Initially then, the cultural-nationalistic role of traditional music appears to dominate both Irish society and its literature; and yet there appears to be a hidden desire for the more European strains of the art music tradition, a desire that is fulfilled in hitherto coded, or secret, ways. But do Beckett's musical texts solely reflect this Keatsian silenced Irish art music tradition, or was there also another aesthetic reason developing in his late work, an aesthetic that many Modernists shared to some degree?

Joyce and Beckett exhibited an affinity for music that resonated with many of their international counterparts to some extent – Pound and Eliot were also experimenting with musical ideas, for instance. In *Listening In: Music, Mind, and the Modernist Narrative* (2002a), Eric Prieto suggests that the Modernists, although divergent in their musical aesthetics, all held the view that music enabled the expression of consciousness. It follows that, as the Irish narrative moved away from objective realism to interior discourse, music was able to assume great structural importance. The ability of Irish literature to harbour musicality, then, was not only culturally conditioned but also historically contingent.

The complex nature of Beckett's musical aesthetic illustrates this phenomenon of music and literature interaction in Irish Modernism particularly well. While Prieto situates Beckett in France, locating the author's place in the Parisian avant-garde, it is also important to recognise the writer's position in a line of Irish writers who engaged with musical ideas. Beckett, therefore,

Musico-literary interaction in Ireland   55

provides us with a useful window through which we can explore the theoretical issues and questions posed by Word and Music Studies.

Beckett was a writer preoccupied with musical ideas. He employed musical devices and techniques progressively throughout his career, but in a more fundamental way he questioned the very nature of music more than any of his contemporaries. The study of music in Beckett's work has attracted notable scholarly attention. Vivian Mercier was somewhat ahead of his time when, in 1977, he noted how "Beckett's visual awareness, developed so cerebrally and almost painfully, could never match his aural awareness, developed so early and, relatively speaking, unconsciously" (Mercier, 1977, 114). Mary Bryden's collection of essays entitled *Samuel Beckett and Music* (1998) and Lois Oppenheim's *Samuel Beckett and the Arts* (1999) have encouraged interdisciplinary Beckett studies, while major studies have been conducted by Eric Prieto (2002a) and Daniel Albright (2003). More recently, the field has benefitted from Franz Michael Maier's German-language monograph *Becketts Melodien: Die Musik und die Idee des Zusammenhangs bei Schopenhauer, Proust und Beckett* (2006), Catherine Laws' *Headaches Among the Overtones: Music in Beckett/Beckett in Music* (2013) and the French-language collection *Beckett et la musique*, edited by David Lauffer and Geneviève Mathon (2014), in addition to the collection *Beckett and Musicality*, edited by Nicholas Till and Sara-Jane Bailes (2014).

In terms of Beckett's musical background, his interest in the artform was the result of an unusual musical upbringing for a child in early twentieth-century Ireland. The Beckett family sent their boys to piano lessons, a practice generally restricted to girls in 1920s Foxrock (Mercier, 1977, 114). John Beckett, Samuel's cousin, became a composer and pianist, while Samuel himself continued his musical education at Portora and emerged an accomplished amateur pianist. He would play duets for hours with his uncle Gerald, an activity that John Beckett recounts:

> My father was a good pianist, a very good sight-reader, but also the sort of person who could go to a cinema and hear a song and come back and play it. The piano was in the dining room of our house and he and Sam would play for hours ... They would have played what we had in the house. We had volumes of Haydn symphonies, Haydn quartets, Mozart symphonies, Beethoven symphonies and our favourites were arrangements for four hands of the late quartets of Mozart.
>
> (Quoted in Knowlson, 1996, 7).

Beckett harboured a great love for Schubert and Beethoven all his life, and this childhood relationship with music would greatly influence his later literary endeavours. James Knowlson, the writer's biographer, documents Beckett's daily playing of the piano (Knowlson, 1996, 191). Beckett's lifelong friend, the poet Thomas MacGreevy, became somebody with whom the writer could discuss musical matters and attend various concerts, particularly when they

56   *Musico-literary interaction in Ireland*

both resided in London in the early stage of their respective careers. Their letters are full of references to music, which along with their interest in Joyce and poetry was a mutual obsession.

One such letter, recounting a Maryjo Prado piano recital, is typical of their musical criticism and illustrative of Beckett's knowledge of performance practice in particular. Beckett writes, "her Chopin and Debussy were dragged out by the scruff of the neck, very disagreeable ... [h]er left hand in the Scriabin was extremely scrupulous and good" (quoted in Knowlson, 1996, 192). The Shavian humorous overtones of the critique, while colloquial, nevertheless exhibit confidence in a particular musical taste and stance as regards "scrupulous" practice.

Beckett's letters continually demonstrate an engagement with music on three levels: as performer, listener and critic. These activities informed one another and played a significant role in the formation of the writer's creative aesthetic. But his enthusiasm for music went far beyond amateur performance and appraisal; instead, it influenced his work at both a structural and a philosophical level. Beckett inserted stage directions that required recorded music – the Schubert lied (D. 827, op. 43, no. 2) that lends the play *Nacht und Träume* ([1982] 2006) its title, for instance, or the specific segments from the second movement of Beethoven's Piano Trio in D Major op. 70, no. 1 ("Ghost") for the television play *Ghost Trio* ([1975] 2006). In the radio play *Words and Music* ([1961] 2006) the respective artforms of the title are personified as two opposing characters, as Beckett effectively plays out the aesthetic problems of musico-literary interaction in dialogue format. *Words and Music* will be further explored in Chapter 5.

The repetitive speech patterns in many of Beckett's plays also contain strikingly musical characteristics. Perhaps the best illustration of this is *Not I* ([1972] 2006), in which a solitary mouth performs the entire monologue, and, which will be discussed in Chapter 6. The lack of any real visual staging in *Not I* foregrounds the aurality of the work as the very process of creating sound and delivering words is prioritised above any other dramatic element. Knowlson recounts how Beckett would actively encourage the musical traits of his work during rehearsals, insisting that the primacy of sound was his aesthetic intention: it was thus his job, he stated, to set the actors on "the right musical road" (Knowlson, 1996, 668). Beckett was known to bring a metronome to rehearsals when directing, and Knowlson describes him more like a conductor than a theatre director, with the author beating out rhythms to the actors' speech, sometimes even prompting the pitch of the actors' speech from the piano (Knowlson, 1996, 668).

The "musical" qualities inherent in Beckett's work have made him particularly attractive to composers from Morton Feldman to Richard Barrett and Scott Fields, whether seeking a text to set or as a general inspiration, as we will further explore in Chapters 5 and 6. Beckett has arguably had as significant an impact on modern music as he has had on literature.

Musico-literary interaction in Ireland 57

What sets Beckett apart from other contemporary writers in terms of the absorption of musical techniques and ideas into his work are his explorations of the philosophy of music. Where the musicality of Joyce's work manifests itself as surface technique, device and quotation, Beckett's writing also involves a philosophical enquiry that operates at a deeper level. His 1931 critique *Proust* ([1931] 1999) (his first published book) displays Beckett's concerns with the meaning of music at an early stage in his artistic awakening. The book recognises the significance of music in Proust's work, going so far as to posit: "music is the catalytic element in the work" (Beckett, [1931] 1999, 92). Proust employs the metaphor of music to symbolise the non-representational aspects of human life; for him, the term "musical" connotes a Romantic spirit or consciousness rather than being a mere technical device. The influence on Beckett is clear. In my analysis and discussion of Beckett's musicality, I therefore do not shy away from the term "musical" in the Scher fashion (discussed in Chapter 1), but rather employ it in the same way that both Beckett and Proust themselves used it as Romantic symbol. Peter Dayan's progressive "On the meaning of 'Musical' in Proust" (2002) has been of great aid in this regard.

What is of particular significance in *Proust* is Beckett's documented understanding, and misunderstanding also, of Schopenhauer's musical thought and its subsequent application in critique of the French novelist. J. D. O'Hara points out that Beckett's Schopenhauer deviates in quite an extreme manner from the philosopher's own writings, and that Beckett's distortion of Schopenhauer's *The World as Will and Representation* ([1818] 1969) is moulded to fit the writer's own musical aesthetic (O'Hara, 1988). Schopenhauer did not posit the puritanical view that opera was a "corruption" of music through the subordination of music to text (as Beckett describes); instead, he viewed it as a combined expression of the same "embodied will" (Pilling, 1998, 176). Schopenhauer did, as we have already discussed, view music as an artform separate from the "other arts", a discrete entity that inhabited a higher realm similar to the one that Walter Pater would later envision. It is these deviations from Schopenhauer's own ideas, however, that best highlight the young Beckett's own aesthetic beliefs and prejudices, and most importantly grant us an insight into his own philosophy of music – further explored in relation to Beckett's later work in Chapter 4. Beckett's praise of the *da capo* form at the end of *Proust* may provide insight into his employment of binary forms in some of his own works. Mercier's famous description of *Waiting for Godot* ([1953] 2006) as a play in which "nothing happens, twice", might be viewed as a kind of mysterious Beckettian *da capo* form, later providing the repetitive structure of *Play* ([1963] 2006)) (Mercier, 1956, 6). Proclaiming "the 'da capo' as a testimony to the intimate and ineffable nature of an art that is perfectly intelligible and perfectly inexplicable", he realised that repetition does not always bring comprehension (Beckett, [1931] 1999, 92). For Beckett, no matter how many times we might hear a piece of music, we can never "comprehend" it "fully"; there is always the "inexplicable" aspect.

58 *Musico-literary interaction in Ireland*

Beckett's writing style, I suggest, evolved towards an aesthetic of intangibility, or a semantic fluidity, attaining a universal quality through which the writer allowed the reader to bring their own connotations and affiliations to the work. As Beckett wrote:

> My work is a matter of fundamental sounds (no joke intended) made as fully as possible, and I accept responsibility for nothing else. If people want to have headaches among the overtones, let them. And provide their own aspirin.
>
> (Beckett, Letter to Alan Schneider, Paris, 12 August, 1957, in Beckett and Schneider, 1998, 15)

Recognising the unattainable nature of definitive meanings, particularly with the developments in structuralism and poststructuralism – Barthes' "The Death of the Author" ([1967] 1977b) with its interrogation of assumptions of "intent", echoing Wimsatt and Beardsley's notion (1954) of the "Intentional Fallacy", for instance – Beckett created worlds with a certain semantic fluidity; the musical text provided the means. This semantic fluidity would not emerge until later, however; Beckett's musical aesthetic took many turns beforehand. Instrumental music went in and out of favour in his stage directions, for instance, as the author grappled with his views on interdisciplinary practice, while Beckett's early novels employ music as metaphor rather than ever granting the work semantic fluidity.[3]

Music and metaphor in Beckett's early fiction

From Beckett's first forays into prose he began incorporating musical ideas. The "Walking Out" chapter of *More Pricks Than Kicks* ([1934] 1993), for instance, contains a reference to one of Beckett's favourite Schubert compositions, *An die Musik* (1817). Mary Bryden has discovered within Beckett's "Whoroscope" notebook, which he carried in the 1930s, the words and music of the Schubert piece copied out. The final lines of "Walking Out" express the same yearning for "better worlds" that the lied does: "They sit up to all hours playing the gramophone, *An die Musik* is a great favourite with them both, he finds in her big eyes better worlds than this" (Bryden, 1998, 29). In the name "Belacqua", the protagonist of *Dream of Fair to Middling Women* ([1932] 1992) and *More Pricks Than Kicks*, itself, there are musical connotations. Belacqua is the indolent lute-maker in Dante's *Purgatorio* (2008); in Beckett he retains this lassitude and wishes for his relations with women to be "like a music", a theme that reappears in *Murphy* ([1938] 2003).

Musicality becomes increasingly significant in Beckett's novels over time as musical devices become more central to a non-representational quality in the text. *Watt* ([1945] 1963) contains much musical discourse, as John Fletcher points out: "the voices play as important a part in Watt's existence as mental retreat plays in Murphy's" (Fletcher, 1964, 65). *Watt* contains

Musico-literary interaction in Ireland   59

Beckett's score for a threnody and the often confusing non-representational nature of the novel has led scholars such as Eric Prieto to view *Watt* as a pivotal novel in Beckett's development of a musical aesthetic, moving towards a more relational artform than a denotative one (Prieto, 2002a, 252). The Trilogy: *Molloy* (1951), *Malone Dies* (1951), *The Unnamable* (1953) (1994) sees Beckett progressively employing musical technique and philosophy, and indeed, as we will see in the next chapter, these elements reach a peak in the prose of the 1980s.

One of the principal techniques in Beckett's fiction is the Joycean "echo" that Knowlson spoke of:

> Beckett may also have acquired from Joyce some of his practice of introducing echoes into his own writing, as if in music. It was a technique that he developed much more fully even than Joyce, particularly in his later prose and theatre.
>
> (Knowlson, 1996, 106)

Take the "duet" of Moran and his son, for instance: "Just listen to what I am going to say, because I will not say it twice ... If you can't find the second hand bicycle buy a new bicycle. I repeat. I repeated. I who said I would not repeat ... It was not the moment to introduce another theme" ([1951] 1994, 143). The epistrophe patterns here (repeated words at the end of sentences) are early signs of a technique that Beckett would build on in later works, and repetition would later become the defining characteristic of Beckett's musical aesthetic, as we will see in the next chapter. Repeated statements are scattered throughout *Molloy*, such as Molloy's exclamation that he is not "hard of hearing" ([1951] 1994, 49), reiterated in Moran's "I have an extremely sensitive ear" ([1951] 1994,128). The act of listening is significant in *Molloy*; while Molloy himself exhibits an outward disdain for music, his ear is always attuned to the sounds around him: "bees hum in various tones" ([1951] 1994, 169).

In *Murphy* ([1938] 2003) we can see Beckett employing music in a number of interesting ways at an early stage in his artistic career. His experiments with the musical text would develop over time as these devices became progressively more pervasive in his work, but it is this work that truly monumentalises his first real musical explorations in fiction. Having written *Proust* in 1931, as mentioned above and to be further explored in the next chapter, Beckett's Schopenhauerian philosophy of music had been well established by the time he began *Murphy*. The sexual metaphor in *Murphy* is in fact one level of this Yeatsian "sensual music" ("Sailing to Byzantium", 1928, in Yeats, 1990), but much more than just a ploy to avert the so-called "filthy censors", those who would not publish Beckett's earlier novel *Dream of Fair to Middling Women* (Beckett, [1938] 2003, 47). Murphy and Celia's relationship is described in musical terms; together they manage to reach a "higher realm" of harmonious, loving music, "their nights were still that: serenade, nocturne and albada" ([1938] 2003, 46). When they are in disagreement, this music is lost: "Celia

60 *Musico-literary interaction in Ireland*

said that if he did not find work at once she would have to go back to hers. Murphy knew what that meant. No more music" ([1938] 2003, 47). This music metaphor spans the theoretical knowledge that Beckett possesses: "He kissed her, in Lydian mode" ([1938] 2003, 82); "A kiss from Wylie was like a breve tied, in a long slow amorous phrase, over bars' times its equivalent in demi-semiquavers" ([1938] 2003, 69).

At one point, Celia describes Murphy's indecipherable speech in musical terms:

> She felt, as she felt so often with Murphy, spattered with words that went dead as soon as they sounded; each word obliterated, before it had time to make sense, by the word that came next; so that in the end she did not know what had been said. It was like difficult music heard for the first time.
>
> (Beckett, [1938] 2003, 77)

Murphy's words, like music, bear little tangible referentiality for Celia, and she is unable to comprehend his outlook on life. Murphy's words sound like "difficult music heard for the first time", as if she was listening to Webern or Berg. White has compared Beckett to Webern, relating their shared concern for the reduction of materials following the encyclopaedic grandeur of their respective "masters", Joyce and Schoenberg. He writes:

> the contrast between Joyce's verbally heroic largesse and Beckett's concentrated parsimony of discourse ... and the messianic compulsion of Schoenberg's reanimation of large-scale musical forms (opera, concerto, cantata) by comparison with Webern's scrupulous reductionism ... On both sides, reciprocity defines the relationship of master-builder (Joyce, Schoenberg) and the "master of undermining" (Webern, Beckett).
>
> (White, 1998, 163)

Schoenberg wrote his first serial compositions in 1923, while Joyce's *Ulysses*, published the previous year, marks what White believes to be "crucial developments in modernist fiction and music respectively" (White, 1998, 163). Beckett himself once wrote: "James Joyce was a synthesizer, trying to bring in as much as he could. I am an analyzer, trying to leave out as much as I can" (19 April 1981, quoted in Gussow, 1981). The famous epiphany that Beckett had, following the death of his father, was to go down the road of reduction and distillation rather than to do battle with Joyce in the epic Modernist tradition.

Music also metaphorically assists Beckett's early fiction in terms of character development or lack thereof. Among Murphy's many erudite accomplishments is his musical education. We know he is a musician of sorts, who has over time ceased to engage with it: "his books, his pictures, his postcards, his musical scores and instruments, all had been gradually

Musico-literary interaction in Ireland 61

disposed of in that order rather than the chair" (Beckett, [1938] 2003, 107). Murphy's personality is entirely out of tune with his surroundings: the "celestial" prescriptions of Suk advise Murphy to "resort to Harmony" ([1938] 2003, 23), but it is impossible for him to ever achieve this. As the narrator writes:

> His troubles had begun early. To get back no farther than the vagitus, it had not been the proper A of international concert pitch, with 435 double vibrations per second, but the double flat of this. How he winced, the honest obstetrician, a devout member of the Dublin Orchestral Society and an amateur flautist of some merit. With what sorrow he recorded that of all the millions of little larynges cursing in unison at the particular moment, the infant Murphy's alone was off the note.
>
> (Beckett, [1938] 2003, 44)

From his very first scream then, Murphy was out of tune with the world. Neary's ability to stop his heart from beating as a method of meditation, something he refers to as "Apmonia" or the "Attunement", is a trick that Murphy fails to master. His personality proves too erratic and unbalanced to achieve such consonance. In a Cartesian sense, and Descartes features heavily in the novel, Murphy wishes to exist solely in the "little world" of the mind, and thus fails to unify the mind/body dichotomy in any harmonious manner. The very first image of the book is of Murphy naked and bound to a chair in an attempt to achieve a possibly maternal kind of peace; the cradle-like rocking is perhaps significant. Murphy views himself as an alien amongst ordinary society; the only people he can truly identify with are patients in the Magdalen Mental Mercyseat – it's no coincidence that the protagonist of Ken Kesey's *One Flew over the Cuckoo's Nest* (1962) is named McMurphy. The fundamental drive of the narrative is the paralysis, or unwillingness, of Murphy to engage with the outside, real world; upon hearing street sounds, he is reminded of his contempt for the outside: "These were sights and sounds that he did not like. They detained him in the world to which they belonged, but not he, as he fondly hoped" ([1938] 2003, 6). In contrast, Murphy's chess-mate, the schizophrenic Mr Endon, possesses an "inner voice" that is "unobtrusive and melodious, a gentle continuo in the whole consort of his hallucinations" ([1938] 2003, 105), perhaps endowing him with the upper hand that enables him to defeat Murphy.

Ruby Cohn writes that *Murphy*'s repetitive nature was one of the reasons why it was rejected in the first place until its eventual acceptance in 1937 (Cohn, 2001, 84). Perhaps these publishers/critics saw only monotony or what they took for a lack of variety and originality, where in fact Beckett was using repetition in a deliberate and complex manner.

There are also many sentences or passages that are repeated discursively (on a more structural level) throughout the book. Murphy's ultimatum to Celia that if he was forced to work in the "mercantile gehenna",

62 *Musico-literary interaction in Ireland*

either she, his body or his mind would have to go: "If you, then you only; if my body, then you also; if my mind, then all" (Beckett, [1938] 2003, 27), for instance.[4] Murphy recollects this later and repeats to himself, "You, my body, my mind ... one must go" ([1938] 2003,107). Other discursive repeats in the book are the "acoustic properties" of the stairwell in the dark, recognised by the prying Miss Carridge as she listens out for Celia's movements upstairs ([1938] 2003, 89), later repeated by the narrator: "that black night so rich in acoustic properties, and on the landing, to the infinite satisfaction of Miss Carridge" ([1938] 2003, 130). Likewise, the directions of Professor Suk constantly reverberate in Murphy's mind, and are also reiterated by Celia: "'Avoid exhaustion by speech', she said" ([1938] 2003, 25); "'Avoid exhaustion', she murmured, in weary ellipsis of Suk" ([1938] 2003, 80). The triple "M" of "Magdalen Mental Mercyseat", Murphy's workplace, soon takes on another meaning for him: "MMM stood suddenly for music, Music, MUSIC, in brilliant, brevier and canon" ([1938] 2003, 132). This alliterative triplet is later echoed as Murphy contemplates his return to Celia: "leaving Ticklepenny to face the music, Music, MUSIC, back to Brewery Road, to Celia, serenade, nocturne, albada" ([1938] 2003, 141). The format is repeated in the rising crescendo of the triplet "all, All, ALL" ([1938] 2003, 135). Other repeats occur several times on a single page, imposing a tempo or rhythm on a passage while also informing us of certain facts: "A lie" ([1938] 2003, 84), for instance, or "In vain" ([1938] 2003, 141). "All out" repeats musematically (locally) six times on the final page ([1938] 2003, 158), calling to a close the park as well as the book – the reader must vacate the premises just as Celia and Mr Kelly do.

Characters are often identified by their own idiosyncratic repeats in leitmotivic fashion: Wylie by his continuous repetition of "The horse leech's daughter is a closed system. Her quantum of wantum" ([1938] 2003, 112), a reference to Proverbs 30:15, and his eloquent way of expressing his theory of covetous greed; Miss Counihan by her stilted "er"s ([1938] 2003, 33); Miss Carridge by her reiterations of "the principle of the thing, the principle of the thing" ([1938] 2003, 85); or Neary as he emphasises intelligibility: "'Outside us', said Neary. 'Outside Us'" ([1938] 2003, 120), or his attempts to comfort with the reassuring lullaby-like "'There there', aid Neary. 'There there. There there'" ([1938] 2003, 150). These leitmotivic repetitions are similar to the "exact clothed repeats" that I discuss in terms of Beckett's later work in the next chapter.

Murphy's rocking is perhaps the most significant act of repetition in the novel, a motif that would reappear most famously in *Rockaby* ([1981] 2006). The rhythm of his rocking chair provides his only method of attaining a peaceful state of mind:

> The rock got faster and faster, shorter and shorter, the iridescence was gone, the cry in the mew was gone, soon his body would be quiet. Most things under the moon got slower and slower and then stopped, a rock

Musico-literary interaction in Ireland   63

got faster and faster and then stopped. Soon his body would be quiet, soon he would be free.

(Beckett, [1938] 2003, 9)

The repetitions of "faster and faster" and "soon his body would be quiet" in just this short passage emphasise the repetitive nature of the ritualistic act. If we compare this early passage to Murphy's final moments, we can see that most of the passage is repeated:

The rock got faster and faster, shorter and shorter, the gleam was gone, the grin was gone, the starlessness was gone, soon his body would be quiet. Most things under the moon got slower and slower and then stopped, a rock got faster and faster and then stopped. Soon his body would be quiet, soon he would be free.
The gas went on in the WC, excellent gas, superfine chaos.
Soon his body was quiet.

(Beckett, [1938] 2003, 142)

When Murphy leaves Celia alone, she in fact repeats his repetitive rocking, and even begins to comprehend the motives behind his strange activities: "Thus in spite of herself she began to understand as soon as he gave up trying to explain ... She could not sit for long in the chair without the impulse stirring, tremulously, as for an exquisite depravity, to be naked and bound" ([1938] 2003, 42).

One of Murphy's "highest attributes", according to the astrologer Suk, is "Silence" ([1938] 2003, 22). In the passage quoted above, Murphy imagines his death in terms of such quietude. I return to the integral role of silence in Beckett's work in Chapter 6, a trait that itself develops in the author's aesthetic. In *Murphy*, pauses or rests often follow passages of intensity, be it a heated debate between Murphy and Celia – "There was a long silence, Celia forgiving Murphy for having spoken roughly to her" ([1938] 2003, 81) – a moment of unease – "There was a silence, Bim liking the look of Murphy less and less, Murphy racking his brains for plausible curiosity" ([1938] 2003, 92) – or when at the morgue, upon the group being asked to identify Murphy's body, "Such a silence followed these words that the faint hum of the refrigerators could be heard" ([1938] 2003, 148). John Cage (1973) observed that true silence doesn't exist; here we have the inescapable sound of a kitchen appliance. Other passages contain musical rests that accentuate the drama while also instilling a sombre tempo to the episode. An abandoned and heartbroken Celia attempts to explain her plight in stilted fashion, as follows:

"At first I thought I had lost him because I could not take him as he was. Now I do not flatter myself."

64   *Musico-literary interaction in Ireland*

A rest.

"I was a piece out of him that he could not go on without, no matter what I did."

A rest.

"He had to leave me to be what he was before he met me, only worse, or better, no matter what I did."

A long rest.

"I was the last exile."

A rest.

(Beckett, [1938] 2003, 130–131)

Likewise, the integral final moments that Murphy shares with the slumbering Mr Endon are enhanced by the use of musical rests:

> Murphy heard words demanding so strongly to be spoken that he spoke them, right into Mr Endon's face, Murphy who did not speak at all in the ordinary way unless spoken to, and not always even then.
>
> > "the last at last seen of him
> > himself unseen by him
> > And of himself"
>
> A rest.
>
> "The last Mr Murphy saw of Mr Endon was Mr Murphy unseen by Mr Endon. This was also the last Murphy saw of Murphy."
>
> A rest.
>
> "The relation between Mr Murphy and Mr Endon could not have been better summed up by the former's sorrow at seeing himself in the latter's immunity from seeing anything but himself."
>
> A rest.
>
> "Mr Murphy is a speck in Mr Endon's unseen."
>
> (Beckett, [1938] 2003, 140)

Beckett's use of epistrophe is clearly apparent here, as are the binaries and chiasmus of the line "The last Mr Murphy saw of Mr Endon was Mr Murphy unseen by Mr Endon". Such wordplay abounds in *Murphy* and is very characteristic of early Beckett. The narrator often interjects with witty wordplay on senses (paronomasia) or repetitions of sentences, such as "He was vigilant and agitated. His vigilance was agitated" ([1938] 2003, 68). Such rhetorical devices become increasingly pivotal in Beckett's musical repetition, as we will see in the next chapter. Mr Endon's condition meant that he never truly saw Murphy as anything but a chess-mate: he was perhaps however, tragically, the closest that Murphy found to a peer or friend, a genuine inhabitant of the "little world" that Murphy so wanted to inhabit. As Murphy sees his own reflection in Mr Endon's eye, the cracked looking glass of a lost mutual recognition, this is the nearest Murphy gets to harmony or unison in a distorted world before his inevitable tragic end. Beckett's musical text would evolve alongside his aesthetic, but its beginnings are clear to see in *Murphy*.

Notes

1 Wagner became a hero to Shaw and the subject of his culminating work of music criticism *The Perfect Wagnerite* (1898). Harry White believes Shaw's "play of ideas", drama of the intellect, was Shaw's only way forward following Wagner's achievements in melodrama. See White (2008, 133–153). Shaw writes: "The drama of pure feeling is no longer in the hands of the playwright: it has been conquered by the musician, after whose enchantments all the verbal arts seem cold and tame. Romeo and Juliet with the loveliest Juliet is dry, tedious, and rhetorical in comparison with Wagner's Tristan, even though Isolde be both fourteen stone and forty, as she often is in Germany ... there is no future now for any drama without music except the drama of thought. The attempt to produce a genus of opera without music (and this absurdity is what our fashionable theatres have been driving at for a long time without knowing it) is far less hopeful than my own determination to accept problem as the normal material of the drama" (Shaw cited in Meisel, 1963, 44).
2 Brown (2007).
3 Lois Overbeck provides a useful overview of Beckett's changing stance on musical collaboration in "Audience of Self/Audience of Reader" (2011).
4 For a detailed explanation of my taxonomy of repetition, see Chapter 4.

4 Beckett's semantic fluidity
Repetition in the later work

One of the most striking features of Beckett's later writing are the persistent repetitions that infuse his prose, repeated sounds that seem to break apart the narrative and move towards a guttural form of enunciation. For a reader hoping for a clear, intelligible story, such stuttering appears like hesitation: a fissure in the flow of information that might suggest an author battling uncertainty or anguish. However, it is precisely within these moments of excessive repetition that the key to Beckett's narratives lies. At first glance, repetition draws the reader's attention away from the story and onto the writing itself, initiating a formal, structuralist materiality; but I will argue that these moments in fact take us further into the Beckettian musical aesthetic, by dissolving explicit meanings that we can grasp, and instead endowing the work with a semantic fluidity. This, I suggest, is due to the inherently musical nature of Beckett's repetition, a result of his philosophical engagement with Schopenhauer.

Beckett's later Schopenhauerian music

Might Beckett's abundant employment of repetitions in his later work be related to a Schopenhauerian philosophy of music wherein the writer attempts to express the Kantian *noumenon* through a musical text: to evoke "the universal in the particular", as Bryan Magee (2000, 170) puts it? For Schopenhauer, the *noumenon* and the *phenomenon* are two sides of the same reality. For him, the unknown *noumenon*, outside of all experiential knowledge and void of material objects as well as time and space themselves, could be reached, if only briefly, through music. An artform not "condemned to explicitness" yet structured within "intelligible", amenable forms – music – represented the highest of the arts for Schopenhauer. Music, he believed, enabled engagement with the "thing in itself", the reality that we cannot comprehend or express in words. Kant recognised that we can only perceive that part of reality that our physical capabilities allow, and for Schopenhauer music offers us a teasing, satisfying, yet unexplained, glimpse of this other side of reality: the *noumenon* –"the world is my representation" (Budd, 1985, 78).

Beckett's semantic fluidity 67

Figure 4.1 The Human Condition (1933) – René Magritte © ADAGP, Paris and DACS, London 2016

This concept can be explained by looking at Magritte's painting *The Human Condition* (1933) (Figure 4.1). A key element of the human condition is, as Kant ([1781] 1998) pointed out, that all we understand as reality is only our perception, a small portion of reality that our senses allow us to view. Magritte's painting inside the room represents the painter's perception or interpretation of the exterior landscape – *sans noumena*. Magritte clearly understood the problems inherent in forms of representation. The landscape may be repeated in canvas, but it is always different as a result of perception. In reality, science tells us, the outside that is depicted here would in fact be blue with ultraviolet light. Our brains compensate for this and decode our surroundings in a manner that makes sense to our understanding and mental

68 *Beckett's semantic fluidity*

capability. As humans, there is indeed a great deal more that we can't perceive than that which we can. Neural Darwinism, the study of brain development in its environment and how it becomes perceptually conditioned as a result of context, explores these issues. At the subatomic level, the world changes upon the gaze of the onlooker (Heisenberg principle); so too does the reception of phenomena in the world of our senses. Schopenhauer's Romantic view actually sounds strikingly similar to how quantum physicists describe our perception of the world; Schopenhauer's "the world is my representation" (Budd, 1985, 78) is echoed in Einstein's "[r]eality is merely an illusion, albeit a very persistent one" (Einstein quoted in Montgomery, 2010, 1), or Plato's allegory of "The Cave" (Plato, *c*.380 BC). Schopenhauer was fascinated with Eastern philosophies, and Buddhism was a major influence on his thought; Buddha's teaching that the universe is itself a concept pre-empts these Western developments. Of course, there is yet another layer to this painting, due to the fact that the whole picture of the room is itself a visual representation on canvas.

Beckett's involvement with the work of Schopenhauer has been well documented and his preoccupation with "the thing itself" is established.[1] In his early essay on Joyce, for instance, Beckett spoke of the *Work in Progress* as not "*about* something; it *is* that something itself" (Beckett, [1929] 1983a 27). The book, Beckett writes, is "not to be read – or rather it is not only to be read. It is to be looked at and listened to" ([1929] 1983a, 27). Joyce himself referred to the book as "pure music" (Joyce quoted in Ellmann, [1959] 1982, 703).[2] The performative musicality of *Finnegans Wake* would influence Beckett's own musical aesthetic.

Beckett was not concerned about incongruities between the philosophies and texts that he read, borrowed from, and incorporated in his own work. Intertextual material abounds in Beckett, and the contradictions that arise employ a postmodern poetic licence. In a letter to MacGreevy (July 1930), he writes: "I am reading Schopenhauer. Everyone laughs at that" (see Knowlson, 1996, 122). But Beckett is not concerned with the problems of the philosopher, nor the futile search for hard truths; instead he seeks "an intellectual justification of unhappiness – the greatest that has ever been attempted" (see Knowlson, 1996, 122).

The writer continued to harbour a love for Schopenhauer throughout his life, and, like Wagner, consistently reread the *The World as Will and Representation*. A convalescing Beckett wrote to MacGreevy of the comfort he found in the work:

> the only thing I could read was Schopenhauer. Everything else I tried only confirmed the feeling of sickness ... I always knew he was one of the ones that mattered most to me, and it is a pleasure more real than any pleasure for a long time to begin to understand now why it is so. And it is a pleasure also to find a philosopher that can be read like a poet.
>
> (See Knowlson, 1996, 248)

Beckett's semantic fluidity 69

Beckett's study *Proust* ([1931] 1999) examines the French novelist from a distinctly Schopenhauerian perspective:

> The influence of Schopenhauer on this aspect of the Proustian demonstration is unquestionable. Schopenhauer rejects the Leibnitzian [*sic*] view of music as "occult arithmetic", and in his aesthetic separates it from the other arts, which can only produce the Idea with its concomitant phenomena, whereas music is the Idea itself, unaware of the world of phenomena, existing ideally outside the universe, apprehended not in Space but in Time only, and consequently untouched by the teleological hypothesis.
> (Beckett, [1931] 1999, 92)

Here, Gottfried Leibniz's notion of a grand order of things – there being a reason for everything, a greater good – is condemned as "occult arithmetic", in the face of Schopenhauer's view of the meaninglessness of reality. For Schopenhauer, music has the ability to express the "Idea" without any of the "concomitant phenomena", the multitude manifestations of the *noumenon* in the *phenomenon* without the baggage. As Magee writes: "[music] is, according to Schopenhauer, the self-expression of something that cannot be represented at all, namely the *noumenon*. It is the voice of the metaphysical will" (Magee, 2000, 171).

Just like his lifelong affinity for Schopenhauer, Beckett's concern with the nature of music never waned. Beckett told Lawrence Shainberg as late as 1987 that he viewed music as "the highest art form" for the very fact that "it's never condemned to explicitness" (see Bryden, 1998, 31), an obvious reference to the following Schopenhauer passage:

> The inexpressible depth of all music, by virtue of which it floats past us a paradise quite familiar and yet eternally remote, and is so easy to understand and yet so inexplicable, is due to the fact that it reproduces all the emotions of our innermost being, but entirely without reality and remote from its pain.
>
> (See Pilling, 1998, 177)

It is this notion of music, never being "condemned to explicitness", not tied down to definitive semantics, that I believe Beckett sought in his own art. In *Proust*, Beckett explores how the novelist achieved this combination of the "intelligible" and "inexplicable" in a work in which music was the "catalytic element" ([1931] 1999 92). Of course, he was a writer first and foremost, and we must read his idealistic proclamation of music as "the highest art form" with some caution. The crucial element that Beckett borrows from music is the possibility of what I refer to as *semantic fluidity*, the creation of a language that is both "intelligible" and "inexplicable" at the same time. Semantic fluidity occurs when an artform disallows any definitive interpretation of the signs involved. Beckett's later writing offers a more universal

70 *Beckett's semantic fluidity*

world in which the reader can, to a certain extent, create his or her own meanings.

Beckett's semantic fluidity stems not only from musical sound, but also from the silences that punctuate and propel it. In a letter to Axel Kaun in July 1937, the author wrote: "Is there any reason why that terrible materiality of the word surface should not be capable of being dissolved, like for example the sound surface, torn by enormous pauses, of Beethoven's seventh symphony" (Beckett, 2009, 518). The relation of the frequent "pauses" and rests in Beckett's work to that of his beloved Beethoven is apt and the use of silence is certainly a central element of Beckett's musical formalism. However, this idea of "dissolving" the word surface, melting its very meaning, presents a fundamental problem. Words will always carry some semiotic content no matter how they are deconstructed. A persistent problem for Beckett was the failure of words to express anything sufficiently: the imperfections of the medium lead to confusion and communication is often stifled by insurmountable gulfs of expression. For him, such problems became the basis for creation itself; focusing upon the issue led to the production of art. Catherine Laws argues that:

> Beckett's work exposes the complexities and deliberate contradictions of the postmodern condition. His assertion of the impossibility of expression is offset by the experience of reading, watching and/or listening, and the paradox of the success of his writing resists simplification and focuses on problematization as a force for creation (without ever suggesting that the problems have been solved)
>
> (Laws, 1996, 254)

The juxtaposition of the "intelligible", distilled, accurate words, alongside the "inexplicable" mysterious quality in his work, then, deliberately foregrounds the very failures of language itself. Adorno touched on this duality when he likened Beckett's work to music. In his notes on *The Unnamable*, written towards an unpublished essay (recently translated), he writes: "In B[eckett] there is, a kind of counterpoint, something like sound common sense. Everything so meaningless, yet at the same time the way one speaks is so normal" (Adorno, [1961] 2010, 175). The paradox of Schopenhauer's philosophy of music is that the philosopher equates music with something that can never be represented; it is a representation of an invisible inner reality, but how can a copy (music) depict the unrepresentable? As Budd puts it, Schopenhauer's music is "the copy of an original that can itself never be directly represented" (Budd, 1985, 86). Budd's devastating critique of Schopenhauer's philosophy of music highlights the contradictions inherent in believing that all music brings about satisfactory conclusions and endings while still evoking endless yearning – how Schopenhauer describes the prelude to Wagner's Tristan, or how a Beethoven symphony could contain all human emotions while music remains "a representation of that which cannot be represented" (1985, 92). Schopenhauer's misunderstandings regarding music and the problems contained in his outdated ideas on representation lead Budd to proclaim: "Schopenhauer's philosophy is not a fitting monument to the art" (1985, 103). The real rub in Schopenhauer's philosophy of music is, as Budd explains, that to access the "will", one must be in a state of pure contemplation, unaffected by emotion; yet Schopenhauer contradicts himself by suggesting that music, an emotional form, is the key to our innermost being. If, in order to access what it represents, we must approach it without emotion, should music then be free from emotion (1985, 101)?

Very few would proclaim nowadays that music represents our innermost being in such a Romantic fashion, just as a repetition can never be exact. But such contradictions were not important to Beckett, who saw the philosopher as a poet; instead, such problems became the focus of his work, material to be employed creatively. The foregrounding of the impossible and futile search for direct representation, mimesis, of communicating exactly and sufficiently became Beckett's life work.

Recognising the unattainable nature of definitive meanings, Beckett created worlds with a certain semantic fluidity. Eric Prieto believes that Beckett's art is music-like in the fact that it is relational rather than denotative – words operate in relation to one another, as notes do in music, without clear relationships to external objects (Prieto, 2002a, 252). Beckett's words do, of course, always contain connotation and meaning, but what Prieto is suggesting here is that Beckett's words are moving towards a non-representational realm similar to that of music. Through the influence of the French Symbolists, the Romantics, and the literary Wagnerism that swept across late nineteenth-century Europe, Schopenhauer's philosophy of music began to take root in numerous artists' aesthetics.[3] Music does contain semantic content obviously, but in this grey area between the two artforms, such metaphor manifests itself as a kind of asymptotic curve, as one reaches towards the other, never to meet fully. Did the language of Beckett's late work become so "dissolved" that the words no longer held any hard objective meaning in relation to the external extra-textual world?

In a 1968 television discussion, Adorno argued that Beckett's musicality is not based on "linguistic imitation of musical effects," as it is in Joyce's work, for instance, but instead on "the way in which linguistic sounds are organised into structures," such that the "prose is not simply organised by meaning" (Adorno, [1961] 2010, 187). If the prose is not "organised by meaning," however, how is it organised, and to what end? Beckett's writing style, I theorise, evolved towards an aesthetic of intangibility, attaining a universal quality through which the writer encouraged readers to bring their own connotations and affiliations to the work. When approaching Beckett, the reader gazes through a kind of filter, like the "attributive screens" proposed by Peter J. Rabinowitz, wherein a person's history of experiences and tastes, their social context and their listening history all imbue their initial experience of the work (Rabinowitz, 1992, 38–56). This is true of all reading experiences, but is

72 *Beckett's semantic fluidity*

particularly emphasised and elevated in Beckett's case. The less that is certain for the reader, the more possibilities there are. By eroding definite meaning and reducing materials to a minimum, Beckett managed to say more with less.

Did Beckett's Schopenhauerian philosophy of music lead to his employment of repetitions that operate in a Deleuzian manner? The repetitions do not help us "grasp" the narrative, in Kivy's manner. Instead, clarity is eroded, dissolved; the repetitions are not the same but evolve on the page and in the ear of the listener/reader. The liberation of repetitions in Beckett's work would seem to deliberately embrace the "absurd" that Shaw suggested earlier would be the result of repetition's proliferation in literature.[4] Beckett's use of repetition is also clearly in opposition to Abbate's categorisations.

Beckett found the semantic fluidity that he sought in the Schopenhauerian Romantic philosophy of music, and this influence manifests itself primarily in the form of repetitions and echoes. As we saw in Chapter 1, Modernist experimentation had reached a point at which Beckett spoke of a "rupture of the lines of communication" and a "breakdown of the object" (Beckett, [1934] 1983b, 70); in Daniel Albright's words, language was beginning to "lose connection to the world of hard objects" and "become more and more like musical notes" (Albright, 2000, 6). Was Beckett employing repetition in a manner that enabled the "intelligible" and the "inexplicable" to co-exist? Ultimately this would always remain an asymptotic curve, as the move towards music in Beckett's language and the development of semantic fluidity in his words always remains a teleology without a finite terminus.

Ill Seen Ill Said ([1981] 1997) is a book haunted by a ghostly music, set in an unearthly realm removed from the spatial and temporal boundaries of reality. Beckett here delves into a base of half-remembered memories and perceptions. Is this female protagonist more than "pure figment" ([1981] 1997, 20)? The time and unspecific location are unknown, while the solitary old woman's faculties of sight and memory continue to fade. Questions remain unanswered; like Beckett's idea of music's virtue, the narrative here is "never condemned to explicitness" (Beckett quoted in Bryden, 1998, 31). Specific details are neither seen nor said.

Knowlson's observation of "echoes" in Beckett's work", seen in Chapter 3, is particularly apt with regard to this book. Within the fabric of *Ill Seen Ill Said*'s staccato sentences lies an interwoven system of motifs, as we can see from this excerpt:

> **1.**Back after many winters. **2.**Long after in this endless winter. **3.**This endless heart of winter. **4.**Too soon. **5.**She as when fled. **6.**Where as when fled. **7.**Still or again. **8.**Eyes closed in the dark. **9.**To the dark. **10.**In their own dark. **11.**On the lips same minute smile. **12.**If smile is what it was. **13.**In short alive as she alone knows how neither more nor less.**14.**Less! **15.**Compared to true stone. **16.**Within as sadly as before all as at first sight ill seen. **17.**With the happy exception of the lights' enhanced opacity. **18.** Dim the light of day from them were day again to dawn. **19.**Without on

Beckett's semantic fluidity 73

the other hand some progress. **20.**Toward unbroken night. **21.**Universal stone. **22.**Day no sooner risen fallen. **23.**Scrapped all the ill seen ill said. **24.**The eye has changed. **25.**And its drivelling scribe. **26.**Absence has changed them. **27.**Not enough. **28.**Time to go again. **29.**Where still more to change. **30.**Whence back too soon. **31.**Changed but not enough. **32.** Strangers but not enough. **33.**To all the ill seen ill said. **34.**Then back again. **35.**Disarmed for to finish with all at last. **36.**With her and her rags of sky and earth. **37.**And if again too soon go again. **38.**Change still more again. **39.**Then back again. **40.**Barring impediment. **41.**Ah. **42.**So on. **43.**Till fit to finish with it all at last. **44.**All the trash. **45.**In unbroken night. **46.**Universal stone. **47.**So first go. **48.**But first see her again. **49.**As when fled. **50.**And the abode. **51.**That under the changed eye it too may change. **52.**Begin. **53.**Just one parting look.**54.**Before all meet again. **55.**Then go. **56.**Barring impediment. **57.**Ah.
          (Beckett, [1981] 1997, 50–51, sentence numbering added)

Even from this one segment of text the use of repetition is striking. If we analyse this single paragraph of the 61 paragraphs in the book, we can begin to realise the extent of Beckett's employment of repetition. Four categories of repetition that I will highlight are labelled as follows:

1. **Exact clothed repetitions** – these are recurrences of the "same" material, always with Deleuze's warnings of the importance of different successive contexts – hence the use of his word "clothed" rather than "naked" repetition – there is always an assimilation of meaning that snowballs with each exact repetition.
2. **Local musematic repetitions**, after Middleton's "musematic" – these are local repeats often with minor variations; position and phonetics are of particular importance here.
3. **Binary oppositional repetitions** – those used to emphasise contrasting themes, contradictions, homonyms.[5]
4. **Discursive repetitions**, again named after Middleton – these are repeats acting on a more architectonic, structural level, often recurring throughout an entire work, coming and going in almost leitmotivic fashion in that these combine and develop over time; also often self-reflexive, like Joycean stream of consciousness, these repeats often direct the narrator.

Close reading No. 1 from *Ill Seen Ill Said*

1. Exact clothed repetitions

Of the 57 lines in this paragraph, there are 53 different sentences, and most of those indeed include segments of others. Four sentences are exact repeats, albeit clothed Deleuzian ones; two of these recur in a row and end the paragraph (40–41/56–57: "Barring impediment. Ah"). In sentences 21/46

74   *Beckett's semantic fluidity*

("Universal stone" – "stone" also appears in sentence 15), both occur after the words "unbroken night" in sentences 20 and 45. The other exact clothed repeat is in sentences 34 and 39, "Then back again". There are 261 words in the paragraph, of which only 130 are unique. This means that the ratio of repetition in Beckett's writing here is almost an exact 2:1, a ratio that can be found in many of his works that I have analysed. The individual words are as follows: back, after, many, winter(s), long, in, this, endless, heart, of, too, soon, she, as, when, fled, where, still, or, again, eye(s), closed, the, dark, to, their, own, on, lips, same, minute, smile, if, is, what, it, was, short, alive, alone, knows, how, neither, more, nor, less, compared, true, stone, within, sadly, before, all, at, first, sight, ill, seen, with, happy, exception, of, lights, enhanced, opacity, dim, day, from, them, were, dawn, without, other, hand, some, progress, toward, unbroken, night, universal, sooner, risen, fallen, scrapped, said, has, change(d), and, its, drivelling, scribe, absence, not, enough, time, go, where, whence, but, strangers, disarmed, for, finish, last, her, rags, sky, earth, barring, impediment, ah, so, till, fit, trash, see, abode, under, may, begin, just, one, parting, look, before, meet, then.

Figures 4.2a and 4.2b set out the frequency of the repetition rate for each word within the paragraph, including the percentage of the entire word count each accounts for and the repetition of the grouping of words into repeated phrases:[6]

2. Local musematic repetition

The position at which Beckett employs these repetitions within successive sentences is important. In the first three sentences "winter" occurs at the end of each, an example of Beckett's use of epistrophe. This endless winter is itself an echo from *That Time*, featuring the line "always winter then endless winter" ([1976] 2006, 393). The word "dark" occurs at the end of sentences 8, 9 and 10 – "Eyes closed in the dark. To the dark. In their own dark." This trio of successive closing words produces striking phonetic rhythms.

Further ternaries can be found in sentences 5 and 6 – "as when fled" closes both ("She as when fled. Where as when fled"), appearing again later, towards the close of the passage, as the complete sentence 49 – while repeats at the end of sentences remain crucial: in sentences 31 and 32, this time in direct succession with the words "not enough" – "Changed but not enough. Strangers but not enough." "Not enough" appears earlier as a complete sentence at 27.

In sentences 35 and 43, a six-word repeated phrase occurs at the end of each sentence with the slight variation of including the word "it" in 43: "Disarmed for to finish with all at last"; "Till fit to finish with it all at last". The title of the book, *Ill Seen Ill Said*, is itself a repeating discursive phrase throughout the book and it appears in this paragraph at the end of sentences as a six-word repeated phrase in sentences 23 and 33: "Scrapped all the ill seen ill said"; "To all the ill seen ill said". There is a shorter echo of the phrase with variation in sentence 16 – "first sight ill seen". It would appear that such expressions of

PHRASE	COUNT	PERCENT
the	13	4.962
again	10	3.817
to	8	3.053
all	7	2.672
as	7	2.672
and	5	1.908
ill	5	1.908
in	5	1.908
changed	4	1.527
back	4	1.527
with	4	1.527
too	4	1.527
of	4	1.527
go	4	1.527
as when fled	3	3.435
not enough	3	2.29
when fled	3	2.29
too soon	3	2.29
ill seen	3	2.29
as when	3	2.29
all the	3	2.29
change	3	1.145
enough	3	1.145
stone	3	1.145
still	3	1.145
first	3	1.145
when	3	1.145
seen	3	1.145
dark	3	1.145
fled	3	1.145
then	3	1.145
more	3	1.145
soon	3	1.145
but	3	1.145
not	3	1.145
day	3	1.145
her	3	1.145
it	3	1.145
on	3	1.145
at	3	1.145
all the ill seen ill said	2	4.58
the ill seen ill said	2	3.817
all the ill seen ill	2	3.817
barring impediment	2	1.527
ill seen ill said	2	3.053
the ill seen ill	2	3.053
all the ill seen	2	3.053
universal stone	2	1.527
then back again	2	2.29
unbroken night	2	1.527
to finish with	2	2.29
but not enough	2	2.29

Figure 4.2a Analysis of segment no. 1 from *Ill Seen Ill Said*

PHRASE	COUNT	PERCENT
seen ill said	2	2.29
this endless	2	1.527
ill seen ill	2	2.29
the ill seen	2	2.29
finish with	2	1.527
has changed	2	1.527
all at last	2	2.29
all the ill	2	2.29
impediment	2	0.763
before all	2	1.527
back again	2	1.527
still more	2	1.527
universal	2	0.763
then back	2	1.527
to finish	2	1.527
unbroken	2	0.763
go again	2	1.527
seen ill	2	1.527
ill said	2	1.527
the dark	2	1.527
endless	2	0.763
barring	2	0.763
but not	2	1.527
the ill	2	1.527
at last	2	1.527
winter	2	0.763
before	2	0.763
finish	2	0.763
on the	2	1.527
all at	2	1.527
night	2	0.763
where	2	0.763
smile	2	0.763
after	2	0.763
less	2	0.763
them	2	0.763
said	2	0.763
last	2	0.763
this	2	0.763
she	2	0.763
eye	2	0.763
has	2	0.763
if	2	0.763
ah	2	0.763
so	2	0.763

Figure 4.2b Analysis of segment no. 1 from *Ill Seen Ill Said*

Beckett's semantic fluidity 77

deficiency or of depletion – dark, winter, fled, not enough, ill seen ill said – all close sentences as their semantic meaning implies, by ending negatively.

At other times, the last word of a sentence becomes the first of the next, the rhetorical figure anadiplosis being a common feature of Beckett's writing.[7] The importance of successive repeats in consecutive sentences is seen in sentences 11 and 12 for instance, where the word "smile" recurs in different positions – "On the lips same minute smile. If smile is what it was." This gives the text an improvisational quality, as if this meticulously crafted prose was through-composed or written automatically as one word creates the next. We will return to this quality of Beckett's writing in Chapter 6. The final word of sentence 13 "less" is repeated as the complete sentence 14, as the words themselves act out this direction – the sentence itself consisting of fewer words. This brings to attention another of Beckett's most salient stylistic traits, showing the influence of Joyce. Like Flaubert, Joyce would often craft words to reflect the content of the prose, with the words becoming more short and agitated for anxious moments or long and meandering to reflect the subject of a river, for instance. Words are also often chosen for their homonyms, or their ability to yield multiple interpretations: take the sentence "Leopold Bloom ate with *relish* the inner organs of beasts and fowl" (emphasis added). Here, the word "relish" could be read as the protagonist's carnivorous nature or as his chutney requirements. Another example is Joyce's use of journalese in the Aeolus chapter of *Ulysses*, with each paragraph having its own headline.

S. E. Gontarski describes a similar effect in another of Beckett's prose pieces, *Company* (1980), that was collected and published as *Nohow On*, with *Ill Seen Ill Said* and *Worstward Ho* (1989) (Gontarski cited in Gendron, 2008, 76). As Sarah Gendron writes: "Far from 'unwording the world,' the technique of repeating a few basic words – 'with only minor variants' – allows for a gradual accumulation of language. In effect, the text produces itself by continuously reusing words and expressions that had previously been employed" (Gendron, 2008, 76).

The verb "change" changes position upon repeating as Beckett employs the word to carry out its own command, as it were, as a kind of internal wordpainting. It occurs at the end, middle and beginning of sentences – "The eye has changed" (24); "Absence has changed them" (26); "Where still more to change" (29); "Changed but not enough" (31). Here the words reflect the content, as we saw with the word "less" earlier. The word "changed" appears many times, in sentences 24, 26, 31 and 51, and as "change" in sentence 38. Another word that moves position is "go", appearing in sentence 28 (mid-sentence) and echoed in sentences 37 (mid-sentence), 47 (at end) and 55 (at end). Similarly, "Too soon", sentence 4, is an echoing motif that recurs later as "no sooner" (middle of 22), and again in its original format but within a longer sentence in sentences 30 (at end) and 37 (in middle).

The word "again" occurs no less than ten times in this one paragraph, (7, 18, 28, 34, 38, 39, 48, 54 and indeed twice in 37), often but not always at the end of the sentence. The densest appearance of "again" is in sentences 37

78 *Beckett's semantic fluidity*

to 39: "And if again too soon go again. Change still more again. Then back again." Here, the very act of repeating is reflected in the frequent appearance of the word "again".

3. Binary oppositional repetitions

Ill Seen Ill Said is full of binaries such as "First last moment" (p. 59), and these binary oppositional repeats are so frequent in Beckett's work that I have categorised them separately. The antiphonal, question and answer trope in Beckett's writing is certainly related to this. Here, Beckett employs binary oppositional repeats in lines 13 and 14, "more nor less. Less!" Line 22 may not repeat a word but the binary of dawn and dusk follows the same idea: "Day no sooner *risen fallen*" (emphasis added). The light/dark dichotomy in this paragraph further manifests itself in the contrast of day and night – "day" (18, 22), "night" (20, 45). Other semantic binaries are "before" (16, 54)/"after" (1, 2) – what is interesting here is that "before" occurs at the end of the paragraph while "after" appears in the first sentence. Beckett plays with time: as tenses shift, the centre is displaced. Similarly, we see the binary of "Begin" (52) with "finish" (35, 43); "still" (29, 38) and "go" (28, 47, 55); sadness versus happiness – "sadly" (16), "happy" (17), "On the lips same minute smile. If smile is what it was" (11–12); parting versus meeting – Strangers" (32), "parting" (53), "see her again" (48), "meet" (54). These binaries all serve to deconstruct the idea of certainty, of creating a greyer world of semantic fluidity, which is what *Ill Seen Ill Said* seeks to achieve and what Beckett's overarching aesthetics gravitate towards. *Ill Seen Ill Said* is, at its core, the story of a woman whose senses are in decline, a process which leads her to question the very nature of reality. In the "winter" of her life the woman progresses, as does the language, through "change".

4. Discursive repetition recurring throughout Ill Seen Ill Said

Some of the phrases that appear in this paragraph repeat elsewhere in the book as a whole. The sentence "Neither more nor less. Less!" appears earlier on page 49 and later on page 57. And the smile motif from sentences 11 and 12 is on page 49 ("If smile is what it is"). "What is the wrong word?" appears on pages 17, 44 and 59.

As previously mentioned, one of the motifs that recurs throughout the book, "ill seen ill said", is present here, fragmented in sentence 16 and fully reiterated in sentences 23 and 33. It also occurs on page 43. Other discursive motifs that are employed throughout the book include "when not evening night" (pp. 25 and 41) and the self-reflexive tropes whereby the narrator seems to self-direct progress – "careful" (pp. 8, 9, 18, 20, 23, 30, 39, 41, 47), "On" (pp. 7, 8, 20), "gently" (pp. 11, 20, 31, 48), "enough" (pp. 10, 50, 54), "question answered" (pp. 9, 29, 37, 38, 41, 47, 48).

Close reading no. 2 from *Ill Seen Ill Said*

1.Times when she is gone. **2.**Long lapses of time. **3.**At crocus time it would be making for the distant tomb. **4.**To have that on the imagination! **5.**On top of the rest. **6.**Bearing by the stem or round her arm the cross or wreath. **7.**But she can be gone at any time. **8.**From one moment of the year to the next suddenly no longer there. **9.**No longer anywhere to be seen. **10.**Nor by the eye of flesh nor by the other. **11.**Then as suddenly there again. **12.**Long after. **13.**So on. **14.**Any other would renounce. **15.**Avow, No one. **16.**No one more. **17.**Any other than this other. **18.**In wait for her to reappear. **19.**In order to resume. **20.**Resume the – what is the word? **21.**What is the wrong word?

(Beckett, [1981] 1997, 16–17, sentence numbering added)

Of the 126 words in this paragraph, only 72 are unique, so that we again approach the ratio of 2:1. Figure 4.3 sets out, as in the previous example, the repeated words and phrases by number and percentage in relation to the word count of the paragraph.

If we include "times" as a slight variant pluralisation of "time", then we can see four repeats of the word in this short paragraph of 21 sentences. There are in this case no exact clothed repetitions, but there are indeed a number of binary oppositional repetitions and positional musematic local repetitions.

In terms of position, the word "time" occurs at different points in four sentences, as again Beckett employs the transience implied by the word to self-command its function. The paragraph opens with "Times" as the first word, while "time" ends sentence 2. In the third sentence time is absorbed into the middle of the phrase before appearing once more at the end of sentence 7. The phrase "one moment" appears in the middle of sentence 8, further emphasising the theme of ephemerality in this paragraph. Many of the sentences close with a word that begins the next consecutive sentence – anadiplosis again. In sentences 8 and 9 we see "no longer there. No longer anywhere", in 15 and 16 "Avow, No one. No one more", in 19 and 20 "to resume. Resume the", and in 20 and 21 "what is the word? What is the wrong word?". The last two sentences are also an example of a binary oppositional repetition as Beckett questions the very existence of a satisfactory and comprehensive word choice, a common theme in his work. "What is the word?" as a phrase itself is in fact the name of Beckett's last written work, a poem. In *Ill Seen Ill Said*, Beckett furthers his long exploration of the failures of language and, as mentioned above, engages in deconstructing the notions of certainty itself. The phrase also recurs discursively throughout *Ill Seen Ill Said*, as previously mentioned (on page 17 as "what is the word? What the wrong word?" and on both pages 44 and 59 as "what is the wrong word").

These examples of musematic repetition, ending one sentence and sparking the next, in anadiplosis, produce a phonetic quality akin to the effect of

80 Beckett's semantic fluidity

PHRASE	COUNT	PERCENT
the	12	9.524
to	5	3.968
other	4	3.175
of	4	3.175
no	4	3.175
by the	3	4.762
time	3	2.381
one	3	2.381
any	3	2.381
on	3	2.381
is	3	2.381
by	3	2.381
be	3	2.381
what is the	2	4.762
nor by the	2	4.762
no longer	2	3.175
any other	2	3.175
suddenly	2	1.587
what is	2	3.175
longer	2	1.587
resume	2	1.587
nor by	2	3.175
of the	2	3.175
no one	2	3.175
is the	2	3.175
would	2	1.587
there	2	1.587
gone	2	1.587
what	2	1.587
word	2	1.587
long	2	1.587
she	2	1.587
nor	2	1.587
her	2	1.587
for	2	1.587
or	2	1.587
in	2	1.587
at	2	1.587

Figure 4.3 Analysis of segment no. 2 from *Ill Seen Ill Said*

conversation or of being through-composed. As with the previous example, this meticulous prose provides at times the illusion of improvised automatic writing of the kind that Yeats experimented with in his esoteric explorations with his wife George that eventually led to *A Vision* ([1925] 2008).

The repeated words here are often self-reflexive, once again in the Joycean fashion. Reminiscent also of Swiftean directions to the "gentle reader", the narrator directs himself during the course of the writing. Of special interest

Beckett's semantic fluidity 81

in this paragraph is the appearance of sentence 13: "So on", another discursive phrase within the book as a whole, having appeared as sentence 42 in the example analysed in the previous section.

To further illustrate how these repeats appear in Beckett's later prose, let us explore a short excerpt from *Worstward Ho* (1983c).

Close reading from *Worstward Ho*

> 1.Less. 2.Less seen. 3.Less seeing. 4.Less seen and seeing when with words than when not. 5.When somehow than when nohow. 6.Stare by words dimmed. 7.Shades dimmed. 8.Void dimmed. 9.Dim dimmed. 10.All there as when no words. 11.As when nohow. 12.Only all dimmed. 13.Til blank again. 14.No words again. 15.Nohow again. 16.Then all undimmed. 17.Stare undimmed. 18.That words had dimmed.
>
> (Beckett, 1983c, 39, sentence numbering added)

Of the 59 words in this paragraph, 29 are unique – thus the $c.2{:}1$ repetition ratio is present again. The individual unique words are as follows: less, seen, seeing, and, when, with, than, dim, there, as, til, then, that, had, not, somehow, nohow, by, all, no, only, all, again, words, stare, shades, void, blank, undimmed.

Figure 4.4 sets out the frequency of each repeated word and phrase.

The theme of this paragraph is most likely the act of writing itself (words) and the common Beckettian trope of "failing better".[8] The protagonist toils with the blank page invoking inspiration in order to assuage the need and obligation to express in the void. "Stare by words dimmed" – the narrator gazes at the page attempting or straining to enlighten, to undim, or know, to somehow remove the nohow and the shade.[9]

Position is imperative in these repeats as we have seen in the previous examples. Anaphora is prominent: "Less" always appears at the beginning of a sentence (4 times) in four successive occurrences (1–4). So is epistrophe: "dimmed" always appears at the end of a sentence (5 times, sentences 6, 7, 8, 9, 18) and twice as "undimmed" (16, 17), its contrasting binary. Sentence 9 in fact consists of the verb "dim" alongside the past participle "dimmed". Beckett was preoccupied with beginnings and endings as much as he was with unendings – we remember his comments on "the long sonata of the dead" (*Molloy*, [1951] 1994, 31–32) – and we are given no better or more succinct expression of this aesthetic than in this paragraph. During the peak section, in terms of Beckett's correspondence with the golden ratio (13–15), three sentences end with "again", producing a distinct ternary ostinato effect. The phrase "when nohow" ends sentences 5 and 11, but upon nohow's reappearance as "nohow again" in sentence 15, its repetition is at the start of the sentence.

It is the middle section of this paragraph that is most repetitive, the syllables holding a pattern before again breaking apart. Between sentences 11

82 *Beckett's semantic fluidity*

PHRASE	COUNT	PERCENT
dimmed	6	10.169
when	6	10.169
words	5	8.475
less	4	6.78
nohow	3	5.085
again	3	5.085
all	3	5.085
when nohow	2	6.78
than when	2	6.78
less seen	2	6.78
undimmed	2	3.39
no words	2	6.78
as when	2	6.78
seeing	2	3.39
stare	2	3.39
seen	2	3.39
than	2	3.39
no	2	3.39
as	2	3.39

Figure 4.4 Analysis of segment from *Worstward Ho*

and 15, each sentence holds a four-syllable metre. The ratio of 11 out of 18 corresponds with the golden ratio (.61%), making this a peak stage within the structure of the paragraph. Sentence length is also of interest in this paragraph. Ironically "less" is additive; four sentences add and extend the material following the repeated word. Further to this, in the four consecutive dimming (6–10) sentences, the verb "dim" takes over rather than fizzling out. "Words" and "nohow" appear throughout, while the contrasting "undimmed" opposes the repeat of dim and combines with "words" to conclude the paragraph. In the last five sentences only three new words are introduced ("then, that, had"), the remainder amounting to entirely repeated material.

In terms of binary oppositions, we see "somehow" (5) versus "nohow" (5, 11, 15), the aforementioned "dimmed" versus "undimmed", "words" (4, 18) versus "no words" (10, 14). Sentence 4 is of particular interest in this regard, as two separate binaries are juxtaposed alongside the dual tense of "seen" and "seeing" – "Less seen and seeing when with words than when not".

Conclusion

If we consider George Steiner's point that where texts abandon the "exactions of clear meaning and syntax" they become musical, we can move one step closer to understanding the nature of Beckett's prose (Steiner, [1961]

Beckett's semantic fluidity 83

1985, 47–48). Clear referentiality and meaning in words is certainly reduced as they instead operate more like musical notes. Beckett manages to maintain a semantic fluidity while at the same time writing with such distilled precision. Prieto suggests that a "work of literature that didn't denote anything would not be abstract, it would simply be unreadable, in every sense of the word" (Prieto, 2002a, 27). The problem of a word's associative content perhaps presented more possibilities than hindrances for Beckett; these attributive connotations were used to great effect by him in the creation of an "intelligible" yet "inexplicable" artwork.[10] While the words will always hold some meaning, in Beckett's late work there exists a semantic fluidity; instead of focusing on definitive detail, the reader perceives the text in a manner closer to music.

Stephen Connor writes: "[t]he most important aspect of being-in-the-world, for Beckett, is being in time" (Connor, 2006, 45). The temporal factor is key to the art. Like Feldman's later music, in which he experimented with extending time, repetitions in Beckett become crucially important. Connor believes that Beckett's writing always imposes particular conditions or limitations – the human condition; we are thrown into life *in medias res*, Heidegger's *Geworfenheit* (Connor, 2006, 44). These limitations are what paradoxically enable freedom. As Goethe wrote, "In der Beschränkung zeigt sich erst der Meister" (It is in working within limits that the master reveals himself); the artist is forced to innovate within constraints, just as humans learn to live in the face of death (Goethe quoted in Wilde, [1891] 1997b, 930).

Like the loop music discussed in Chapter 2, Beckett would embrace technology in his work,[11] in the many media for which he wrote. *Krapp's Last Tape* ([1957] 2006), uses loops in order to explore the nature of memory and the recorded text. As Krapp listens back to these documents of any earlier self, he undergoes a Proustian journey through a painful past. The novel *Molloy* is also a kind of loop, ending where it began but transformed to some degree. Indeed, the entire series of novels from *Murphy* to *The Unnamable* are a kind of recapitulation of the same story.

In the theatre, the precision of Beckett's stage directions might prevent errors of direction, but the fact remains that while the codes of production might be clear, the codes of reception are certainly not. The author plays with expectation, meanings and symbols. It would seem futile to seek out Beckett's own intention of meaning in his writing (he himself avoided discussions of meaning, or indeed any exegesis of his work at all cost throughout his career), for the very structures of the work itself defies and deconstructs clear and definite meanings.

As mentioned in Chapter 2, Hegarty describes noise music as being based on an aesthetic of failure. This is also an apt description of Beckett's aesthetic. The writer's famous dictum "Try again. Fail again. Fail better" (*Worstward Ho*, 1983c) is manifested in the "fundamental sounds" of repetition (letter to

84 *Beckett's semantic fluidity*

Alan Schneider, Paris, 12 August, 1957, in Beckett and Schneider, 1998, 15). As the word "Fail" is repeated anaphorically, so Beckett's repetition of words, themes and familiar characters and situations perennially bemoan the short-falls of language in fully expressing the human condition. Daniel Albright views Beckett's theatre as "the dramatic equivalent of the music of John Cage" (Albright cited in Abbott, 2004, 716). In the final chapter I will explore how Beckett experimented with chance procedures. The complex dialectic of meaning and erosion of meaning does echo Cage's views on the removal of extramusical meaning, and indeed his emancipation of sounds for their own sake. For Cage (1973), natural sounds did not require added connotations, or metaphors, in order to be viewed as "music": they already were music. Beckett's "fundamental sounds" have much in common.

For Cage, the fact that nothing was being symbolised in sounds made them no less important as "music", while Beckett's words – free of absolutes – never render the work anything less than literature. Instead, his work has reached out to audiences and readers because of this factor. As Wilde believed that openness bred longevity, a new King Lear or Hamlet for audiences, so Beckett's semantic fluidity, his theme of the human condition and his avoid-ance of exegesis help to ensure the lively interpretation of his work. (Wilde, [1891] 1997b, 965–1016). As Beckett himself wrote: "All I know is what the words know, and dead things, and that makes a handsome little sum, with a beginning and a middle and an end, as in the well-built phrase and the long sonata of the dead" (Beckett, *Molloy*, [1951] 1994, 31).

Notes

1 Scholars who have claimed the importance of Schopenhauer to Beckett include: Harvey, Hesla, Märtens, Cohn, Pilling, Rabinovitz, Knowlson, Maier, Moorjani, Rabaté, Acheson, O'Hara, and Büttner.
2 "Pure music" is of course untenable as a term today. Perhaps Joyce meant an unproblematised "absolute" music or maybe "instrumental music" – that the work acted as a performative text exhibiting musical qualities, or this may even be an example of the common Hiberno-English practice whereby a noun is preceded by the attributive adjective "pure" to emphasise quality. Beckett did occasionally use the unproblematised expression "pure music" subsequently.
3 A fine example is Mallarmé's "Un coup de dés" (1897).
4 The term "absurd" was famously applied to Beckett much later, notably by Martin Esslin, but in a different sense. See Esslin, *The Theatre of the Absurd*, Third Edition ([1962] 2004).
5 I owe a debt to Elisabeth Bregman Segrè for her conceptualisation of oppositional poles in Beckett's prose (Segrè, 1977).
6 The software that I used for counting these repetitions was developed by Steven Whitney, at http://25yearsofprogramming.com/perl/phrasecounter.htm (no longer available). Whitney explains that the percentage is = ([# of repetitions of the phrase] * [# of words in the phrase] / [total word count of the text]) * 100.
7 See http://rhetoric.byu.edu/Figures/Groupings/of%20Repetition.htm [accessed 14 August 2013].

Beckett's semantic fluidity 85

8 The famous Beckett quote – "Ever tried. Ever failed. No matter. Try Again. Fail again. Fail better" – occurs in *Worstward Ho* (1983c).
9 *Company, Ill Seen Ill Said* and *Worstward Ho* were later published together in a collection called *Nohow On* (1989).
10 The terms "intelligible" and "inexplicable" are the ones Beckett borrows from Schopenhauer in the quote above, taken from Beckett ([1931] 1999, 92).
11 Beckett's *All that Fall* ([1957] 2006) was a pioneering work for the BBC Radiophonic Workshop – for more see Porter (2010).

5 Beckett and Feldman
Time, repetition and the liminal space

Beckett's semantic fluidity was deeply informed by his exploration of the philosophy of music. But how might such repetitive, fluid texts be translated into music? How have the repetitive qualities of Beckett's literary texts been transmitted from text to sounding objects? And what happens to the notion of intermedia when another author, or composer, is involved in the transformation?

Beckett's work has been very influential on modern music. His extensive use of silence and repetition and his experimentation with indeterminacy are interests that he shared with contemporary composers such as John Cage, while Beckett's interest in the distillation of material is echoed in the reductive pieces of György Kurtág and Earl Kim, and the repetitive complexity would greatly influence composers such as Brian Ferneyhough.[1] Other notable Beckettian compositions include Roger Reynolds (*Ping*, 1968); Philip Glass (*Company*, 1984, *Mercier and Camier*, 1979); Luciano Berio (*Sinfonia*, 1968, containing fragments of *The Unnamable*); Richard Barrett (*stirrings*, 2001); John J. H. Philips (*The things one has to listen to* ... (1990); Wolfgang Fortner (*That Time*, 1977); Heinze Hollinger (*Come and Go*, 1977; *Not I*, 1980), Michael Nyman (*Act Without Words 1*, 2001); Antonio Giacometti, *Le allucinazioni di Watt* (1982), based on *Watt*; and the piano interpretations of experimental composer John Tilbury.

But it is perhaps in the work of American composer Morton Feldman that Beckett's influence – and his desire for semantic fluidity in particular – can most clearly be seen. Feldman was attracted by the intangibility of the author's repetitive writing, and sought to transform this musicalised literature, this intense textual recurrence, into an instrumental soundworld. Feldman viewed repetition itself as a kind of translation, and his Beckettian work witnesses the translator (Beckett often self-translated his own work into French and vice versa) translated, via an intermedial slippage, into another artform – music.

Beckett engaged in collaboration with only a couple of composers. He often showed disdain for proposed musical settings of his works, but was also known to encourage the composers whom he respected.[2] Beckett's letters display responses ranging from benevolence (he allowed a young Gerald Barry to use his text) to blunt refusal (he deterred Edouard Coester from setting one of his texts and Werner Egk from composing stage music for *Godot*). In a letter to Coester dated 11 March 1954, Beckett explains his feelings about musical settings and responses to his work in some detail:

> I have already publicly expressed my opposition to any stage music (Werner Egk had thought of writing some). For me that would be an awful mistake. A very different case would be music inspired by the play and I would be greatly flattered by any venture in that direction. But, in saying that, I have in mind instrumental music, no voices. To be quite frank, I do not believe that the text of *Godot* could bear the extensions that any musical setting would inevitably give it. The piece as a dramatic whole, yes, but not the verbal detail. For what is at issue is a speaking whose function is not so much that of having a meaning as of putting up a struggle, poor I hope, against silence, and leading back to it. I find it hard to see it as an integral part of a sound-world. But this drama which you seem to have felt so keenly, if you thought fit to translate it, however freely, into pure music, that would interest me a great deal and give me great pleasure. And then what about silence itself, is it not still waiting for its musician?
>
> (Beckett, 2011, 475–476)

Beckett's position at this stage in his career echoes many of the author's sentiments explored in Chapter 4: namely that a Schopenhauerian "pure music" (see Chapter 4, note 2) should not be corrupted by words (we saw this in our examination of *Proust* ([1931] 1999) in particular); and that his dramatic works "could not bear the extension" that a literal musical translation may afford them.

We must remember, however, that Beckett, always one for contradictions, would later embrace music in many of his plays, including the Schubert lied (D. 827, Op. 43, No. 2) that lends the play *Nacht und Träume* ([1982] 2006) its title, for instance, while Schubert's "Death and the Maiden" (String Quartet No. 14) features in the radio play *All that Fall* ([1956] 2006), or the specific segments from Beethoven's Piano Trio, Op. 70, No. 1 chosen for the television play *Ghost Trio* ([1975] 2006).[3] He would also go on to collaborate with composers, the radio play *Words and Music*, offering his most distilled and thorough philosophical interrogation of the interrelationship of both artforms, music and literature, Beckett's cousin John providing the original score. In 1961 the composer Marcel Mihalovici became quite close to Beckett and wrote a small opera inspired by *Krapp's Last Tape*, entitled *Krapp, ou, La dernière bande*. John Calder has described how Beckett would sit alongside Mihalovici at the piano, actively involved in the arrangement and narrative development of the opera (Calder, 2001, 75). The partnership proved successful; Mihalovici later composed the original music for Beckett's radio play *Cascando* ([1962] 2006). But by far the most fruitful musical collaboration

88　*Beckett and Feldman*

was that between Beckett and Morton Feldman. Feldman composed an anti-opera to Beckett's libretto *Neither* (1977), a new score for Beckett's *Words and Music* (1987), and the last piece that Feldman ever wrote was dedicated to the author, *For Samuel Beckett* (1987). Though Feldman had spent his life exploring temporality, sadly he himself ran out of time before he could compose the intended score for *Cascando*.

I will examine the ways in which Feldman's repetitive music shares many qualities with the author's own aesthetic. But why did such collaboration arise? And what was it in Feldman's work that opened up the possibility of such creative audio-textual exchange, something Beckett had repelled in the past? From the 1950s onwards, and under the influence of John Cage, Feldman began experimenting with open works that incorporated a measure of indeterminacy. Cage's rebellion against previous compositional traditions excited the young Feldman a great deal. Feldman met Cage when both attended a performance of Webern's twelve-tone Symphony, Op. 21; both left before the Romanticism of Rachmaninoff's Symphonic Dances, Op. 45 dared taint their evening of High-Modernism. And yet, Feldman's aesthetic differed a great deal from that of Cage, in that he shared little of his fellow American's interest in musical tricks and grandiose, conceptual statements such as those promoted in *4'33"*. Feldman preferred to stick to traditional instruments and, though he remained a staunch avant-gardist throughout his life, he would often defend those derided by the trend followers (Alex Ross points out Feldman's praise for Sibelius in this regard; Ross, 2006). Feldman once remarked on Cage's influence on his music as follows: "I owe him everything and I owe him nothing" (Feldman in interview with Alan Beckett, 1966).

Feldman's first music after meeting Cage bore the influence of the new artistic circle to which Feldman had been introduced. The New York intellectuals and artists of the 1950s that Feldman knew best included Jackson Pollock, Robert Rauschenberg, Mark Rothko, Franz Kline, Earle Brown and Christian Wolff. In particular, the work of painters Rauschenberg and Rothko exerted a profound influence on his musical ideas. Rauschenberg's early monochromatic work, *White Paintings* (1951) for instance, has clear parallels with Cage's silence, emphasising an ambient environmental engagement with shadow.

This visual influence can be seen most clearly in the employment of patterns as a compositional device, a creative prompt that became a salient characteristic of Feldman's music. The scores for early pieces such as *Projection 1* (1950), for instance, look like paintings themselves, as Feldman developed his idea of graphic scores that allowed the performer certain creative freedoms. Written for solo cello, Feldman left pitch undetermined and to the performer's discretion, within the broad register categories of high, middle and low. Other symbols in the grid include the directions *pizzicato*, *arco*, harmonics (the three performing modes), while the duration of each box is depicted by the amount of space within it. The individual boxes are made up of icti that each account for a 72bpm pulse. In John P. Welsh's analysis of the piece, he

Beckett and Feldman 89

astutely points out that "silence is present far more than sound in each of the three performing modes" (Welsh, 1996, 23).

But Feldman would soon tire of graphic scores that allowed so much indeterminacy, and his later music evolved to be much more specific, only allowing freedoms with regard to durations – the extension of which, playing with time, became a key focus for him. Late works such as String Quartet No. 2 (1983) can last as long as six hours, putting a deliberate amount of strain on performers and listeners alike. In a conversation with Howard Skempton in 1977, Feldman explained that he was trying to "hold the moment":

> I don't think any composer really wants variation, though variation might be a marvellous technical device to achieve the maximum unity of the moment. I don't even like variation as a musical device. I'm trying to hold the moment with the slightest compositional methodology. The thing is how do you sustain it, how do you keep it going? There are many ways you can keep it going. You can become a composer and that's easy! I think that Beethoven's big problem was how not to be just another composer.
>
> (Feldman quoted in Skempton, 1977, 6).

Feldman's desire to stop time, and to "hold the moment" is reminiscent of Beckett's concept of time. This suggests a concord between the two artists that was emerging independently of one another, and from very different sources. In her work on Feldman's concern for the sustainable moment, Catherine Laws posits the composer's intent in terms of an ungraspable narrative:

> To create a purely static spatial object would, therefore, be no more appropriate than the "measuring out of time" that Feldman finds in most Western musical composition. Feldman's undertaking is more complex; the attempt to hold the moment is the attempt to capture time – an impossible task – but in the attempt Feldman exposes the *experience* of the attempt, taking us close to grasping the ungraspable.
>
> (Laws, 2013, 284)

Feldman's later works play with and interrogate the nature of time. Not a great deal changes in the almost static environment of String Quartet No. 2, and while the listener may slip in and out of focused attention, as they might when viewing a painting in a gallery – only occasionally "grasping" the piece – Feldman's music has the power to immerse the listener: suspending redundancy, these small changes mark enormous moments. In the opening bars of the quartet a single pulsing chord is heard 36 times, the only variation being dynamic, although, in the absence of any rhythmic, motivic or harmonic change, the changes in volume become highly noticeable and serve to "keep it going". The stillness of the static chords is reminiscent of Rothko's vertical paintings or Beckett's insistent repetitions. Feldman writes: "The degrees

90 *Beckett and Feldman*

of stasis, found in a Rothko or a Guston, were perhaps the most significant elements that I brought to my music from painting" (1981, 149). The composer would often move between sections, without any kind of development, juxtaposing blocks music, like Rothko's blocks of colour.

Another example of Feldman's use of repetition, this time employing exact clothed repeats in a single part, is *The Viola in My Life (3)* (1970). Here, riff-like ostinato motifs recur throughout the piece. This particular viola run occurs three times in the short composition, each time being preceded and followed by a single bar of silence in the viola and piano line. For the fourth piece in the series of *The Viola in My Life*, Feldman reused the material from the first three, describing the piece itself as a "translation" (1971–1972, repr. 2000, 90). Here, the composer, much like the revisional music of Meredith Monk, wherein the composer often reworks older pieces to form new music, echoes Beckett's process of returning to the same themes and characters in his work (Monk, 2013). Feldman's description of translating his own work is apt considering his relationship with Beckett – the self-translator – but also when exploring whether or not interdisciplinarity involves a kind of translation.

String Quartet No. 2 and *The Viola in My Life (3)* also clearly display how central repetition became to Feldman's approach to composition in his later work, a focus that we will return to shortly.

It was not just his American contemporaries in the visual arts that inspired Feldman: the composer was also greatly influenced by Cézanne's portrayal of time. The composer wrote that Cézanne's concern was "not how to make an object, not how this object exists by way of Time, in Time or about Time, but how this object exists as Time … Time as an Image … This is the area which music, deluded that it was counting out the seconds, has neglected" (Feldman quoted in Laws, 1996, 202). Laws emphasises this idea of "experiential time" in Feldman's music:

> All music creates a kind of virtual experience of time, but Feldman sees this as a mere falsification: the focus should instead be upon the very point of intersection or collision of the two temporal experiences: "real time" and musical time. While music must be played through actual time, he requires it to reveal the experiential nature of time.
>
> (Laws, 2013, 283)

We previously encountered Max Paddison's description of Adorno's sense of "experiential time", in which a Bergsonian ([1946] 2002) understanding of time is divided into "interpretative experience" (*Erfahrung*) and "lived experience" (*Erlebnis*).[4] For Feldman, such a form of "experiential time" is necessary in order to perceive time itself, for time to reveal itself as a creative medium.

Jonathan Kramer's ideas of "vertical musical composition" and "stasis" in non-teleological works make a great deal of sense when considering Feldman's music in this way. Kramer defines "vertical musical composition" as follows: "In music without phrases, without temporal articulation, with total consistency, whatever structure is in the music exists between simultaneous layers of sound, not between successive gestures. Thus, I call the time sense invoked by such music 'vertical'" (Kramer, 1988, 55). He gives, as an example of "vertical time", Terry Riley's *A Rainbow in Curved Air* (1969), in which the composer overdubbed improvisations on top of droning textures. According to Kramer, this provided the "most radical of the new temporalities", with links to the "process" music of Reich and Rzewski (Kramer, 1988, 57):

> Listening to a vertical musical composition can be like looking at a piece of sculpture, we determine for ourselves the pacing of experience: We are free to walk around the piece, view it from many angles, concentrate on some details, see other details in relationship to each other, step back and view the whole, contemplate the relationship between the piece and the space in which we see it, close our eyes and remember, leave the room when we wish, and return for further viewings. No one would claim that we have looked at less than all of the sculpture (though we may have missed some of its subtleties), despite individual selectivity in the viewing process. For each of us, the temporal sequence of viewing postures has been unique. The time spent with the sculpture is structured time, but the structure is placed there by us, as influenced by the piece, its environment, other spectators, and our own moods and tastes. Vertical music, similarly, simply *is*. We can listen to it or ignore it. If we hear only part of the performance we have still heard the *whole* piece, because we know that it will never change.
>
> (Kramer, 1988, 57, original emphasis)

There are, of course, metre changes in Feldman, but in many ways his works do act on this surface level akin to the sculpture that Kramer describes. Significantly, the composer liked to refer to his music as "time canvasses" (Feldman quoted in Laws, 1996, 212). If we return to Lessing's categorisations, it is possible to see that a merging of temporal and spatial artforms is at play in Feldman's spatial "canvasses". But Kramer's assertion that "if we hear only part of the performance we have still heard the *whole* piece" is clearly problematic. Kramer suggests that the general idea of a piece can be grasped from an encounter with only part of the work; and yet Kramer misses the significance of this type of music, it seems. Such an idea is not operable in Feldman's music, which can progress almost like a mantra, rather than via the teleological forms to which Kramer is referring. Feldman's music is meditative, and to appreciate the stillness of such music, the ways in which he holds "the moment with the slightest compositional methodology" requires more than just a few moments. Of course, to suggest an amount of time that a listener must submit to, or whether or not an entire piece must be experienced, is pure conjecture (or is at least well beyond the scope of this chapter, as is the vast amount of nascent research

92   *Beckett and Feldman*

on listening and reception post-Adorno's expert listener).[5] If we consider Kramer's ideas in relation to Gérard Genette's notion of "discourse time" and "narrative time" introduced earlier, we can see that, rather than stepping into a piece and "grasping" its structure, one must engage and submit to the lengthy "discourse time" of Feldman's music in order to fully appreciate its coherence in terms of "narrative time". How would repetition apply in Kramer's static "vertical" music then? The temporal nature of music will always mean that repetitions will remain Deleuzian. Repetitions that seem exact can never be the same at the reception level. As Sarah Gendron puts it: "In repetition, the only certainty is the impossibility of *exact* repetition" (Gendron, 2008, 7, original emphasis).

As it did for Beckett, then, repetition provided Feldman with a method for undermining clear semantics. The composer strove for the same fluidity in music that Beckett sought in literature: a way in which he could negate function and form, in order to reveal sounds in and of themselves. If we return to the analytical categories outlined in the previous chapter, we can usefully unpack Feldman's use of recurrence as an example of what I termed "clothed exact repetition" after Deleuze. For this category, I noted that Beckett would often reiterate the same word or phrase in texts, but their appearance in different contexts and in different time frames brought about change at the reception level. In music, such repetition may manifest itself as recurring motifs. Feldman himself seems to describe his method of "sustain through stasis" in terms of clothed exact repetition, as he finds, at times, old-fashioned ideas of replication to be flawed: "there is a suggestion that what we hear is functional and directional, but we soon realize that this is an illusion: a bit like walking the streets of Berlin – where all the buildings look alike, even if they're not" (Feldman, 1981, quoted in Benson, 2005, 174). If we return to the example of String Quartet No. 2, these repetitions, these literal reiterations, cannot be called exact repeats in terms of reception.

Walter Zimmerman's interview with the composer gives us a unique insight into Feldman's Deleuzian understanding of clothed exact repetition and its importance in his work:

> **Zimmerman**: I see in your pieces that every chord which follows [*sic*] tries to establish a completely different world from the former one.
> **Feldman**: Yes. Actually now [in the later music] I just try to repeat the same chord. I'm reiterating the same chord in inversions. I enjoy that very much, to keep the inversions alive in a sense where everything changes and nothing changes. Actually before I wanted my chords in a sense to be very different [one] from the next, as if almost to erase in one's memory what happened before. That's the way I would keep the time suspended ... by erasing the references and where they came from. You were very fresh into the moment, and you didn't relate it.
> (Zimmermann, 1985, 229, quoted in Hirata, 2006, 215)

Beckett and Feldman 93

Feldman's desire to create music in which "everything changes and nothing changes" also underpins another talk, this time given as part of the Darmstadt lecture held in July 1986 at the 33rd International Summer Courses for New Music. Here, Feldman elaborates on his use of repetition by discussing the influence on his music of Turkish rugs, another form of static, spatial recurrence akin to the work of Rothko, Rauschenberg and Cézanne mentioned above. In a similar way to Kivy's later discussion of carpets and patterns in music, Feldman explains that:

> Another very interesting man, the father of cybernetics, of the computer, had a marvelous phrase. Norbert Wiener. "Hardening of the categories." You know hardening of the arteries? Hardening of the categories. And that's what happens. They get very hard. Which gets us, believe it or not, to why I use the spelling, more microtonal spelling. The hardening of the distance, say, between a minor second. When you're working with a minor second as long as I've been, it's very wide. I hear a minor second like a minor third almost. It's very, very wide. (Laughter). So that perception of hearing is a very interesting thing. Because, conceptually you are not hearing it, but perceptually, you might be able to hear it. So it depends upon how quickly or slowly that note is coming to you, like McEnroe. I'm sure that he sees that ball coming in slow motion. And that's the way I hear that pitch. It's coming to me very slowly, and there's a lot of stuff in there. But I don't use it conceptually. That's why I use the double flats. People think they're leading tones. I don't know. Think what you want. But I use it because I think it's a very practical way of still having the focus of the pitch. And after all, what's a sharp? It's directional, right? And a double sharp is more directional. But I didn't get the idea conceptually, I got the idea from Teppiche, from rugs. (Walter already told you about my interest in Teppiche). But one of the most interesting things about a beautiful old rug in natural vegetable dyes, is that it has "abrash." "Abrash" is that you dye in small quantities. You cannot dye in big bulks of wool. So it's the same, but yet it's not the same. It has a kind of microtonal hue. So when you look at it, it has that kind of marvellous [*sic*] shimmer which is that slight gradation.
>
> (Feldman, 1986, quoted in Ozment, 2011, 15)

So, Feldman's shimmering repetitions are like the patterns in the old rugs that he so admired, with their "microtonal hue" and "slight gradation" achieved thought the process of "abrash"; both "the same" and "not the same"; or rather, the same but ever-changing. His compositions continually play with this idea of difference in order, paradoxically, to "hold the moment"; no repeat ever seems the same for the listener. Feldman achieves his "marvellous shimmer" in a variety of ways, whether it be the abrupt dynamic changes in the opening pulse of String Quartet No. 2, or the recurring squares that populate the graphic score of *Projection 1* for solo cello, which invite the performer

94   *Beckett and Feldman*

to rethink the same image from a number of angles and spatial levels. In both cases, exact repetitions remain perennially "clothed" in the Deleuzian sense. As the natural dyes produce minor variations in colour, so the contextual clothed repetitive patterns of his music produce the "slight gradation" that ensures that his music holds "the moment with the slightest compositional methodology". Deleuzian repetition, where a repeat is never *just* the same, manifests itself nowhere better than in Feldman's music. When Feldman repeats a chord in a different inversion, or when he simply repeats a note at a different time and context, these repetitions take on new and powerful affiliations. A repetition is, as we have seen throughout the previous chapters, never simply an exact repetition, but is instead a much more complex process of creation and reception.

Another passage further equates the colour patterns of rugs with his musical aesthetic and demonstrates the ways in which he observes a connection between his patterns and the technique of "abrash":

> I'm being distracted by a small Turkish village rug of white tile patterns in a diagonal repeat of large stars in lighter tones of red, green, and beige. ... Everything about the rug's coloration, and how the stars are drawn in detail, when the rectangle of a tile is even, how the star is just sketched (as if drawn more quickly), when a tile is uneven and a little bit smaller – this, as well as the staggered placement of the pattern, brings to mind Matisse's mastery of his seesaw balance between movement and stasis. Why is it that even asymmetry has to look and sound right? There is another Anatolian woven object on my floor, which I refer to as the "Jasper Johns" rug. It is an arcane checkerboard format, with no apparent systematic color design except for a free use of the rug's colors reiterating its simple pattern. Implied in the glossy pile (though unevenly worn) of the mountainous Konya region, the older pinks, and lighter blues – was my first hint that there was something there that I could learn, if not apply to my music. The color-scale of most nonurban rugs appears more extensive than it actually is, due to the great variation of shades of the same color (abrash) – a result of the yarn having been died in small quantities. As a composer, I respond to this most singular aspect affecting a rug's coloration and its creation of a monochromatic overall hue. My music has been influenced mainly by the methods in which color is used on essentially simple devices. It has made me question the nature of musical material. What could be used to accommodate, by equally simple means, musical color? Patterns.
>
> (Feldman quoted in Ozment, 2011, 9)

Orchestration, instrumentation and small timbral changes become pivotal in Feldman's aesthetic of repetition and his search to emulate "the great variation of shades of the same color" found in old rugs. Feldman's reductive, repetitive approach, especially in his later work, has sometimes led to him being mislabelled a "Minimalist" composer, a problematic term even for those within its remit, such as Philip Glass, John Adams, Le Monte Young and Michael Nyman. But despite its manipulation of small motivic cells, Feldman's music occupies a very different world from that of the Minimalists: indeed, he situated himself within the avant-garde, considering himself a highly experimental composer of complex music to the last.

As Nyman's seminal text on "Experimental Music", instilled, however, in discussion of Feldman's work, the important cross-pollination of all these twentieth-century Americans should not be underestimated. As we saw previously, it may even be possible to locate a common driving force behind all of these composers. Nyman suggests that the Minimalists actually drew inspiration from European serialism to some extent. He writes:

> The origins of this minimal process music lie in serialism. La Monte Young was attracted by aspects of Webern's music similar to those that interested Christian Wolff. He noticed Webern's tendency to repeat pitches at the same octave positions throughout a section of a movement, and saw that while on the surface level this was a "constant variation" it could also be heard as "stasis, because it uses the same form throughout the length of the piece ... the same information repeated over and over again".
>
> (La Monte Young quoted in Nyman, [1974] 1999, 139)

So, perhaps the Americans and Europeans were not as aesthetically divided as one might think. Feldman was also indebted to the European tradition and wrote serialist pieces in his formative years of study with Stefan Wolpe. The silence, lyricism, and repetitive nature of Webern's music, then, attracted not only Feldman, but also many of his American peers. Nyman describes this attraction as oppositional to how Webern was being perceived in more conservative ways in Europe (Nyman, [1974] 1999, 38). For Feldman, the reduction of materials led to an approach to composition that again echoes Goethe's maxim that the master reveals himself/herself within limits.[6] By fixing certain parameters, Feldman's creativity was pushed to new heights. As this quiet, slow music hangs static, an infinite sonic world is created. With this in mind, it becomes even clearer how Kramer's ideas of "vertical time" and musical "stasis" are useful to an understanding of Feldman's extended, repetitive works.

Both Feldman and Beckett were greatly concerned with the treatment of time and stasis. As we have seen, Feldman's music, with its clothed exact repetition, evolves towards extended time as his vast temporal canvasses unravel like the shimmering gradation of colours on an old Turkish rug, presenting a sonic world that the listener can inhabit. Ruby Cohn considers Beckett's work along similar lines, suggesting that his "plays are unfinal. Rather than Aristotelian beginning, middle, and end, Beckett's plays are endless continua; his protagonists are in the tradition of the Wandering Jew, the Flying

96   *Beckett and Feldman*

Dutchman, the Woman without a Shadow – cursed to endure through time" (Cohn, 1980, 35). William Barrett believes that the idea of beginnings and endings was no longer the focus for the Modernists, an idea most clearly evident in James Joyce's *Ulysses*, as Bloom, the "Wandering Jew" of Dublin meanders the streets (Kramer, 1988, 202). While Beckett's Molloy may have declared his praise for the "long sonata of the dead" with its "beginning, middle and end", his own work clearly contradicts such clear structures (Beckett, [1951] 1994, 31). In fact, Beckett's writing abounds with abandoned beginnings and unresolved endings, from the *da capos* of *Godot* ([1954] 2006) and *Play* ([1963] 2006), to the continuity invoked in the final line of *The Unnamable* ([1953] 1994): "I'll go on." Beckett's works, like the characters within them, perpetually "go on". Working according to similar aesthetic beliefs, Feldman also considers such narratives to be lacking in possibility: he even told Everett Frost in relation to *Words and Music* that "[t]he whole idea of beginning, middle, and end ... would not help as an emotional structure. And so I dipped into it all the time. I learned a lot about Beckett by reading his very early study on 'Remembrance of Things Past [Beckett's *Proust*]'" (Feldman quoted in Frost, in Bryden, 1998, 51).

As we have seen in the previous chapters, Beckett's obsession with time manifested itself in fascinating linguistic and structural ways. In *Proust* ([1931] 1999), for example, Beckett describes time as "that double-headed monster of damnation and salvation" ([1931] 1999, 11). Indeed, the very concept of time pervades the work as both symbol and device. Cohn points out the abundance of clock imagery in Beckett's texts, from Pozzo's watch, given to him by his grandfather (*Godot*), to Krapp's silver watch, and the alarm clock belonging to Clov and Hamm (*Endgame*) (Cohn, 1980, 38). Such imagery also extends into productions of his work. The DVD recording of Sarah Leonard's performance of *Neither* (Radio Sinfonie Orchester Frankfurt, conducted by Zoltan Pesko, DVD 1990 issued from 1977 recording, reissued 2011) is a useful example of this. Clocks are employed as a dominant dramatic feature in this staging, as the static score plays out in real time to a prominent, ticking timepiece. Cohn believes that, in Beckett's work, "time becomes the subject of dramatic dialogue" (Cohn, 1980, 36), in a way similar to the expansive spatial time created by the shimmering repetitions that drive much of Feldman's music. From the "inbetween" text of the *Trilogy*, *Malone Dies* onwards, Beckett would abandon any kind of traditional character development or plot. His non-teleological texts often include characters from previous works, such as Watt, Molloy or Belacqua. Such repetition of characters and references might lead to the notion that Beckett, in one sense, did not compose individual works, but rather one vast canvass that eternally returns to the same theme. For Cohn, *Happy Days* "denies time" (Cohn, 1973, 184) in a way akin to Feldman's search for a "vertical temporality". One is reminded of Walter Benjamin's explorations of the "original" in an age of mechanical replication (Benjamin, [1936] 1973). With such repetition, the very notion of "original" loses meaning; yet, as Benjamin pointed out, the "original" was always greatly indebted to the copy for survival and success. An icon of a famous painting in the format of a postcard, for instance, ensures that the art is preserved in the onlooker's memory. As we saw previously, the recurrence of theme and character intertextually in Beckett's work somewhat negates the idea of "original", and in some ways his *oeuvre* can be seen as a vast, connected canvas.

The reduction of materials, the use of silence and, most of all, the employment of repetition in their work meant that both artists, Beckett and Feldman, were charting similar territories in the latter half of the twentieth century. But initially, the composer's work was unfamiliar to Beckett, as Knowlson reminds us:

> Beckett did not know Feldman's work at all when he wrote the text for him. But, by a strange coincidence, only a few days after posting "Neither", and in London by this time, he was listening to Patrick Magee reading his own *For To End Yet Again* on BBC Radio 3, when he noticed that, in the second part of the "Musica Nova" concert that followed the reading, there was an orchestral piece by Morton Feldman. He listened to it and found he liked it very much.
>
> (Knowlson, 1996, 632)

Feldman quickly found in Beckett a peer who welcomed contradictions: as the composer explained, "it's so universal – that so many people find things in Beckett to relate to on a very personal and emotional level. That's one of the wonderful contradictions in him" (Frost, 1998, 51):

> It's beyond Existentialism, you see, because Existentialism is always looking for a way out, you know. If they feel that God is dead, then long live humanity. Kind of Camus and Sartre. I mean, there's always a substitute to save you in Existentialism. And I feel that Beckett is not involved with that, because there's nothing saving him. For example, the opera that we (it really wasn't an opera; it was just a poem that I extended into an opera length) ... The subject essentially is: whether you're in the shadows of understanding or non-understanding. I mean, finally you're in the shadows. You're not going to arrive at any understanding at all; you're just left there holding this – the hot potato which is life.
>
> (Feldman quoted in Frost, 1998, 51)

Feldman's evocation of the "shadows" between "understanding or non-understanding" provides one of the many points of similarity that exists between the aesthetics of the two artists. Liminality was very appealing to both men, who situated their work in the space between conventional beginnings, endings and dramatic arcs. With reference to the work of Philip Guston, for instance, Feldman once said that the art is not imprisoned in a "painting space" but instead inhabits "somewhere in the space *between the canvas and ourselves*" (Feldman, 1967, repr. 2000, 76). Thomas DeLio

98   Beckett and Feldman

describes Feldman's work along similar lines, describing the composer as "revelling in the inbetweeness" (DeLio, 1996, 149). In this "unspeakable home", no teleology, development or resolution exists. Derrida described this liminal space, this threshold between meanings, as Sarah Gendron writes relating Mallarmé and Derrida: "if one is looking for the meaning of the Mallarménian text, one should not seek it in the extreme points of the text: at the beginning or the end. As Derrida might say, the signification of his text, like the signification of all texts and all words, lies in the ambiguous space of the 'in between': the 'entre de Mallarmé'" (Gendron, 2008, 25).

Other prominent connections between Beckett and Feldman include their penchant for pushing the listener and performer to their limits. While *Not I* ([1972] 2006) might push an actress to emotional turmoil, for example, Feldman's extended works require audience members and performers with both stamina and diligence. Both artists also experimented with aleatoric procedures, leaving certain parameters open to interpretations (as we'll see in the next chapter) in order to include performers and the audience in the construction of a work. Laws finds, along with Derval Tubridy (2012, 151), that translation in Beckett bears a similar aesthetic function to the unique forms of repetition that propel Feldman's music (Laws, 1996, 211). The composer once described translation as "a kind of repetition that incorporates difference", for instance (Feldman quoted in Tubridy, 2012, 151). He also compared the repetitious nature of composition to Beckett's translation of his own writing. In an interview with Everett Frost, for example, Feldman explains that:

> He [Beckett] probably does it in a way that would be very surprising, like saying it to himself in French and then saying it to himself in English. I'm quite sure that many times his way of arriving at something could be absolutely much more clinical, almost pedantically so, than one would think. But the end results are what we're involved with here. So, I understand him to some degree as an artist. I know that there is a clinical approach and then he's learned how to lose it, or to work with it, or to change it. I know that he did tell me that he says things over to himself over and over. I work the same way. I play things or look at things over and over and over.
>
> (Feldman quoted in Frost, 1998, 51)

Describing his compositional process in more detail, Feldman also explained:

> What I do then is, I translate, say something, into a pitchy situation. And then I do it where it's more intervallic, and I take the suggestions of that back into another kind of pitchiness – not the original pitchiness, and so forth, and so on. Always retranslating and then saying, now let's do it with another kind of focus.
>
> (Feldman quoted in Tubridy, 2012, 150)

Beckett and Feldman 99

But while the ideas of translation, interactivity, liminality, the reduction of artistic material and the desire to fold all within a static form of temporal flow create an aesthetic that draws together the work of Feldman and Beckett, perhaps the most significant link between the two for this study is the fact that Feldman also endowed his work with a form of semantic fluidity. As we have seen in previous chapters, semantic fluidity emerges when words or music are repeated to such an extent that meaning or signification, typically brought about through connected affiliations, begin to dissolve. In both Beckett's and Feldman's work, explicit meanings are avoided at all costs, as the artists instead seek creative forms that express the complex, unresolved nature of the human condition. The longing, the unanswered questions, the mystery, the heavy weight of time are all themes favoured by Beckett and Feldman and both employ repetition to explore them. What is especially interesting is how musematic, discursive, binary oppositional and exact clothed repetition (our categories from the previous chapter) can translate from text to instrumental music, and at the same time maintain this semantic fluidity. While Beckett found the inspiration for his semantic fluidity in music and music philosophy, how these ideas get retranslated back into music can be highly revealing.

Neither

Sebastian Claren provides us with a valuable chronology of events around the Beckett/Feldman collaboration, the composer beginning work on the score in Spring 1976 and completing it on 30 January 1977 (Claren, 2000, 521–544). Feldman first met Beckett while the latter was rehearsing *Footfalls* and *That Time* in Berlin on the 20 September 1976 (Knowlson, 1996, 630). Feldman later recounted the episode to Skempton:

> He [Beckett] was very embarrassed – he said to me, after a while: "Mr Feldman, I don't like opera". I said to him, "I don't blame you!" Then he said to me "I don't like my words being set to music", and I said, "I'm in complete agreement. In fact it's very seldom that I've used words. I've written a lot of pieces with voice, and they're wordless". Then he looked at me again and said, "But what do you want?" And I said "I have no idea!" He also asked me why I didn't use existing material … I said that I had read them all, that they were pregnable, they didn't need music. I said that I was looking for the quintessence, something that just hovered.
> (Skempton, 1977, 5)

As Feldman notes, Beckett had little time for opera. His first published work, the critique *Proust* ([1931] 1999), went so far as to label the form a corruption of the Schopenhauerian will, as if by attaching words to "pure music", some of its intangible ideal beauty was tarnished (Beckett, [1931] 1999, 92). But Feldman also disliked opera and rarely set music to texts, something that makes his work with Beckett even more remarkable (a notable exception was

100   *Beckett and Feldman*

his *Four Songs to e. e. cummings* written in 1951). Feldman explained his aversion to opera in a conversation with Everett Frost in 1987:

> the first thing he [Beckett] said to me was that he hated opera. And so did I. I mean, I'm not an opera goer; I hardly ever go to the opera. I just don't experience what exactly, what is meant theatrically [by opera]. If I would have to talk about it, because there's something about, there's something in the world of, uh – I wouldn't want to use a term like prosaic or clichéd, but it's something to some degree related.
>
> (Feldman quoted in Frost, 1998, 50)

According to James Knowlson, Feldman then produced a drafted score that he had written up on some lines from Beckett's *Film* ([1964] 2006), before the author declared that there was but one theme in his life:

> "May I write it down?" [asked Feldman]. (Beckett himself takes Feldman's music paper and writes down the theme ... It reads "To and fro in shadow, from outer shadow to inner shadow. To and fro, between unattainable self and unattainable non-self") ... "It would need a bit of work, wouldn't it? Well, if I get any further ideas on it, I'll send them on to you."
>
> (Knowlson, 1996, 631)

Knowlson recounts that Beckett did indeed send a card to Feldman's home in Buffalo by the end of the month, with the following note attached: "Dear Morton Feldman. Verso the piece I promised. It was good meeting you. Best. Samuel Beckett" (Knowlson, 1996, 631). The text, *neither*, was on the rear of the postcard. Knowlson reminds us that Beckett never thought of it as a poem – he actually considered it short prose – and that the text itself was influenced by his rehearsals in Berlin of the play *Footfalls* ([1975] 2006), owing "one striking image to the play on which he was working so intently: 'unheard footfalls only sound'" (Knowlson, 1996, 632).

Recalling his first encounter with the repetitive libretto, Feldman describes a perplexed and transitory reaction: "I'm reading it. There's something peculiar. I can't catch it. Finally, I see that every line is really the same thought said in another way. And yet the continuity acts as if something else is happening. Nothing else is happening. What you're doing in an almost Proustian way is getting deeper and deeper saturated into the thought" (Feldman, 1985, 185).

Of the 87 words in *neither*, 60 are unique. Figure 5.1 sets out the frequency of repetition in the words and phrases. The text itself isn't as repetitve as other Beckett texts we have seen, but the subject or theme, however, is. The text is full of Beckettian oppositional binaries, of the kind we explored in the previous chapter. The binaries of "to and fro", "self" and "unself", "back and forth", "neared" and "turned away", all present a state of consciouness that yearns for explanations, for answers before death, the final "halt for good". It

PHRASE	COUNT	PERCENT
from	4	4.598
and	4	4.598
gently	3	3.448
the	3	3.448
to	3	3.448
impenetrable	2	2.299
shadow from	2	4.598
for good	2	4.598
neither	2	2.299
turned	2	2.299
shadow	2	2.299
sound	2	2.299
other	2	2.299
self	2	2.299
once	2	2.299
away	2	2.299
good	2	2.299
then	2	2.299
way	2	2.299
for	2	2.299
on	2	2.299
of	2	2.299

Figure 5.1 Analysis of *neither* text

is a text that explores the nature of self-knowledge, a dialectical subject that can only be examined through antithesis. The elusiveness of human perception in the Kantian and Schopenhauerian sense, its flawed and limited capability, is touched on in the final lines, "unspeakable home". As Art Lang writes: "Transformation, then, is not a recovery, but a revealing. The eternal present exists in the space between the familiar and the unfamiliar. Which is real? Neither" (Art Land, 1997, liner notes, *Neither*, Radio Sinfonie Orchester Frankfurt).

Feldman developed this short text, scrawled on the back of a postcard, into an hour-long opera for full orchestra and soprano. The work traverses many terrains, from complex and dense *tuttis* to fragile and ethereal solo passages. So far, we have seen how Beckett included a silenced music in his writing but how does this change when the patterns of repetition are sounded, when silenced music becomes audible once again? *Neither* best embodies all of the tropes discussed thus far.

Feldman does not really depict the words as such, but instead he creates an equivalent soundworld or landscape of consciousness. Unable to "catch" the fleeting, ever-morphing recurrences, Feldman realised that Beckett was effectively repeating the same idea over and over in the libretto: the theme that he spoke of – the impossibility of knowing the self/unself. It was clear to the

102   *Beckett and Feldman*

composer, then, that a suitable musical response might be to write a score that reflected this repeated idea. The chords shift gradually but only in subtle ways, as Feldman's inversions, instrument swapping and transpositions continually play out the same concept. The "comings and goings" of Beckett's aesthetic are thus reflected in the "to and fro" of Feldman's musical response. Far from a standard operatic format, *Neither* is one act with no characterisation or drama. Along the lines of Kramer's ideas on non-teleological music, Feldman deliberately avoided "continuity" so as to fit the Beckettian aesthetic, as he remarked to Skempton: "I didn't want a cause-and-effect continuity, a kind of glue that would take me from one thought to another. I wanted to treat each sentence as a world" (Skempton, 1977).

If we return to the modes of analysis outlined in the previous chapters, we can see some profound intermedial blending occurring. The movement of the position of the chords in the bars ensures that Feldman maintains the "unspeakable home" of the piece. The "to and fro" of the changing time signatures is also an important feature of this Deleuzian repetition. Never is the music exactly the same, but instead Feldman is offering us a slightly manipulated version of previous material, whether it be through transposition, clustering or swapping the accents of the rhythmical patterns. This is very much like Beckett's binary oppositional repetition, as seen in the previous chapter. Where Beckett might use anadiplosis, beginning a sentence with a repeat of the end of the previous sentence, or manipulate the iambs and dactyls rhythmically as binary oppositions, here Feldman applies a similar idea in music. The importance of recurring motifs and note clusters becomes immediately apparent in the score and for this reason a motivic form of analysis is chosen rather than a harmonic one. The repetitive parameters that we applied to Beckett's work in previous chapters offer insights into Feldman's approach, heralding a new kind of intermedial study. As we will see, Feldman's response to the text is both a translation, the term he himself used to describe such Deleuzian repetition, and also an extension of Beckett's text through collaboration.[7]

The static nature of the piece is immediately apparent in the elongated drone of the wind section (Figure 5.2).

Musematic repetition abounds, as Feldman manipulates certain sonorities that may at first seem the same. The soprano line, for instance, has three specific musematic motifs that iterate chosen words alongside other wordless verbal ideas. The first of these vocal ideas (Figure 5.3), which I call V1, occurs with the first entrance of the soprano just before Feldman's figure 15.

On the words "To and fro in shadow, from inner to outer shadow", the first two lines of Beckett's text, the soprano repeats a G^2 note for each syllable. The accompaniment here consists of droning elongated static chords in the wind section, cellos and basses with some interweaving repetitive textures in the percussion and harp lines. The first five syllables, from "to" to "sha", all consist of a minim tied to a dotted crotchet, with each bar beginning with a triplet crotchet rest. Conversely, this changes on the syllable "dow", to become a

Figure 5.2 Neither, bars 1–12

Figure 5.3 Neither, excerpt from figure 14

Figure 5.4 Neither, excerpt from figure 15

Figure 5.5 Neither, excerpt from figure 18

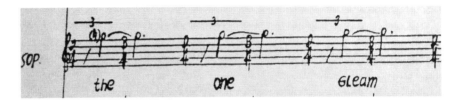

Figure 5.6 Neither, excerpt from figure 59

triplet crotchet rest followed by a crotchet tied to a dotted crotchet. Beginning just before figure 16, we see this idea over the words "from inner to outer shadow", but with the time signatures reflecting a bar of $\frac{2}{4}$ (a crotchet rest and crotchet G tied to a dotted crotchet in $\frac{3}{8}$) (Figure 5.4). This rhythm of the triplet crotchet rest followed by minim tied to dotted crotchet reappears on all words, moving between $\frac{2}{4}$ and $\frac{3}{8}$. Here, repetitive timpani fill in for the lack of winds. Once again, Feldman employs different instrumentation to add variety and colour to repetitive material.

A slight variation of V1 occurs around figure 19, for the line "from impenetrable self to impenetrable unself". Here, the rhythmic material changes to fit the staccato syllables (Figure 5.5)

Feldman again plays with the time signature in the next appearance of V1 in figures 59/60 with the words "the one gleam or the other". A repeated G^2 in the soprano (Figure 5.6) this time moves from $\frac{2}{4}$ to $\frac{3}{4}$ marked by a triplet of a crotchet rest and minim tied over the bar to a dotted minim.

So the time signatures reflect this "to and fro" in the text, and the penumbra of self-knowledge is equally depicted in Feldman's unclear teleology. The

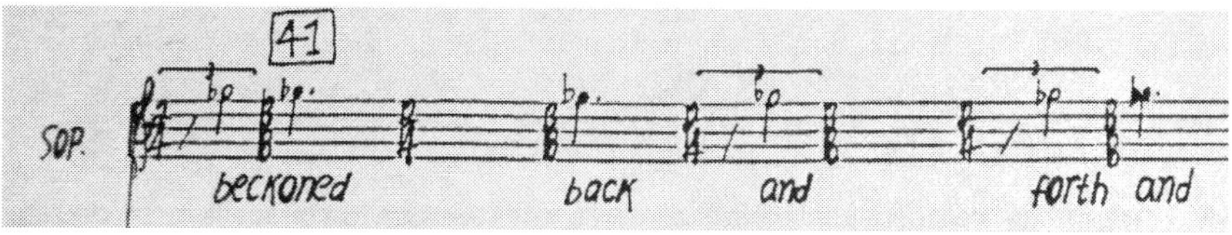

Figure 5.7 Neither, excerpt from figure 41

elusive environment of the text is being recreated in the music itself. Feldman's music "shimmers" in its stillness, reflecting traits of Kramer's vertical time

A variation of V1, recurring $G\flat$ notes on the words "beckoned back and forth and turned away", occurs at figure 41. This time, the V1 in the soprano is adumbrated by its occurrence in the preceding bars of the cello part. A bar of $\frac{2}{4}$ is divided into a triplet of a crotchet rest and a minim, before the next bar of $\frac{3}{8}$ features a dotted crotchet. Here (Figure 5.7), the bars are not tied. For the words "back and forth and" Feldman essentially inserts a palindrome in the soprano rhythm, like Beckett's binary anadiplosis, with "and" and "forth" each in $\frac{2}{4}$. The accompanying percussion mirrors this echoing. As Laws (1996, 202) suggests, the "concern is with keeping the piece going; his [Feldman's] interest lies with the process of duration extended by means of change and reiteration".

At figure 91 the soprano returns with the line "unheard footfalls only sound", employing yet a further variation of V1 (Figure 5.8). This time, staccato quavers are followed by staccato crotchets before a longer emphasis on the word "sound". Feldman marks out this word "sound" for special repetition, repeating it another two times, but these echoes are pluralised to "sounds" in elongated musematic fashion (Figure 5.9). The composer emphasises the dominance of music over text here by deliberately altering the text, an aesthetic choice furthered by the obscured rendition of the words by the high-registered tessitura of the soprano. Significantly, every syllable is set on the dominant D^2 note, as the music metaphorically claims its higher, more semantically fluid, place in the arts. The line of text "unheard footfalls only sound" is sounded out three consecutive times from figures 91 to 93, and the repetition of this line is clearly also due to its reference to footsteps and sound itself.

Neither, V2

The second main musematic vocal idea is one that first appears at figure 25 (Figure 5.10) and continues through figure 27. Where before the soprano stuck to one individual note, here a three-note motif is introduced, while the cello, basses and violas hold static chords.

106 Beckett and Feldman

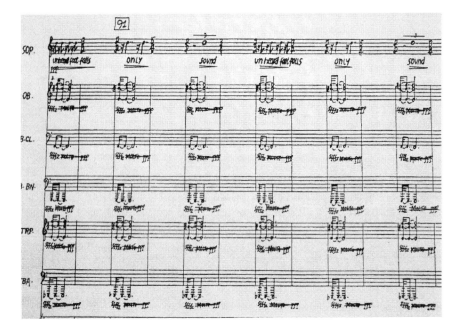

Figure 5.8 Neither, excerpt from figure 91

Figure 5.9 Neither, excerpt from figure 92

Figure 5.10 Neither, excerpt from figures 25/26

On the word "doors", we see an F#, G, A♭; three quavers in $\frac{3}{8}$. The A♭ is tied into the following bar, which consists of a triplet of a minim and crotchet rest in $\frac{2}{4}$, extending the final utterance in a way similar to that of motive V1. The tied notes, time signatures and the triplet make this idea, which will be referred to as V2, quite similar to V1, but the occurrence of this three-note motif on each syllable makes it notably separate and distinct. This motivic development or extension of V1 introduces a neighbour note on either side of the V1 motif. The metaphor of Feldman's chromaticism matches Beckett's dark subject matter in a way that does seem to imply certain affiliations. Semantic fluidity cannot always be maintained completely; some meaning will inevitably be consensually grounded, pinned down rather than left afloat for the listener to gather. The insistent repetition of this chromatic run of three pitches soon becomes chant-like against the alternating textures of the accompaniment. The binary of self/unself in the text is matched by the soprano's stillness in relation to the other instruments.

An elongation of this V2 rhythm is found on page 30 (Feldman, 1977), beginning in figure 49 on the word "heedless" (Figure 5.11). Here we have a bar of $\frac{3}{8}$ consisting of a dotted crotchet on the note F# tied into the next bar of $\frac{2}{2}$ containing three minims in a triplet on the notes F#, G, A♭ that seem to "hold the moment".

The A♭ is tied over into the next bar of $\frac{3}{8}$ with a dotted crotchet. Essentially, then, this variation inserts an extra syllable marked by the dotted tied crotchet on the beginning of the V2 idea seen previously on pages 17–19. At figure 63 we can see a wordless variation of the V2 motive, and once more, but this time elongated, around figure 71. If we recall Feldman's assertion above that "by erasing the references and where they came from ... [y]ou were very fresh into the moment, and you didn't relate it", we can see that, here, such minor variants can achieve a great deal of change over such vast canvasses of static material.

Another variation of V2, amounting to a combination of V1 and V2, or in another way an elongation (like that around figure 71) of V2, can be seen six bars before figure 95, with the words "till at last halt for good" (Figure 5.12).

As we can clearly see, Feldman uses the same rhythmic material, as V1 appears, this time a semibreve triplet rest, before the triplet minim in $\frac{2}{2}$ is tied over the bar to a dotted crotchet in $\frac{3}{8}$. The same three-note sequence as the

Figure 5.11 Neither, excerpt from figure 49

Figure 5.12 Neither, excerpt from figure 95

V2 motif recurs here, but now further spread apart (F#, G, A♭). By extending the words over repeats of three notes instead of single notes, Feldman enlivens the piece, adding an extra layer of colour, or rather, another "shimmer" or shade to the same colour. The repetitive V2 ostinato clashes with the accompanying atonal textures somewhat reflecting the futility of death, the "halt for good".

Neither, V3

The third main soprano musematic motif is the four-note idea seen at figure 128 (Figure 5.13). Like V1, this idea consists of one note per syllable; but this time, instead of a repeated single tone, a four-note sequence of notes repeats after every four syllables, on the rotating note pattern B♭, A♭, A♮, B♮.

On page 71, from figure 129, we see the word "neither" repeated six times in this high register (Figure 5.14), and then another two times in figure 131.

This is an important moment; and one in which Feldman's logic departs from the simple, single utterance offered by Beckett. The last three utterances of the word "neither", however, break from the four-note sequence and instead condense the second half into a single bar that is repeated two bars into figure 131. Like "neither", the final line – "unspeakable home" – repeats eight times, beginning on figure 135 (Figure 5.15), bringing the opera to a close. At a tempo change of 42bpm, Feldman makes the soprano line much denser and highly melismatic. Significantly, variations of elements of the previous V1, V2 and V3 motifs can be seen in the changing contours of this melodic material.

The homophonic texture in the accompaniment further emphasises the intensity of the soprano's futile despair in these final moments, while the interweaving repetitive patterns from V1, V2 and V3 almost approach regularity without ever truly achieving it, and in the end fall apart. Repetitive textures further emphasise the melismatic soprano's high, abrasive tessitura.

Figure 5.13 *Neither*, excerpt from figure 128

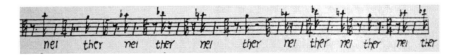

Figure 5.14 *Neither*, excerpt from figures 129/130

Beckett and Feldman 109

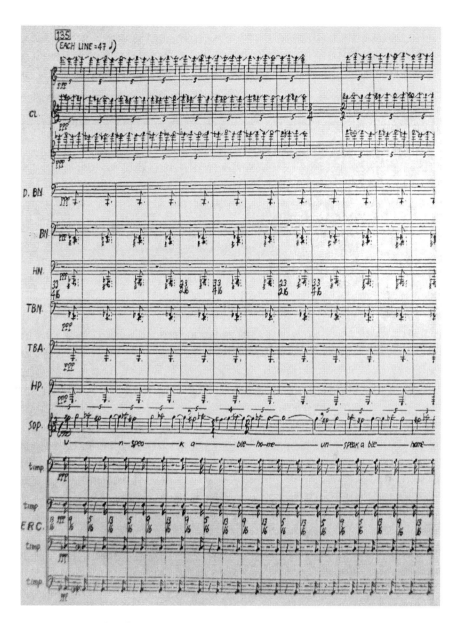

Figure 5.15 Neither, figure 135

In Beckett's letter cited earlier, he had written in relation to *Godot*: "I do not believe that the text of *Godot* could bear the extensions that any musical setting would inevitably give it. The piece as a dramatic whole, yes, but not the verbal detail." Yet here, Feldman's music really furthers the longing of

Figure 5.16 *Neither*, figure 46

Beckett's verbal text – both arts work together in symbiosis to create a work that offers more than the sum of its parts.

The nine-note interlocking texture

Discursive repetition also features in Feldman's treatment of *Neither* in repetitive phrases that recur structurally throughout the work. Acting like a fanfare, the nine-note wordless motif first appearing around figure 46 (Figure 5.16) is a particularly memorable discursive repetition that at first glance appears to be a question followed by an answer, a very Beckettian use of musical theory, perhaps. But on closer inspection, what these two bars amount to is a rearticulated question. Just like Beckett's text, Feldman's music reiterates the question in numerous ways. He told Frost that "[i]t was wordpainting" (Frost, 1998, 54); but of course, in Feldman's aesthetic word painting was something quite unique, something more akin to the forms of representation found on the canvasses of Rothko or Pollock. Just as the questions remain unanswered in Beckett's words, so too do they go without response in Feldman's sounds. The music responds to, and reflects, the longing and yearning of the human condition, the theme of the libretto. Non-developmental in nature, Feldman sought and found a musical parallel to Beckett's non-specific Schopenhauerian text, a libretto that leaves any further interpretation open and fluid.

At figure 46, although all instruments are in unison, the phrasing makes this texture especially alluring. Each instrument has different articulations in their respective phrasing of the part. The horn and bass clarinet are in unison, for example, but the horn is phrased in 6s while the bass clarinet moves in 7s.

Beckett and Feldman 111

The three trombones are likewise grouped in opposing clusters of 4s, 3s and 5s respectively. Following twelve bars of this texture, Feldman changes the instrumentation to three trumpets grouped in 6s, 4s and 3s, a cello grouped in 7s, two violas grouped in 8s and 2s alongside the same contrabassoon bass stabs. The employment of such articulations and in such a repetitive interlocking fashion produces a consistent throb from the different timbres. The lack of accents or dynamics bar the *ppp* at the start of each system suggests a more *fluid* voicing where the only emphasis is one of articulation, a static colour, like that of the painters he so admired. The change or variation comes about through the different orchestral timbres introduced, an alteration of shade and texture rather than motive or harmony. Here the notes are repeated, but the instrumentation changes, a common characteristic of Feldman's Deleuzian repetition, like Beckett's exact clothed repeats seen in the previous chapter.

At figure 48, we see that the cello continues the motif in groups of 7s, while the only other instrument playing the motif is the solo violin, which changes its articulations from 2s to 3s, 4s, back to 3s in bar 468, then 5s, back to 2s in bar 472, then 6s, 3s, 5s, 4s and finally 7s. Significantly, the accompanying timpani and cymbal rolls remain static and unchanging. Feldman is, by playing the same motif through different instrumental combinations and articulations, essentially looking at the same object from different perspectives. This parallax effect is reminiscent of Joyce's Dublin in *Ulysses*, as the individual characters view the same events unfolding concurrently from different viewpoints in the city. Vertical time and stasis are the real goal here, rather than any traditional teleological development.

When the soprano re-enters at figure 49, with the V2 motif repeating melodically the line "Heedless of the way, intent on" (Figure 5.17), Feldman breaks up Beckett's line; the remainder of the phase, "the one gleam or the other" (Figure 5.18), appears later on (page 36, figure 59), but this time with the V1 motif. Here, any sort of teleology breaks apart: V2 – an extended variant of V1 – begins the phrase, reducing down to V1 almost 100 bars later for the development of the text, in a sense, preventing any semantic continuity. But does this suggest a disregard of Beckett's text by the composer; or is he pulling out something that is lying silenced in the libretto? Is Feldman composing not just with words, but also with that which lies within the "shadows" between verbal "understanding or non-understanding"?

The three bassoons here provide accompaniment (Figure 5.17). As we can see, the third bassoon comes in with F♮ held *ppp*, dying to nothing, and is quickly joined by the second bassoon on F# at the same dynamic. A cluster is formed by the first bassoon at the end of the bar on the note G. All three notes are contained in the nine-note interlocking section preceding this. This nine-note riff becomes refrain-like in *Neither*, in the Poe-like manner that we spoke of in Chapter 2. It enlivens the opera with a memorable discursive repetitive melody and texture, somewhat like a *ritornello* or fanfare. Of course this is not a tonal melody, but instead a chromatic contour that suits

Figure. 5.17 Neither, excerpt from figures 49/50

the libretto well: universal, dark and moving. The refrain thus serves as an interlude, and practically speaking, it offers a rest for the soprano from the strenuous demands of the work.

Bassoons follow by playing the same idea again but in a different order: F# for a bar, then the first bassoon adds its G, while simultaneously the third bassoon adds its F♮. The soprano enters with her F#, ensuring a close jar. When she finishes, there is a bar of silence before she re-enters alone with the V2 motif again. Like in *Projection 1*, Feldman uses silence here to great effect in *Neither*. But while this is happening, violin, viola and cello appear on the rising part of the soprano notes. The strings play clusters including every single chromatic note except, C, A and G#. A repetitive texture follows on page 31, 5 bars into figure 50 (Figure 5.19), where parts are shared between the voices – what I refer to as the shared dialogue section. Each instrument has its note and that does not change until we return to the interlocking nine-note idea at figure 52/53.

Here, the solo violin plays double-stop perfect fourths, grouped in 2s, this time accompanied by its stringed peers – the viola phrased in 3s, third violin in 4s, and the second violin in 5s. At the same time, this is supported by

Beckett and Feldman 113

Figure 5.18 Neither, excerpt from figures 59/60

rhythmic interjections in the percussion – from timpani, consistent repetitive rolls on the tam tam, and alternate bars of silence and marimba shimmers. This injection of rhythm provides a build before the return of the nine-note motif. The vibraphone and piano also play the motif, the piano grouped in

114 *Beckett and Feldman*

Figure 5.19 Neither, excerpt from figure 50

6s. The harp is playing in the same bars as the marimba but a triplet later. In contrast to the first appearance of the nine-note interlocking texture, here the soprano enters with the V2 motif and light accompaniment, followed by 18 bars of pulsing shared voices for a second time, implying some concordance in the soundworld. The nine-note texture is on this second discursive, repetitive appearance much lighter and even somewhat consonant on account of the added perfect fourths in the solo violin.

The nine-note interlocking texture returns for a third time on page 40 at figure 69 (Figure 5.20). This time, the shared dialogue section, seen earlier, is combined with the nine-note texture. The soprano sings the motif as a wordless instrument before returning to a V2 variation, 2 bars before figure 71, also wordless. Semantic fluidity has reached a peak here. Words are no longer present, as the voice becomes an instrument like any other in the orchestra. The V2 motif does, however, retain its musematic affiliations gathered from its previous appearances, though it may now be textless.

Repetitive droning cymbals and gongs in rising fifths accompany this elongated variation of the V2 motif, while the other instrumentation is sparse. The tuba, harp and D♭ bassoon offer occasional stabs, whereas the violins and violas accompany the soprano's A♭, with a clashing A♮, a minor second

Beckett and Feldman 115

Figure 5.20 Neither, excerpt from figure 69

so characteristic of Feldman. Following this utterance, we don't go into the shared dialogue idea as before, but instead we are offered an extended drone section with wordless soprano variations. The instruments, including the voice, converse by way of music alone, something Beckett would no doubt have enjoyed.

Two bars before figure 79, the soprano again sings wordless variations of the V1 motif before the final discursive return of the nine-note interlocking

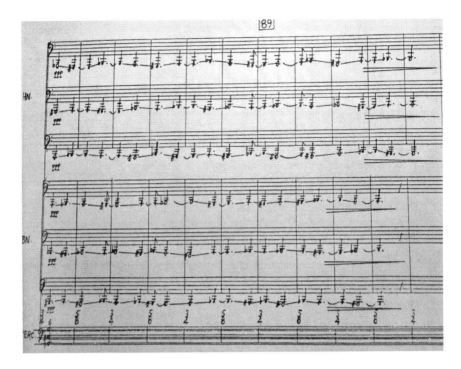

Figure 5.21 Neither, excerpt from figure 88

texture at figure 86. All instruments are now playing the motif in unison, each with their own articulation grouping as before. Coming out of the texture this fourth and final time, we have a melismatic texture of three horns, three trombones and percussion (4 bars into figure 88 – Figure 5.21). This fits with the yearning and longing expressed in the libretto, before we enter the insistent exclamation of "unheard footfalls only sound", discussed above.

As we have seen, Feldman's music for *Neither* displays the use of interspersed motifs and silent space, rhythmic interlocking and manipulations of accents and time signatures that keep the music going "back and forth" – depicting those very lines in the libretto and the central theme of the text. The repetitive nature of the libretto and, in particular, Feldman's belief that Beckett reiterates the same idea in various ways, is matched by the music composed: not in a literal way, but by suggestion and the recurrent manipulation of the material. In sum, *Neither* provides us with a complex example of music and literature interaction through the employment of semantic fluidity, achieved through repetition at both the textual and musical levels, even if the types of repetition do not always coincide. This non-teleological, non-developmental music achieves stillness through its use of repetition and the refrain-like nine-note interlocking motif. Feldman's music is at times static, reflecting the influences of the painters he so admired alongside the ancient methods of dying wool and weaving rugs. Yet at other times the vast temporal canvas of the music emphasises the fact that time plays such an important role in this artform. In terms of intermediality, Feldman's music cannot be separated from the libretto. Rather, the words and music have fused together at such a level that intermedia is established; to tear them apart would detract from the elusiveness forged by semantic fluidity.

Words and Music

Although we do not know how Beckett reacted to Feldman's treatment of his text, it would seem that the writer was not disappointed, for, nearly a decade later, Feldman was invited to write a new score for *Words and Music*. First published in 1962 and broadcast on the BBC Third Programme on 13 November that year, the play featured music by the author's cousin John Beckett. The score was subsequently withdrawn, supposedly on the grounds that John Beckett was never entirely pleased with it – there is no actual evidence to show that Samuel disliked John's score. Feldman's score takes a very different approach to John's in that the Irish composer provided much more in the manner of Romantic-tinged textures in response to Beckett's textual directions. An archival production by Beckettian Katharine Worth, with music by Humphrey Searle, was performed for the University of London Audio-Visual Centre in 1973, but it was not until Everett Frost's production in 1985, for the Festival of Radio Plays, that the Beckett/Feldman *Words and Music* came about.

The context of the play is vastly different from *Neither*, as is the result. The latter is a complex one act anti-opera lasting an hour, versus *Words and Music*, which is a radio play with 33 brief snippets of music, each lasting from as little as a few seconds up to three minutes. This huge difference has much to do with the fact that *Words and Music* is intended for radio rather than the concert hall. The score calls for seven players: two flutes, vibraphone, piano, violin, viola and cello. Marjorie Perloff called the work an opera (Perloff, 2003), and, though it may be short, it actually does adhere more to an operatic aesthetic than *Neither* does; there is drama, emotion, dialogue and characterisation. But what is particularly innovative about this play and is indicative of Beckett's aesthetic involvement in the philosophical relationship between music and literature is the *dramatis personae*. The play is set for three characters, Bob (music), Joe (words) and Croak (the master). The character Bob is played entirely by instrumental music, whose every utterance is, in this case, composed by Feldman. A dialogue ensues between Joe and Bob, with a master figure, Croak, referred to as "my Lord" by Joe, running the proceedings. The play has echoes of courtly entertainment as the two "comforts", words and music, serve their master by acting out his requests.[8]

Although Feldman's approach to the music differs from his previous setting of Beckett's text, there are nevertheless certain continuities. Deleuzian

118 *Beckett and Feldman*

repetition is again present here, as Feldman repeats material in a transformative fashion. Laws writes that Feldman's music gives a:

> sense of encountering the material repeatedly but slightly differently each time – of being taken further into the thought and working at it from different perspectives without conclusion.
>
> Laws (2013, 348)

This "encountering the material repeatedly but slightly differently each time" is reminiscent of the mechanics of *Neither*, as Feldman approaches Beckett's repetitive texts in a manner that perennially poses queries from different angles without cadence.

Beckett's script includes verbal musical descriptions or directions for Bob, and Feldman's music, unusually for him, corresponds in a loose way to the significations of the scripted words, such as "great expression", "spreading and subsiding music" and "Love and soul music". For Feldman, a composer who avoided expression and traditional notions of "beauty" and melody, as we have seen, this was a venture not be taken lightly. In fact, it is a testament to his respect for Beckett that he even agreed to the collaboration. As a result of these suggestions for expressive music, Feldman wrote uncharacteristically evocative snippets that connote emotions unlike any of his earlier works, though still a far cry from consonant, harmonious tonality. This was one of Feldman's last works before his death in 1987, and in the remaining two works that he composed, this emotive quality seemed to prevail. The last, we remember, was dedicated to the author, entitled *For Samuel Beckett*.

Words and Music also brings to the fore more Beckettian contradictions. As we saw previously, Beckett's sentimental Romantic view of music may seem contradictory, given his general aesthetic belief that there is "nothing to express". Yet here, the author includes directions for "expressive music". We must also remember that such contradictions would not have worried him, and were perhaps the prerogative of the postmodern artist. The Feldman collaborations also manifest a change of perspective on Beckett's part in terms of musical collaborations. Where earlier, in *Proust*, he had viewed the pairing of words with music as a corruption, after his work with Mihalovici and the success of *Neither*, the author seemed more positive about intermedial synthesis. *Words and Music* is a direct result and "metamedial" (Wolf, 2005, 150) dialogue of such an approach. As Stephen Benson points out, both Feldman and Beckett shared disdain for functional form – the composer famously declaring that "polyphony sucks" due to its favouring of structure over sound – while the writer had a distaste for Bach for similar "mechanical" reasons, mainly that form was not in itself a satisfactory teleology (Benson, 2005, 170). Both Beckett's Joe and Feldman's Bob, iterate repetitive material that is close but never exactly the same, a near miss that Brian Ferneyhough refers to as "slight phrase decoupling" (quoted in Benson, 2005, 175). This decoupling relates to the phenomenon of Deleuzian musematic repetition that we have

Beckett and Feldman 119

been exploring in Beckett and Feldman thus far. Joe, the words character, parodies functional rhetorical devices in his language; his speech on "sloth" is virtually identical to that on "love", with the respective word for the subject matter only swapped. Joe even slips up and says "sloth" when he means love at one point; his incantation of the memorised form overbears the content:

> "Sloth is of all the passions the most powerful passion and indeed no passion is more powerful than the passion of sloth, this is the mode in which the mind is most affected and indeed"
> "Love is of all the passions the most powerful passion and indeed no passion is more powerful than the passion of love"
> "Of all these movements then and who can number them and they are legion sloth is the ... LOVE is the most urgent and indeed by no manner of movement is the soul more urged than by this".

These words seem tautologous and meaningless, as Joe (words) uses the same rhetoric to express different subject matter. As we saw in the previous chapter, Shaw believed that literature requires more variation than music does, and here Joe's insistent banal ravings simply do not suffice to express such subject matter. Beckett is deliberately foregrounding the failures of language and the insincerities of rhetorical devices, including repetition. Werner Wolf points out the text operates in a self-enclosed manner in this fashion: "the discourse thus appears to be constructed according to internal self-referential principles rather than being an attempt at transmitting referential meaning" (Wolf, 2005, 153). Of course, Beckett had long left the goal of "transmitting referential meaning" behind, or at least explicit meaning, in his pursuit of semantic fluidity, and *Words and Music* displays this aesthetic "metamedially" better than any. The play offers an unparalleled philosophical debate on the respective artforms.

Beckett once said when discussing the play that "music always wins" (quoted in Worth, 1998, 16), and certainly in this battle within the play in which Joe (words) is constantly interrupting Bob (music) and pleading with him to stop, Joe eventually succumbs and even seems to enjoy the music. At the end, Joe finally invites music to play before sighing in acceptance. Words and music eventually collaborate successfully, for the appeasement of Croak, and perform a song that brings together these discrete mediums, in the Lessing sense, in a kind of mutual respect. I wouldn't say music wins necessarily; perhaps nobody wins in the end, as there is no resolution or "home" reached. The fact that music finishes the play seems to conform more to standard song structure, with a musical outro, than it does any distinct victory.

After analysing the textual repetitions in *Words and Music*, including stage directions, from a word count of 1,779 there are only 447 unique words. This yields an especially high ratio of repetitions, *c*.4:1. Figure 5.22 outlines the repetitions of words and phrases in *Words and Music*.

Joe's tautologous mechanical rhetoric is clearly based on repetition, as Beckett continues to erode meaning through recurrence. Many of the

PHRASE	COUNT	PERCENT
the	96	5.396
pause	80	4.497
words	53	2.979
of	51	2.867
and	48	2.698
music	42	2.361
to	37	2.08
is	36	2.024
croak	35	1.967
in	32	1.799
this	28	1.574
no	26	1.461
a	21	1.18
or	20	1.124
that	18	1.012
my	18	1.012
as	18	1.012
trying to	17	1.911
to sing	17	1.911
trying	17	0.956
sing	17	0.956
as before	16	1.799
before	16	0.899
thump	16	0.899
love	16	0.899
by	15	0.843
in the	14	1.574
suggestion	13	0.731
with	13	0.731
sing this	12	1.349
my lord	12	1.349
lord	12	0.675
more	12	0.675
soul	12	0.675
all	12	0.675
age	12	0.675
for	12	0.675
club	11	0.618
bob	11	0.618
of club	10	1.124
then	10	0.562
than	10	0.562
violent thump	9	1.012
thump of	9	1.012
a little	9	1.012
violent	9	0.506
little	9	0.506
is the	9	1.012
face	9	0.506
on	9	0.506
the ashes	8	0.899
the face	8	0.899

Figure 5.22 Analysis of *Words and Music*

Figure 5.23 Words and Music, 2 bars

repetitions are indeed due to the practice of learning through mimesis that Joe displays when repeating the pitched lyrics of the song, "then down a little way, through the trash". Other examples of his repetitive language include the phrase "in the ashes", which occurs three times in the final song, and "that clarity of silver", repeating twice on page 292 (segments 5–6; see Figure 5.23).

In Feldman's score, his "same but different" approach is clearly evident again in *Words and Music*. Much of his music repeats the same ascending scale pattern, and characteristic minor seconds, but in slightly varied ways. On the first page, for the direction "As before", the composer does not merely replicate the previous segment (no. 5) but he instead writes a new segment (no. 6) that, in his own way of varying repetition through orchestration, moves the top melodic idea into the piano part. For segment no. 7, again under the direction "As before", Feldman's Bob is somewhat disobedient, as the composer introduces a new piece of music. In contrast, when Joe (words) is given the same direction, "As before", he repeats the words, "My Lord" exactly.

Later on, Bob (music) begins suggesting melodic lines for Joe (words) to pitch his utterances to. Here, didactic repetition, music teaching words,

Figure 5.24 Words and Music, 7 bars

requires repetitive suggestions from Feldman. It would seem that, here, his "crippled symmetry" (Feldman, 1981, repr. 2000, 134–150) takes a back seat in place of his respect for Beckett's requests. For "repeat suggestion", 2 bars of music are repeated exactly by Feldman (segments 19–20), albeit an exact clothed repeat at the reception level (segments 19–20; see Figure 5.24). Feldman, however, adds another 3 bars on to segment 20.

Likewise, in segment 21 under the direction "repeats end of previous suggestion", Feldman does just this, repeating the added 3 bars at the end of segment 20. Here, we see that Feldman the collaborator is unafraid to embrace exact clothed repetition. This eventually leads up to the climactic collaboration where both characters engage in a song. For the directions "statement with elements already used" (segment 35) and "As before or only slightly varied" (segment 36), Feldman repeats previous motivic musical ideas and closes the play in contemplative fashion.

So what this means is that, in this radio play itself, we see in collaborative format the kind of translation that Feldman's opera employs and, as we shall see in the next chapter, is also evident in the Beckettian jazz improvisations of Scott Fields. Joe (words) repeats what Bob (music) suggests and both repeat themselves extensively. Rather than a composer taking Beckett's text and writing music inspired by it, in this case the composer reacts to the musical suggestions of the text and actively becomes a collaborator in the original document. One might say that the opera is the same kind of collaboration, but we must remember that in that case Feldman had the initial idea before approaching Beckett, and perhaps, as a result, music is far more dominant in *Neither* than it is in *Words and Music*. *Words and Music* is much more Beckett than Feldman due to the limitations that Beckett imposed, even though Feldman's contribution is the most successful musical contribution to the play.

Conclusion

Producing an hour of music from nine lines, Feldman's non-developmental, non-teleological anti-opera, *Neither* is one in which an abundance of clothed repetition renders a static texture full of "to and fro"s, "comings and goings", pulse changes, timbral juxtapositions and colour manipulations. *Words and Music*, although composed in a much more confined format and operating on a more literal level, shares a similar concern for semantic fluidity. Like

Beckett's semantic fluidity, Feldman's music both "comes and goes" and is never quite the same. The music is free from definite semiotic interpretations. In the ultimate manifestation of a metamedial dialogue between words and music, free of semantic shackles, both artforms ride the contour of an asymptotic curve, as they approach one another, yet, in the end, reach "neither". Just as the "self" never reaches an explanation as to its existence, so the "back and forth" of the libretto, static chords and recurring motifs are never fully resolved, but resound perennially.

Both collaborative pieces embody a twentieth-century turn away from clear semantics, goals and answers, instead offering the Ivesean "unanswered question". The indefinable becomes acceptable, not in a sublime way, as perhaps Schopenhauer or the Romantics and Symbolists would have it, but rather in a manner that reflects the complexity and diversity of modern life. In a world with as many musics as there are languages, each with its own system, an acceptance of the unbridgeable gulfs in communication became important to Feldman. Perhaps the greatest gulf between the composer and Beckett was that the author was never able to abandon the quest for answers as easily, and would remain steadfast in search of such a bridge. Feldman seems more comfortable with the "not knowing" than Beckett did. While Beckett's works would become increasingly short and focused exercises in intensity, Feldman's music became progressively vast and expansive, as in String Quartet No. 2.

Notes

1 The next chapter explores this Beckettian indeterminacy.
2 Lois Overbeck provides a useful overview of Beckett's fluctuating stance on musical collaboration in "Audience of Self/Audience of Reader" (2011)..
3 For more discussion on the evolution of Beckett's musical quotations, see Maier (2008).
4 See the contributions by Paddison (2004) and Kivy (2004) in the special issue of *Musicae Scientiae* devoted to time.
5 The previous chapters engage with such questions somewhat in terms of Kivy's "grasping".
6 "In der Beschränkung zeigt sich erst der Meister" (In the limitation, the master) (Goethe quoted in Wilde, [1891] 1997b, 930).
7 I say "collaboration" in its broadest sense. Both certainly worked alone, and with little discussion. Yet the result is nevertheless double-authored.
8 Werner Wolf (2005) reads music (Bob) and words (Joe) as the "comforts" of the master figure.

6 Improvising Beckett

Chance, silence and repetition

Ruby Cohn speaks of an "improvisational quality" in Beckett's writing, wherein the meticulously crafted texts seem through-composed (Cohn, 1980, 135). The language is self-reflexive, directing itself somewhat in the same way that Flaubert's and Joyce's styles would often mirror word content. Beckett enjoyed employing number games and permutations in his work, the famous "sucking-stones" episode in *Molloy* ([1951] 1994) for instance, in which the protagonist attempts to logically formulate a method of manoeuvring through each of the 16 stones in turn from his four pockets. But might such an "improvisational quality" in the author's work account for a previously unexplored reason for so many musicians and composers being attracted to Beckett?

Perhaps exploring the work of a Beckettian improviser serves our purposes best. Building on several ideas introduced in the previous chapters, it is possible to develop a theory of improvisatory semantic fluidity that oscillates between, yet transforms, Beckett's work and the live interpretation of a jazz performer. This chapter will situate the Beckettian jazz of Chicago-born composer and improviser Scott Fields, after first investigating Beckett's own explorations in indeterminacy. It explores how improvisation and indeterminacy might be compared and investigates how a semi-improvised avant-jazz composition based on Beckett's *Not I* transforms the protagonist's self of the play. By exploring this "illusion of improvisation" in Beckett's work and examining how it has been incorporated in improvised music, this chapter further investigates the transmedial translation of repetition from musicalised literature into music itself.

Fields' Beckettian jazz differs a great deal from Morton Feldman's approach to composing music inspired by or using Beckett texts. While one may find similarities in terms of the freedom given to the performer of Fields' and Feldman's music; Michael Nyman reminds us that Feldman "had never thought of the graph as an 'art of improvisation' but more as 'a totally abstract sonic adventure'" (Nyman, [1974] 1999, 70). Feldman experimented with innovations in graphic scores early in his career, but gradually grew weary of abandoning such elements of control, as we saw in the last chapter.

Improvising Beckett 125

Lessness

Beckett experimented with aleatoric methods in the short prose piece *Sans* from 1969 (later translated by the author into English as *Lessness* in 1970 (Beckett, 1995). *Lessness* builds on the musical repetition of previous short prose works like *Bing* from 1966 (English translation by the author as *Ping* in 1967) – Cohn called *Ping* "a tantalizing echolalia" (Cohn, 1973, 256). The word "white" alone repeats a total of 88 times in this short text, while "almost" appears 37 times, "ping" 33 times, "light" 31 times, "only" 31 times, "one" 30 times, so repetition is central to the piece. In fact, out of the 934 words in *Ping*, only 126 are unique. Unlike the single block of text in *Ping*, *Lessness* is divided into 24 paragraphs. Cohn suggests that the structure of *Lessness* mirrors humanity's obsession with time:

> the number of sentences per paragraph stops at seven, the number of days in a week. The number of paragraphs reaches twenty-four, the number of hours in a day. The number of different sentences is sixty, the number of minutes in an hour. But the repetition of the sixty sentences in a different order suggests the capricious arrangement of passing time.
>
> (Cohn 1973, 263)

Beckett explained that he composed the 60 sentences based on six different images, and subsequently put all of these into a container from which he randomly picked them out in the order that they appear in the text (Cohn, 1973, 265). *Lessness* comprises 120 sentences, each sentence repeated in another position in the second of two sections. Once again, as we saw in *Godot*, *Play* and *Molloy*, Beckett's use of the *da capo* device is evident. The author further explained the process of composing *Lessness* to John Pilling as the arranging of 60 sentences "first in one disorder. Then in another" (Knowlson and Pilling, 1979, 173). Beckett then allocated paragraphs lengths of 3, 4, 5, 6 and 7 sentences in random order to give the final text its structure.

This piece has been well analysed. Susan Brienza and Enoch Brater, for instance, distinguish the six images that make up Beckett's sentences as being:

> 1. the ruins as "true refuge" 2. the endless grey of earth and sky 3. The little body 4. The space "all gone from mind" 5. Past tenses combined with never 6. Future tenses of active verbs and the "figment" sentence about dawn and dusk.
>
> (Brienza and Brater, 1976, 245)

Once more the Beckettian trope of binary oppositions returns – the "dawn" and "dusk", "figment" versus reality. For Brienza and Brater, the "steady repetition of the images, not on the sequence in which they appear" is of the utmost importance (Brienza and Brater, 1976, 246). Might this repetitive indeterminacy account for a new attempt by Beckett to find a method

126 *Improvising Beckett*

to "accommodate the mess" (quoted in Cohn, 1980, 96), that he spoke of in reference to the role of the modern artist; one influenced, perhaps, by Dada and the chance operations that underpin much of John Cage's compositions? Or was *Lessness* an exploration by Beckett to achieve a timelessness in short prose through the use of extensive repetition, omission of tensed verbs, connectives and subordinate clauses (Paton, 2009)?

Cohn writes that Beckett explained the aleatoric composition of *Lessness* as being "the only 'honest' ... thing to do" (Beckett quoted in Brienza and Brater, 1976, 246). As the French language had earlier allowed Beckett a stylistic freedom in which his creations were liberated from the stranglehold of indigenous syntax and habit, now aleatoric methods enabled a mode of composition that produced an "honesty" of chance. During their study of the final published version of *Lessness*, however, Brienza and Brater question just how neatly the text worked out; in fact, the tidy finality of the closing section is, according to them, glaring evidence of posthumous tampering. Might Beckett have doctored the results of chance to some extent in an aesthetic adjustment that produces the cadence? It certainly seems possible given Brienza and Brater's analysis, but such a practice would only maintain Beckett's persistent faith in contradictions, a notion itself oxymoronic in nature. The chance procedure was a means, not an end in itself. The interplay between "chance and choice" is perhaps another Beckettian binary opposition, manifesting itself again in *Lessness* (Brienza and Brater, 1976, 244–258).

A collaborative project based at Trinity College Dublin was developed in 2002 by Elizabeth Drew (English) and Mads Haahr (Computer Science), resulting in a website – www.random.org/lessness/ – that enables users to create new versions of *Lessness*. Software facilitates random permutations of the sentences and paragraph lengths according to Beckett's criteria. Their method of obtaining this randomness comes from software that takes atmospheric noise as its starting point, an organic, more natural type of indeterminacy than that used by most computerised programs, according to Drew and Haahr. Beckett continually documented the human condition, and in *Lessness* the fact that we can never predict the next sentence brings with it a strange form of realism.

For Drew and Haahr, *Lessness* is "a precisely calibrated exercise of indeterminacy", and they emphasise the fact that the published version is only "one of the 1.9 x 10176 possible arrangements of its sentences" (Drew and Haahr, 2002, 3). Each version should hold equal value, it seems, and Drew and Haahr feel that Beckett's use of indeterminacy here highlights "human orientations towards possibilities over the actual" – the order is of less importance than the continual repetition of the material: the final product, in other words, is less important than the process. Recognising Beckett's goal of creating a work without "an obvious determinism", Drew and Haahr write: "[t]he absence of an obvious determinism guiding the flow provides a gap in understanding that spurs the reader's interaction with the piece. The sense of patterning in the chaotic sequence of sentences entices the reader to untangle the random arrangement and attempt to piece together an elusive storyline" (2002, 2). Yet,

Improvising Beckett 127

while we can make our own *Lessnesses* with the program, we are unlikely to achieve the finality of the published version without Beckett as editor.

Another interesting feature of the work is the fact that each half of the text amounts to 769 words, a figure that Matthew May points out is only irreducible to factors other than itself and the number 1.[1] Such mathematics would not have been a coincidence in Beckett's search for semantic fluidity; the self is not easily reducible.

This aleatoric work has resonated throughout twentieth-century literature. For his Ph.D thesis, for example, J. M. Coetzee, another Nobel prize-winning novelist, used computer software to produce a statistical analysis of Beckett's prose. In "Samuel Beckett's *Lessness*: An Exercise in Decomposition" (1973, 196), Coetzee, like Drew and Haahr, also identifies repetition as "the basic principle of construction in Lessness". Writing in 1973, Coetzee seems unaware of Beckett's procedures (having not heard of the conversation with Cohn): and yet he succeeds in describing how it was composed by deciphering the constituent parts of the text. In his painstaking analysis, he highlights 106 different phrases that range in length from 1 to 12 words occurring on average 5.7 times, and settles on a count of 166 "lexical items" (1973, 195). His subsequent realisation that "[w]ords 770–1, 538 of the text turn out to be nothing but words 1–769 in a new order", lead him to see the text as a "linguistic game rather than linguistic expression" (1973, 195). The Beckettian *da capo* is, for Coetzee, a means of cancelling through repetition the initial idea, a retracing that leaves a significant residue: each contrasting pair of oppositions – whether it be the characters Molloy and Moran, Sam and Watt, or the temporal regions of dawn and dusk – initially override one another; and yet in the end, each produces more than an absence, or nothing, reaching instead towards a higher understanding of the futility of certainty (1973, 198). Coetzee describes *Lessness* as a work that is "dismissing its own invention" (1973, 198). With this in mind, Beckett's aesthetic statement in the *Three Dialogues* that "[t]he expression that there is nothing to express, nothing with which to express, nothing from which to express, no power to express, no desire to express, together with the obligation to express", perhaps makes sense in terms of this dismissal [1949] 1999, 103). Process had become the centre of Beckett's aesthetic at this stage in the late 1960s and early 1970s, a trajectory that, alongside his use of silence and repetition, was echoed in many corners of modern music.

Silence and indeterminacy

One of the most prominent binary oppositions in Beckett's aesthetics is that between sound and silence. The space between the notes is of equal importance as the notes themselves, something that Beckett was keenly aware of and is evident from *Murphy* onwards. These gaps on the page are what Iain Sinclair refers to when he writes of Kötting's admiration for Beckett: "that's why he loved Beckett: the white spaces" (Sinclair 2015, 51).

128   *Improvising Beckett*

In *Texts for Nothing*, Beckett writes that "there is silence and there is not silence" ([1946] 1995, 115). Just as the "intelligible" and the "inexplicable" provide a balanced dichotomy, Beckett's employment of silence is equally dialectical.[2] In his attempt to find a form to "accommodate the mess" of modern life, the noise of infinite disparity, Beckett's aesthetic of reduction and distillation pushes silence to the foreground. Beckett admired Beethoven's approach to silence, writing: "Is there any reason why that terrible materiality of the word surface should not be capable of being dissolved, like for example the sound surface, torn by enormous pauses, of Beethoven's seventh symphony" (Beckett, 2009, 518). Taking musical silences as inspiration for an approach to silence was especially apt: Beckett once even asked Stravinsky for his thoughts on formulating a way of precisely timing pauses in *Waiting for Godot* in a manner resembling musical notation.

A history of silence in music and literature falls outside the scope of this chapter, but insofar as Beckett's aleatoric explorations are concerned, the aesthetic connections here with John Cage need to be addressed.[3] Cage was perhaps that very composer that Beckett prophesised, or at least yearned for in a letter to Coister in 1954, when he wrote: "[a]nd then what about silence itself, is it not still waiting for its musician?" (11 March 1954 in Beckett, 2011). Dirk Van Hulle writes that *Lessness* "was partly inspired by John Cage and other experimental music of the 1960s".[4] Perhaps such an influence was not only aleatoric but also concerned with silence and nothingness. Adorno's belief that all art was driving towards silence, that it was moving further into an obscure esoteric niche, unheard by greater and greater numbers, describes a modern world in which Beckett was paradoxically well equipped. After all, Beckett described his being awarded the Nobel Prize for Literature to James Knowlson as being "damned to fame".[5] The silence in his work was matched by his own silence in exegesis of his writing. David Metzer's article "Modern Silence" (2006) contextualises a modern turn towards unsound as indicative of a new perspective on sound's "intimate relationship" to silence, by analysing its importance to Anton Webern, Luigi Nono and Salvatore Sciarrino; but Cage was the true pioneer in silence's apotheosis – while also recognising its fundamental impossibility (Sciarrino quoted in Metzer, 2006, 332).

In "Experimental Music" (1957, in Cage, 1973), the composer speaks of sounds in a fashion very similar to Beckett's notion of "fundamental sounds". Written a year after Beckett's *Texts for Nothing* (Kim-Cohen, 2011, 2), Cage recognised the impossibility of pure silence: following his experience in an anechoic chamber, he realised that a person cannot escape the recurring murmurs of their central nervous system and heartbeat even in such a quiet space. Sounds will go on perennially, as Beckett's characters do. If any sound is liberated to become music – another Cagean idea – so too might silence, or the lack of sound, assume a musical role. *4'33"* is, in a way, the first ambient composition; the silence invites audiences to listen to the indeterminate ambient sounds of coughing, ambulances, creaky chairs and so on – creating a composition that is never the same but unique and always asking us to contextualise sounds as music.

There is no such thing as pure silence, or "black silence" as Beckett describes it in *The Unnamable* (Metzer, 2006, 354). There are, however, many grey silences. Like Deleuze's clothed repeats, silence is always filtered through affiliations and contexts. Silence becomes codified, attached to particular meanings in its reception, and the listener later decodes such signs – the silence of horror and tension, for instance. When Beckett described Joyce's *Work in Progress* as not "*about* something; it *is* that something itself" ([1929] 1983a, 27, original emphasis), he was referring to the performative quality of the work, the sounds produced, the fact that the words themselves reflected the content and were sufficient in themselves rather than evoking underlying conventional narratives. This liberation of words to be sufficient in themselves, to become "that something itself" is very similar to Cage's ideas on emancipating all sounds from the tyranny of the term "music". Cage writes, "I have nothing to say and I'm saying it" (Cage, 1973, 109), while for Beckett "there is nothing to express, nothing with which to express, nothing from which to express, no desire to express, together with the obligation to express" ([1949] 1999, 103).

While for Pater literature might have aspired to the condition of music, in the twentieth century literature was, for Ihab Hassan, aspiring to silence (Hassan quoted in Lodge, 1968, 85). Of course, silence is entirely linked with the inexplicable aspect of Beckett's aesthetic, as, for him, to say less is to say more. In the end, silence is yet another Schopenhauerian Romantic ideal – never possible yet perennially desired. Like the asymptotic curve between music and language, or between sameness and uniqueness, silence and sound represent a Derridean non-limit: one that can never be reached but perpetually yearned towards (Kim-Cohen, 2011, 20).

Georgio Agamben writes of Glenn Gould's intuition for knowing what *not* to play (Kim-Cohen, 2011, 3). In Cage's explorations of Zen Buddhism, he would have come across similar ideas: that true power lies in the volume held in reserve rather than at full *fortissimo*, in the crouching tiger rather than in open attack. Like the Trinity College Dublin *Lessness* project, it is the possibilities inherent that imbue such power, the affordance of the text. The paradoxical Cagean notion of turning towards the unintended is exemplified in the binary opposition between chance and choice discussed in *Lessness*. Of course, to intend to un-intend is a contradiction in terms, as to choose to allow certain parameters a "freedom" merely sets up another set. As mentioned above, Beckett told Cohn that this approach was the only "honest" method, as if chance procedures could remove the aesthetic prejudices of the author. But does using a different method of organisation render sincerity? What truth exists in randomness? On the one hand, what is commonly understood as a "truth", that the universe is "organised chaos", might fit nicely with Beckett's claim: yet on the other hand, such a decision is simply another aesthetic choice and no more "honest" than any other. In the *Decay of Lying*

130   *Improvising Beckett*

([1891] 1997b), Oscar Wilde lamented the contemporary focus on realism rather than the imaginative, and here Beckett seems to equate deconstructing the author, a kind of Barthesian removal of self, with verisimilitude. Beckett, we remember, turned to writing in French for similar reasons – to escape the stranglehold of prescribed style that had been engrained in him within the English or Hiberno-English tongue.

There are, of course, huge differences in Cage's and Beckett's respective aesthetics. Perhaps the most salient is that Cage seemed more comfortable with unknowing. Stephen Benson (2012, 227) suggests that although Beckett wrote tirelessly about the subject, he seemed to yearn for answers at times – if not in his work, in life. Cage, on the other hand, maintained a kind of Keatsian "negative capability", a peaceful understanding that one could not understand everything, and one was never going to possess the faculties for such understanding. Benson puts it well when he writes: "an unlikely duo, so the story goes, because Beckett knew too much, although he was a quick unlearner, while Cage was too comfortable in his apparent unknowing" (2012, 227).

The final section of Cage's "Experimental Music" resembles something Beckett could have written, as does "Lecture on Nothing". Cage writes:

> Where do we go from here? Towards theatre. That art more than music resembles nature. We have eyes as well as ears, and it is our business while we are alive to use them.
>
> And what is the purpose of writing music? One is, of course, not dealing with purposes but dealing with sounds. Or the answer must take the form of paradox: a purposeful purposelessness or a purposeless play. This play, however, is an affirmation of life – not an attempt to bring order out of chaos nor to suggest improvements in creation, but simply a way of waking up to the very life we're living, which is so excellent once one gets one's mind and one's desires out of its way and lets it act of its own accord.
>
> (Cage, [1957] 1973, 227, 5)

Here, Cage imagines a theatre of "purposeful purposelessness", and who better to achieve it than Beckett. Indeed, as Emilie Morin has pointed out, indeterminacy has grown popular in contemporary British theatre from Sarah Kane to Martin Crimp and Tim Crouch (Morin, 2011, 71). The idea that such a method invokes the chaos of nature, acting as an affirmation of life, reminds us of Beckett's perpetual portrayal of the repetitious nature of life, and the cyclical daily routine of the human condition.

These ideas take on another layer when we consider how attractive Beckett's texts have been to improvisers. But how can we compare or contrast aleatoric or indeterminate music with improvisation? What differentiates the two is, I suggest, really a question of timing – at what point in the compositional process the choices are made. In aleatoric music, the

Improvising Beckett 131

composition sets the parameters within which certain processes will play out, while in improvised music the choices are made in real time during the performance/composition. Limits are set beforehand in improvisation too, of course, whether they are deliberate or not. The style in which a performer is participating, for instance, will set up a certain set of parameters. Fred Frith might approach a guitar instrumental improvisation with no idea whatsoever how it will play out, without a single note pre-planned or composed, and yet the end result will undeniably resemble a Fred Frith sound. Such parameters are the result of learning, an individual's aesthetic, their taste, their physiology, their instrument, their capability to listen and respond, and, of course, their musical intuition. The type of improvisation I am referring to here, rather than blues or traditional jazz improvisation over composed heads (the tune), changes, chord structures, or even any kind of tonality, is of the free improvising school. Derek Bailey preferred the term "non-idiomatic improvisation", but inevitably his own style also became itself an idiom fairly quickly. All is eventually codified and commodified in the market of cultural capital.

Repetition has a complex relationship with improvisation: on the one hand, a repeated phrase, or idea can emphasise a particular aesthetic intent, but on the other hand, it runs the risk of negating the very idea of improvisation itself. The guitarist, improviser and composer Elliott Sharp once joked that no improvisation can ever be fully free unless the performers suffer from amnesia.[6] Within any musical context there are certain aesthetic parameters that a musician must negotiate, and improvisation of any kind has such limits. Whether it be the knowledge of specific scales that work well over certain changes or chord progressions, or just a particular sound or technique that an improviser is drawn to through experience, all improvisation has an "anxiety of influence", a system of expectations, and can therefore never be "free"; repetition is always present.

Many modern musics appear under the rubric of "improvisation". Bailey's landmark lateral survey of various improvised musics, *Improvisation: Its Nature and Practice in Music* (1980), includes studies of Indian music, Flamenco, Baroque, Organ, Rock and Jazz, reminding us that the first music ever produced had to have been an improvised utterance – Mithen's singing Neanderthals or not. Traditional standard-based jazz improvisation, whereby a musician plays "over changes", or solos over chord progressions employing suitable scales, is very different to what developed during the 1960s to become termed "free improvisation". Musicians such as Cecil Taylor, Bailey, Frith, Evan Parker and Anthony Braxton all contributed to a new aesthetic of improvisation, a music composed entirely in the moment and unchained by harmony, a move beyond Ornette Coleman's so called "free jazz" that was still bound to structure and tune.[7] A major institution in this regard was the Art Ensemble of Chicago and the Association for the Advancement of Creative Musicians (AACM) in Chicago. In the UK, the improvising network centred around the group

132 *Improvising Beckett*

AMM, and key pioneers like Keith Rowe, Gavin Bryars, Bailey and Eddie Prévost. Free improvisation exemplified a meeting point for art music and popular music at this time, as followers of Cage, Stockhausen, La Monte Young, Cornelius Cardew, Henry Cowell, rock and jazz all found common experimental ground. Later musicians, including Morton Feldman, Elliot Sharp, John Zorn and Pauline Oliveros, began to experiment with new ways of combining composition and improvisation. Scott Fields, the musician and composer on whom I will concentrate in this chapter, was, growing up in Chicago, greatly influenced by the vibrant scene propagated by AACM.

We have spoken of the illusion of improvisation, the employment of aleatoric devices and the almost through-composed features of Beckett's writing, but what happens when an improviser takes Beckett's texts as inspiration for their own instrumental music and improvisations? And what does Beckett have to do with jazz? The two might seem unlikely bedfellows initially, but aligned with the fact that he became hugely influential on modern music, Beckett also translated two pioneering jazz-related pieces in 1934 for Nancy Cunard's anthology *Negro*. The two jazz texts were "The Best Negro Jazz Orchestra", a survey by early jazz critic Robert Goffin, and a poem by Ernst Moerman entitled "Louis Armstrong".[8]

Scott Fields, a Chicago-born avantjazz guitarist, now based in Cologne, has composed two albums based entirely around Beckett texts, *Beckett* (2007) and *Samuel* (2009). Together the two albums offer instrumental interpretations of *Breath*, *Play*, *Come and Go*, *What Where*, *Rockaby*, *Not I*, *Ghost Trio* and *Eh Joe*. Fields approaches the Beckett plays seeking structure for his semi-improvised compositions and each setting incorporates the repetition, word painting and character of the original text.

Fields is active in a number of musical projects including his acoustic guitar duo with Elliott Sharp, his freetet, his string quartet and octet, a duo with Matthias Schubert, and his early music–modern music fusion group counterpart:counterpart, with lutenist Stephen Rath, New Music flautist Angelika Sheridan and early music flautist Norbert Rodenkirchen. Fields has led over 24 recordings and has appeared on many others, including collaborations with Tortoise's Jeff Parker. These two Beckett albums feature a quartet named the The Scott Fields Ensemble, consisting of drummer John Hollenbeck, cellist Scott Roller and tenor saxophonist Matthias Schubert.

Fields is a composer and improviser predominantly occupied with ways of organising improvisation into structures. His musical language has developed to include the post-tonal, non-linear scales of Professor Stephen Dembski, with whom Fields has studied and performed, since meeting him at the University of Wisconsin. If we analyse one text, *Not I* ([1972] 2006), comparing Beckett's text and Fields' instrumental interpretation of the piece, incorporating improvisational sections, it will enable us to explore these questions further.

Figure 6.1 The Scott Fields Ensemble – photo credit: Stefan Strasser

Beckett's *Not I*

Not I foreshadows many of the qualities described in *Ill Seen Ill Said*. The personal pronoun is avoided at all costs, as the protagonist's sense of self is always left ambiguous. The emphasis on sound in the work is foregrounded, as a single "mouth alone" utters the text alongside a mysterious listener, the Auditor. Aurality is paramount, leading Enoch Brater to refer to the play as "not eye" (Brater, 1975, 50). The Auditor has often been removed from stage productions, many directors, including Beckett himself, deeming it too difficult to execute successfully. Clarity is once again eroded as Beckett's cyclical repeats reflect the "maddening", seemingly automatic or spasmodic utterances of a woman who has undergone a significant traumatic event. This untold event at "Croker's Acres" sparks a logorrhoea wherein the woman replays and repeats the trauma, much in the same way that Freudian psychoanalysis documents patients' negative cyclical repetitions (repetition compulsion) (Freud, 1961). We see the word "unintelligible" once again, this time in Beckett's stage direction for an acousmatic voice at the opening of the play. The voice must reflect the "unintelligible" as the curtain rises and falls.

As "the mouth alone" yearns for silence, the repetitive trauma disallows any respite. Right from the beginning we can see an epistrophe repeat with "into this world … this world". Local musematic repeats at the start include "before its time" and "tiny little thing" with its anaphoric variant "tiny little girl". In many cases Beckett interpolates a word in-between two repeats, often with the recurrence emphasised with an apostrophe. The word "imagine" is

134   *Improvising Beckett*

used seven times in this way, perhaps a particularly Hiberno-English colloquial choice in such exclamatory form:

> "Imagine!" in between repeats – "what position she was in … imagine!..
> what a position she was in!"
> "not suffering … imagine! ... not suffering!"
> "words were coming … imagine! ... words were coming"
> "no idea … what she was saying … imagine! ... no idea what she was
> saying!"
> "no idea what she's saying … imagine! ... no idea what she's saying!"
> (occurring twice)
> "her lips moving … imagine! ... her lips moving!"
> "now can't stop … imagine! … can't stop the stream"

The phrases "all right", "ha!" and "so it reasoned" are also used to similar effect:

> "nothing she could tell? … all right … nothing she could tell"
> "so far … ha! ... so far"
> "that April morning … so it reasoned ... that April morning"

"April morning" repeats another two times in the text as a sentence itself and
another time with the musematic development to "all that early April morning light", making it repeat a total of five times throughout.

Other musematic local repeats[9] include:

> "which had first occurred to her" recurring later as "first occurred to her"
> "it can't go on" appearing later as "can't go on"
> "all silent as the grave" and "sweet silent as the grave"

Position remains important. Often sentences end with the same words
repeated in consecutive sentences:

> "when suddenly she felt … gradually she felt"
> "admit hers alone … her voice alone"

But we also witness mirror images as the words are swapped, the rhetorical
device of chiasmus: "so that not only she had … had she … not only had she".

Binary oppositions

In terms of binary oppositional repeats in *Not I*, the Beckettian trope of day
and night is again present here. In the "April morning light" the woman "found
herself in the dark". Likewise, we see the familiar comings and goings: "a ray
of light came and went ... came and went". Of particular interest in *Not I*
is the dichotomy of screams and silence. As we saw earlier, Beckett's use of

Improvising Beckett   135

silence is key to his aesthetic and nowhere is it more apparent than in this play. The two are always coupled, as silence follows the outburst of scream, as the tormented woman listens in vain for any response:

> scream ... [*Screams.*] ... then listen ... [*Silence.*] ... scream again ... [*Screams again.*] ... then listen again ... [*Silence.*] ... no ... spared that ... all silent as the grave

Discursive repetitions

Many of the discursive repeated phrases, those repetitions acting on a structural level recurring throughout the text, are also exact clothed repeats of sentences. It should be remembered that these categories of repetition can and do overlap with one another:

> "all the time the buzzing" occurring four times
> "always winter some strange reason" three times
> "brought up as she had been to believe" two times
> "God is love" three times
> "sudden flash" eight times
> "steady stream" three times
> "tiny little thing" three times
> "once or twice a year" three times
> "nothing but the larks" three times
> "so on" nine times, including one following another consecutively and beginning a sentence – "so on ... so on it reasoned"

Discursive repeats also occur over groups of sentences:

> "what? ... seventy? ... good God!" occurs twice
> "what? ... the buzzing? ... yes" occurs seven times
> "what? ... who? no! she!" occurs five times, each time signalling a movement that follows a pause. On the fifth and final occurrence "she!" is followed by another, this time shouted as "SHE!". All instances are exact clothed except for this final musematic variant.

Figure 6.2 (first page of analysis) sets out the repeated words and phrases in *Not I*. This analysis does not include the stage directions for laughs, screams and silences, instead only including the scripted verbal text. Of the word count of 2,329 words, only 534 are unique, reflecting a repeat rate of 4.36:1.

In considering the performative nature of *Not I*, we must remember that it is a play, and is therefore, primarily intended to be performed. It immediately becomes clear that the abundant repetition is even more striking on the stage than on the page, an aspect that becomes further apparent in Scott Fields' recorded performance of *Not I* explored below.

PHRASE	COUNT	PERCENT
the	122	5.238
she	73	3.134
in	51	2.19
on	46	1.975
all	44	1.889
to	44	1.889
not	42	1.803
no	39	1.675
what	37	1.589
that	37	1.589
of	37	1.589
and	35	1.503
her	35	1.503
it	32	1.374
so	31	1.331
a	30	1.288
in the	24	2.061
then	23	0.988
had	23	0.988
or	23	0.988
-	23	0.988
but	22	0.945
was	22	0.945
as	22	0.945
could	18	0.773
this	17	0.73
something	16	0.687
time	16	0.687
for	16	0.687
buzzing	15	0.644
the buzzing	14	1.202
nothing	14	0.601
after	14	0.601
long	14	0.601
she was	13	1.116
like	13	0.558
yes	13	0.558
at	13	0.558
she had	12	1.03
stop	12	0.515
any	12	0.515
out	11	0.472
up	11	0.472
all that	10	0.859
sudden	10	0.429
back	10	0.429
oh	10	0.429
be	10	0.429
oh long after	9	1.159
long after	9	0.773
she could	9	0.773
imagine	9	0.386

Figure 6.2 Page 1 of *Not I* analysis

Improvising Beckett 137

Due to production delays in London, *Not I* was premiered in the Lincoln Center, New York on 22 November 1972. Beckett allowed his friend, director Alan Schneider, the right to perform it with actress Jessica Tandy. In their correspondence at the time, Beckett suggests to Schneider that the audience should "share her [the protagonist's] bewilderment".[10] Beckett encouraged the director to emphasise the fast-paced unintelligible panic of the woman rather than overthink the plot. He writes to Schneider: "All I know is in the text ... I hear it [*Not I*] breathless, urgent, feverish, rhythmic, panting along, without undue concern with intelligibility ... [to be a]ddressed less to the understanding than to the nerves of the audience".[11] Beckett's semantic fluidity in theatre works here as a means of eroding and dissolving meaning rather than the repetition reinforcing meaning. Here we also see Beckett speaking of his will for the words to act more like unsettling, high-tempo sounds than as clear intelligible language. The actress chosen by Beckett to perform the play, and who is generally acknowledged to have given the definitive performance, is Billie Whitelaw. She first performed the play at the Royal Court Theatre, London on 16 January 1973 under the author's direction. A filmed version of this production was recorded on 13 February 1975. Where Tandy had employed a teleprompter as an aid, Whitelaw instead memorised the lines and focused entirely on the unsettling elements that the director desired. If we compare Whitelaw's filmed performance to the cinematic staging of Neil Jordan's *Not I*, featuring Julianne Moore from the 2000 *Beckett on Film* production, a number of differences arise. Such is the nature of performance. Interpretation and artistic directions lead to significantly altered zones. The text of the play is extremely precise, allowing for no improvisation – the illusion of it yes, lending it a through-composed quality. Yet nuances do differ from actress to actress.

First, Whitelaw sits in darkness, with her face painted black, as the camera zooms in on the "mouth alone", murmuring below her breath before the first audible words arise. Moore, on the other hand, arrives at the chair in full view, in a lit room; a visible young woman, far from the old Irish crone that the play supposedly portrays – Whitelaw's English accent of course also negates this. Whitelaw's delivery is far more rhythmical than Moore's, sounding like a stream of frantic schizophrenic stuttering. Whitelaw is faster and her exclamations are more dramatically emphasised, the result of incessant tongue-twisting, and even though she holds the instructed pauses of silence for longer than Moore, she still manages to finish earlier – in my analysis, Whitelaw's performance from the opening word "out" to the closing word "up" takes 11 minutes 42 seconds; Moore's, on the other hand, takes 12 minutes 33 seconds, a difference of 51 seconds. As a result, Whitelaw's performance does produce more of an air of panic and menace – thus unnerving the audience.

Fields' 200bpm is actually quite close in tempo to Whitelaw's delivery. Beckett, as was mentioned earlier, was known to bring a metronome to rehearsals; but Whitelaw's performance does fluctuate in places, possibly deliberately gaining pace along with the increasing panic. Fields' recording

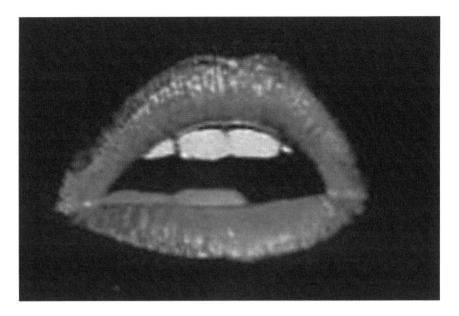

Figure 6.3 Billie Whitelaw in *Not I*

of *Not I* amounts to some thirty minutes, however, on account of the added solo interludes – "a real test of endurance"[12] as the composer puts it. This is significantly shortened for live performance, however.

Without the words being sounded in Fields' *Not I*, the speaker is silenced almost completely; her frantic utterances take the form of a repetitive dissonant music that repeats exact pitch and duration rather than words alone. Where Whitelaw and Moore might vary a word's inflection, Fields scores words to recur as close to each other as possible. The voice remains as residue.

At a further level of abstraction, a text influenced by musical ideas becomes music alone in adaptation. Fields' score takes its form from a text instead of a text taking its form from music, the more common phenomenon within Scher's three categories of word and music relations – music in literature, music and literature, and literature in music. Fields' approach reflects the latter of these categories, literature in music, but his is a literature in music that is actually more complex given Beckett's musicality; instead, it is more like literature (music in literature) in music. This is a more complex layering of phenomena than the music in literature of, say, Joyce's attempt at a fugue in the "Sirens" episode of *Ulysses*. The text of the translator, Beckett, is further translated into instrumental music, without the vocal that Feldman had.

Fields' score follows the directions, words and characterisation meticulously, paralleling, for the most part, Beckett's text rather than any kind of Eisensteinian cognitive dissonance or counterpoint. The solo interludes are the exception to this, and it is interesting that Fields expresses regret regarding

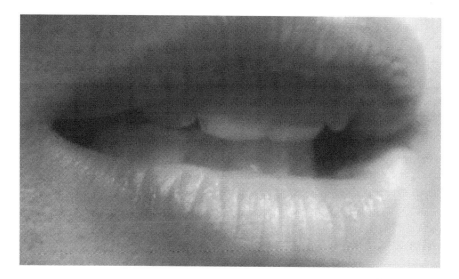

Figure 6.4 Julianne Moore in *Not I*

this decision.[13] Another major departure is the fact that he didn't score it for a solo instrument, instead utilising the full "Beckett" ensemble that plays on both albums – John Hollenbeck, Scott Roller, Matthias Schubert and himself. Given the presence of the quartet, however, it does make sense that each exhibits in turn their own expression of frantic nervous energy following the "movement" indicated after the four points of pause in the play. For the audience, it may seem that the woman is spouting out intuitively while thinking, a through-composed verbal improvisation, an entirely illusionary interpretation. Fields presents a mix of improvised and composed elements, all tied to Beckett's words.

Fields' *Not I* is scored for four voices, a quartet of tenor saxophone, electric guitar, cello and drums: perhaps *Not 1* or even *Not 4* might have been a more playful but apt title. Instead of a solitary woman we hear a tenor line sounding the rhythms of the words, but without any of their remaining semantic content alongside three accompanying improvisers. In this regard Fields' approach is a further extension of Beckett's semantic fluidity: now we have none of the word content, beyond their musical interpretation by Fields and the less tangible residue of their musical incarnation. Instead of many fragmented selves, the three other musicians comment on the urtext or ground bass of the tenor line. Fields chooses to omit the first few lines of the text and begins at the sentence "to make a ball". When I asked him about this in a Skype interview, he suggested that this was "most likely a mistake",[14] something I find difficult to accept given the meticulous care and attention to detail of the text that the score reflects. In my view, it was most likely an editing decision due to the length of the piece, a practice that Fields continues in live

140   *Improvising Beckett*

performance, as we will see. From here on, each note in the melody line corresponds directly to each and every word of the text. In setting each phrase, Fields assigns a number of beats that then form the pattern of time signatures. The first sentence "to make a ball" is scored in $\frac{4}{4}$, while the second bar changes to $\frac{5}{4}$ for the sentence "a few steps then stop". Fields inserts a crotchet rest in place of the ellipses between sentences in Beckett's text. In bar 4, the line "then on" is written in $\frac{3}{4}$ in order to accommodate a crotchet rest, and this practice continues throughout. As a result, Fields' score reflects the same staccato quality as Beckett's text.

Beckett's words act as musical directions in Fields' score. At bar 6, for the line "stop and stare again", a stop sign is introduced in the three lower parts. This sign recurs each time the word "stop" recurs, and indicates (according to the legend at the top of the piece) that the musicians "lay out" or stop playing suddenly. The instruments not carrying the melody line are to improvise throughout, and following such pauses they are to resume improvising at the arrows, the first of which occurs at bar 7 in the guitar and cello lines. This binary of structure and improvisation is what defines Fields' style of music, and finding ways to bring form to improvisation is an ongoing obsession for the composer.

Following the first occurrence of the "what? ... who? ... no! ... she!" discursive phrase (bars 14–17), in place of the movement indicated in the stage directions, Fields' score introduces a seven-bar improvisatory interlude. The melody line returns to the text in $\frac{7}{4}$ at the line "found herself in the dark" (bar 25). Interlude sections appear at each occurrence of this discursive phrase but extend to varying lengths of time. The second time is from bar 254 to bar 330, the third from bars 590 to 659, the fourth from bars 761 to 821 (moving between solo tenor and written parts). Do Fields' series of interludes adhere to Beckett's directions that each movement become less perceptible? As the directions tell us:

> Movement: this consists in simple sideways raising of arms from sides and their falling back, in a gesture of helpless compassion. It lessens with each recurrence till scarcely perceptible at third. There is just enough pause to contain it as MOUTH recovers from vehement refusal to relinquish third person.

There is no interlude following the fifth appearance of the phrase, in line with the stage directions; instead we are given a crescendo fade and a bar pause (bar 900) before returning to the text. When I asked Fields about these improvised interludes, he explained his slight regret regarding the decision as follows:

> In *Not I*, there are four pauses in the script. Since I had four musicians that gave them all a chance to lead on it. I slightly regret the way I handled that, because the way it's written, it's really meant as a kind of breather, I think, for the actress, so she makes it through the monologue. And it might be meant as relief for the audience, even though that doesn't seem very much like Beckett to give them a break. So I think it's really for her.

Figure 6.5 Fields' *Not I*, page 1

But I instructed the musicians to try and keep up the pace of the music rather than feel like a pause, and I sort of regret that. I don't think I really got it right. I especially regret it because they kept dropping the energy during those sections and I would stop them and make them do it right, but they may have been right.

142 *Improvising Beckett*

On the fourth interlude, Fields explained that at the time he had also wanted the tenor solo to continue for longer, but physical limits of the recording session made this impossible – the players had been playing non-stop for over four hours:

> I would like to have had him [Matthias Schubert] solo for a longer time but the problem was that he'd been playing through-composed music at 220 beats a minute for, by the time it was over, 26 minutes. But we didn't do it in a continuous take, so by the time he got to his solo, he had been playing at 200 beats a minute for 4 hours.

In any case, Fields' interludes are by no means less perceptible towards the end, as Beckett had directed. Does this aesthetic decision on the part of Fields represent an unfaithful manifestation of the text? It seems that Fields was straddling the conventions of two media with very different expectations, jazz improvisers on the one hand and a meticulous text for theatre on the other. In dealing with the practicalities of performance, Fields was forced to make certain compromises. The silence of the play is not as present in Fields' *Not I*, but the frantic unnerving quality is perhaps stronger as a result.

At over thirty minutes long, the recorded version of *Not I* presents stamina challenges for both players and listeners. Fields explains: "for live performance, I've cut out about 300 bars of *Not I*. So it's maybe 20 minutes instead of 30." In live formats, *Eh Joe* is also shorter than the recorded version. Fields is less extreme in what he will inflict on his performers and listeners than Beckett, then – or indeed than Morton Feldman.

It is clear from the very beginning that Fields recognises and follows the repetitive nature of Beckett's work. On what attracted him to Beckett he explains:

> His [Beckett's] writing is so stylised, so formal. He does use pauses in ways that I thought I could fill them … there's room to occupy and a good reason to do it. You're not just inserting sounds because you want a chance to play.
>
> In terms of setting any of the writers I have set, I look for rhythm and repetition. The first playwright I set was David Mamet. Rhythmically he's great. He uses a lot of speech patterns that I'm familiar with because he grew up near where I did in Chicago, just a couple of miles south from me in the city. But still his writing is not at all naturalistic; the beats are really great. The same goes for Charles Bukowski; he uses a lot of repetition and rhythmically he's really great as well. So, I wasn't really thinking thematically; it's really just based on repeated phrases and the rhythmic material, and with Beckett it's nice that he had so many short plays … I tried to set Pinter but it didn't work for me. It's sort of the opposite to rhythmic and stylised.

Improvising Beckett 143

Repeated words are repeated as the same pitch and duration:

> If a word is repeated, of course, I would use the same pitch and rhythmic value. So that means a phrase would be the same. But I also look for rhymes. Now this doesn't occur so much in *Not I*, but for the Bukowski poems I might make them into a musical rhyme like a third or fourth, or if it's a near rhyme it might be a flat five or something like that … within my tonal sets I make up these rules too.

In bar 4, the line "then on", is written in $\frac{3}{4}$ as a D followed by a B and crotchet rest. Bar 7 contains a similar phrase – "so on" – and this word "on" is also a B. This holds for all discursive and musematic repeats throughout the piece, indicating the meticulous lengths that Fields underwent in the composition of the melody line. Debussy set Baudelaire's "Harmonie du soir" in a somewhat similar fashion, but with the added dimension of transposition. As Dora A. Hanninen (2012, 279) writes, "Shaping each line of text into distinct musical phrase, Debussy matches structural line repetition in the text with literal, transposed, or modified melodic repetition in the voice."

Fields employs word painting on a number of occasions. Even though the words may not be sung, some of their inevitable semantic content is evoked and repeated. When a word indicates a sound, the instruments attempt to recreate it. The word "buzzing" in bar 29 includes the melody moving to the cello line for that single word, while the guitar and drums must stop.

Likewise, in bar 557 we see the phrase "dull roar" reflected by a *crescendo* followed by the descending *glissando* line that matches "like falls", evoking a waterfall sound in the drums. In bar 843, for the line "half the vowels wrong", the saxophone is instructed to vary the vowel sound applied to the written melody. In bar 338 the same instruction to "vary vowel sound" occurs at the word "vowel", but at the word "sounds" the three lower instruments play staccato flickering notes. This occurs almost every time the word "sound" appears in the text, as in bars 180, 181, 334, 477, 478 and 538. The laughs indicated in the stage directions are scored as cello scrapes, as in bars 70 and 72. Likewise the screams are scored as high-pitched, loud saxophone cries, as in bars 185 and 189. Here, the players are expected to imitate such sounds as for the buzzing mentioned above. The silences that follow these screams in the text are written as full bar-length pauses for all instruments. Where Beckett had yearned for specific periods of silence in his texts – we remember his appeal to Stravinsky for such a method – Fields scores such a distinct pause. The freedom that Fields offers the players in this aspect of word painting is also reminiscent of the power with which Cage endowed his performers. The players have the words on the score accompanying each of their parts when performing, and Fields desires that they individually respond to the words affecting the notes.

Dynamics in the music also reflect punctuation in the text; for instance, in bar 390 the exclamation mark at "her lips moving!" includes an *fff* dynamic

Figure 6.6 Fields' *Not I*, page 2

mark. For the word "sounds", a flickering staccato is indicated, leaving a certain amount of interpretative freedom open to the instrumentalists to employ rhythmic scraping or flutter-tongue techniques, for instance. Any sentence ending in a question mark is given an upward inflection in the score.

The word "God" is deliberately written as a dominant chord. In bar 674, a "sudden flash" is represented by the flashy technique of a multiphonic in the tenor. Fields emphasises the importance of interpretative engagement with the text in performance:

> You have to adjust to him [the tenor] because of the structure of the piece. You're improvising almost entirely in the beginning. And then as phrases recur, the musicians will one at a time play this phrase with the tenor player, even though it's not a matching phrase. But it's one that will repeat. And so, after the tenor solo, every phrase in the piece has recurred a number of times. And so everyone is playing written music by the end.
>
> You really have to be able to read the tenor part while improvising, and my instructions are to improvise in a way that makes it unclear whether you are improvising or reading along badly.

The Beckettian "illusion of improvisation" has here been translated by Fields into improvised music that at times attempts to feign being scored, for the player to sound like they are "reading along badly". To return to the concepts of Deleuzian repetition discussed in previous chapters, the improvised explorations offered by Fields' repetitions of Beckett's texts are Deleuzian in nature. Adrian Parr writes that 'in terms of discovery and experimentation; it [Deleuzian repetition] allows new experiences, affects and expressions to emerge" (Parr, 2005, 223.) Far from tautology then, perhaps through Beckett, Fields finds "a form that accommodates the mess", as his Deleuzian exploration of Beckett's world manifests itself as this complex music. (Beckett quoted in Cohn, 1980, 96). Fields' improvisational structures somewhat echo Beckett's concern with aleatory methodology in the composition of *Lessness*. Improvisation more widely might be seen as a distinct move beyond such notions of denotative expression, as are the slurred words of John Martyn or the low vocal mix in Shoegaze music. If there is no content per se in improvisation – besides the dialogue of tradition and creation, between notes and other notes, with no narrative or pre-planned content at all, only intuitive Bergsonian response, a conversation, even with oneself – how does Fields' music interact with the "self" in Beckett's work? Improvisation is often equated with self-realiation, an idea backed up by recent research into the creative activity in the brain during such a practice. A project led by Charles Limb, for instance, involved getting jazz pianists to improvise while inside an fMRI scanner. The resultant scans clearly showed that the same parts of the brain that relate to self-consciousness and the willingness to take risks and make mistakes in the frontal lobe lit up whilst improvising (Limb,

146   *Improvising Beckett*

2010). On the other hand, others speak of losing oneself as the true pull of improvising. As John M. Carvalho writes:

> The improviser must give musical sense to a form that comes with few cues about how to take it. Again, this frees the improviser from habits, good and bad, and from remembered history of improvisations on the standard forms, and it challenges the improviser to lose herself in the form and experiment with provisional solutions to the problems posed by the form.
>
> (Carvalho, 2010, 289)

Though Carvalho here speaks of the kind of improvisation in modal jazz from the late 1950s through the 1960s, including Miles Davis' seminal *Kind of Blue* (1959) and *In a Silent Way* (1969), this idea of an improviser losing his- or herself certainly persists in descriptions of the phenomenon by artists themselves. Indeed, as an improviser myself, the energy that such quick decisions require means that all else is necessarily sidelined. The best improvisers react instantly and don't even seem to make conscious decisions. Carvalho writes further: "In the repetitive drone of the rhythm, he precisely loses his Ego, his Self, and identifies with a principle of selection that guides him to his goal, more entelechy than telos, and that goal is what we hear as melody" (Carvalho, 2010, 289). Quoting Frederic Rzewski, Carvalho equates this self-realisation, while improvising over the repetitive backgrounds of modal jazz, with Lacanian psychoanalytic concepts:

> The pleasure that accompanies these improvisations, "a state of perception in which one seems to be outside oneself, or to be in more than one place at the same time", is precisely the ecstasy, the *jouissance*, associated with the death drive. The improviser realizes this pleasure in herself and her listeners and realizes in this *jouissance*, drawing on a form of repetition modelled on this drive.
>
> (Carvalho, 2010, 289)

Both Beckett and Feldman's concern for the self and the human condition is therefore brought to another level in Fields' Beckettian jazz when we consider this connection between selflessness and improvisation. The title of the piece explored above, *Not I*, is of course particularly apt in this regard. Beckett avoids the personal pronoun in an exegesis of a frantic, unsettled self while Fields quarters this self into an even less tangible and silent entity. The "loss" associated with *jouissance*, which Carvalho relates to improvisation, perhaps provides a further loss of the negated self, the protagonist's self in Fields' *Not I*.

Notes

1 See http://matthewemay.com/doubling-down-on-lessness/ [accessed 25 March 2013].
2 For more on Beckett's use of silence, see Bryden (1998).
3 There is extensive literature on the matter; see for instance Susan Sontag, "Aesthetics of Silence" ([1967] 1994), David Metzer, "Modern Silence" (2006), Mary Bryden, "Beckett and the Sound of Silence" (1998).
4 Dirk Van Hulle, "Sans", in *The Literary Encyclopaedia*, 1 March 2004, www.litencyc.com/php/sworks.php?rec=true&UID=2307 [accessed 25 March 13].
5 Knowlson's biography of Beckett is entitled *Damned to Fame: The Life of Samuel Beckett* (1996).
6 Elliott Sharp interviewed by Joe Gore, in "Where Order Meets Chaos", in *Guitar Player* Vol. 3, no. 1, January 1997.
7 Other pivotal free jazz musicians include Albert Ayler, Sun Ra and Pharoah Sanders.
8 These were reprinted in 2000 in *Beckett in Black and Red*, edited by Alan Friedman.
9 Please refer to my taxonomy of repetition in Chapter 4.
10 Beckett, letter to Alan Schneider 16 October, 72, quoted in Harmon (2000, 283).
11 *Ibid.*
12 Fields, quoted in liner notes to *Samuel* (2009, 7).
13 This and all following Fields quotes are from an interview I conducted with him on 12 September 2012.
14 See www.ted.com/talks/charles_limb_your_brain_on_improv.html [accessed 13 August 2013].

Conclusions

Beckett is a rarity in that his innovative use of music is primarily at the philosophical level, and is therefore not always explicitly visible, or audible. In creating a semantic fluidity in prose that resonates an intangible, non-explicit meaning, his later work can be read in a manner similar to music. In Beckett's later prose, we are not engaging with a plot wherein a piece of music is mentioned, or in which a sonata sparks a memory for the protagonist. Instead, the prose itself has been composed under the influence of music. Such a structural use of music ensures that the musical elements will always, however, be metaphorical in nature: a written text is not composed according to melody or vertical intervals, it is not informed by textures or harmonies, and it cannot be varied through instrumentation or volume when read silently. Repetition and silence can be employed transmedially and indeed provide the salient factors of such a prose style. Where Beckett differs from many of the other musically influenced writers, then, is that his very style of writing – the composition – is musically infused with repetitions and silences as well as music philosophy, while others may refer to mere surface devices.

Beckett achieved a semantic fluidity in his work through the employment of repetition informed by a Schopenhauerian philosophy of music, but in the end the Romantic application of musical devices to his work will always remain metaphorical. Like the themes and subject matter that Beckett's work repetitively explores, the author's musical prose could never fully reach the condition of music. Music and literature strive towards one another without ever truly converging, as though tracing an endless asymptotic curve. The philosophical intangibility of music is also a literal intangibility, unreachable through words alone. Such a yearning and longing between the artforms is echoed in the longing of Beckett's characters, his expression of the human condition and in the author's application of musical ideas. This futility is not to be regarded negatively however: such a Beckettian "failure" is, in a very real sense, the whole point of his musico-literary exercise. The Derridean liminal space is where both Beckett and, as we have seen, Feldman operate: in between meanings, space and time itself. Although Beckett's semantic fluidity displays musical qualities, a certain degree of meaning remains as residue: words will always hold a certain amount of affiliated and snowballed

Conclusions 149

meaning. In *Molloy*, Beckett writes: "the words I heard were sounds ... free of all meaning" (Beckett, [1951] 1994, 50). And yet, in truth, there is always *some* meaning as the author later concedes: although these words are free of explicit definition, they are nevertheless "sounds unencumbered with precise meaning" (Beckett, [1951] 1994, 50).

Though Beckett explores various musical devices such as the *da capo* repeat in *Play* ([1963] 2006), he can "never get there", argues Paul Lawley in relation to the musical qualities of the work (Lawley, 1984, 25). For him, these musical qualities have:

> the effect of pushing the language to the borders of abstraction. On the first run-through the heads' speculations about the nature and meaning of their present state do seem, despite the specified tonelessness of delivery and uniform tempo, evidence of "how the mind works still to be sure!" (p. 18), but in the repeat our sense of this diminishes drastically: everything now seems fixed, absolutely cyclic, and our already considerable awareness of words as opaque blocks or aural artillery is made even more acute than it was during the initial run-through. What we are witnessing is not a quest for "truth" (of whatever kind) but a frantic struggle for survival against the light. Yet although for the heads the words they speak are stone-dead, entirely without semantic "charge" (the toneless delivery seems to confirm this), for the audience the words can never empty themselves entirely of meaning – even second time round. The *Play* tends towards the condition of music but, as far as we are concerned, can never get there. For the heads communication is never a concern, since each is apparently oblivious of the presence of the others.
>
> (Lawley, 1984, 25)

Beckettian contradictions abound in various ways, from his changing position on instrumental music being used in his work, to the ways in which composers are encouraged to set his words. Perhaps this is part of the postmodern condition as Laws would have it, but lying at the core of the matter is the fact that Beckett is an artist, and for art to be interesting (according to him), contradictions are necessary. A Schopenhauerian approach would suggest that artists could bypass and transgress such contradictions and offer greater insights through such juxtapositions. A poet should never have to explain or show his or her licence (here we can recall the pedantry of Baricelli's criticism of the *Four Quartets* in Chapter 1). The fact that Beckett was an avant-garde author with a predilection for Romantic music and its philosophies might confuse some, but such a clash was more generally a part of Modernism, a binary illustrated earlier through reference to Picasso's inclusion of a bull from the oldest cave drawing in Europe in *Guernica* (1937). Beckett was far from alone in this Romanticism. Hans Werner Henze and Helmut Lachenmann were modern European composers who also looked to the Romantics for their inspiration rather than to the Darmstadt School or Boulez.

150   *Conclusions*

In the end, the semantic fluidity created during Beckett's search for a way of unwording the word achieves an intangible universality, itself a repetitive theme in his *oeuvre*. Just like the theme of winter and silence that resonates in his favourite *Winterreise* (1828), this Schubertian longing in Beckett's work challenges the reader to "make sense who may" (Beckett, 1983, 476). Discussing *What Where* ([1983] 2006), White suggests that while the play might posit that nothing else is happening ("Time passes. That is all"), in fact "this representation of passing time is its most disturbing feature" (White, 2008, 194). Rather than a representation of specifics, the refrain of passing time is a thematic reiteration of semantic fluidity, a leitmotif particularly befitting the temporal unravelling of words through music.

Play is an example of *da capo* form, like *Godot* and *Lessness*, as previously mentioned; but it also exemplifies Beckett's obsession with failure. The repeats are directed to decrease in volume and speed alongside diminishing lighting in order to highlight the play's primary theme of degradation. As Martin Esslin writes of *Play*:

> These three parts are repeated, and the play ends, as it began, with the Chorus. But, Beckett explained, there must be a clear progression by which each subsection is both faster and softer than the preceding one.
>
> (Esslin quoted in Cohn, 1980, 125)

Such inferiority in imitation – the notion that we lose something with each repeat – echoes Plato's views on the lesser nature of mimesis, but also the erosion of meaning in semantic fluidity. What it also shows is that Deleuzian discursive repetition, positive transformation, can also be used to emphasise failure. The famous line from *Worstward Ho* (1983c) is itself, aptly enough, as if in Flaubertian or Joycean style-mirroring-content, a fine example of Beckettian anaphora and epistrophe: "Ever tried. Ever failed. No matter. Try Again. Fail again. Fail better" (*Worstward Ho*, 1983c).[1]

All of these traits in Beckett's work have attracted and influenced so many contemporary composers. Beckett's curious mixture of Romantic and Modernist ideals was highly influential on both contemporary and subsequent artists. György Kurtág is perhaps, after Feldman (himself a strong advocate of Sibelius, we must remember), the composer who works most closely with Beckett's aesthetic, and continually demonstrates the author's influence in his reduction of materials, short fragmentary compositions and his setting of Beckett's last poem in "What Is the Word?" (1990–91). Earl Kim is another highly Beckettian composer, having composed minimal, quiet and reductive music to a great many Beckett texts including ...*dead calm*... (1961) and *Now and Then* (1981). Other noteworthy Beckettians are Richard Barrett and Michael Finnissey, whose approaches to Beckett are from another side, instead drawing inspiration for complex compositions like Barrett's *stirrings* (2001), based on *Stirrings Still* (Beckett, [1988] 1995), and Finnissey's *Enough* (2001).

Conclusions 151

By exploring two very different musicians, from very different genres, backgrounds and aesthetics, we saw just how important both repetition and silence are in modern music. Feldman and Fields offer two contrasting types of Beckettian music, yet both display a focus on transmedial repetition. While Feldman's works inhabit Scher's "music and literature" category, Fields' instrumentals fall within the category of "literature in music", or even perhaps "literature (music in literature) in music", as mentioned in Chapter 6. Both composers, like Beckett, employ musematic, discursive, binary and clothed exact repetition throughout their work. Both translate the repetitive qualities of Beckett's texts into music. Feldman famously grew tired of allowing much indeterminacy in his work and his exacting, precise work has, as we have seen, much in common with Beckett's own aesthetic, not least his serialist-like precision of movement and gesture (*Film*, 1964, for instance), and structure (*Quad*, 1981; *That Time*, 1976), as White would have it. Fields, on the other hand, creates structures for his improvisations, but these are interspersed with lengthy and meticulously composed sections. Taken together, Fields' and Feldman's music is certainly repeating Beckett in the Deleuzian sense – "in terms of discovery and experimentation; it allows new experiences, affects and expressions to emerge" (Parr, 2005, 223).

Like Beckett, in his employment of semantic fluidity Feldman plays with the "to and fro"s, exploring the grand themes of time, stasis and waiting in ways similar to Beckett's investigations in *Godot*, *That Time* and many other works throughout his career. Feldman's music is also, like Beckett's later prose, free from explicit, definite meanings. Instead of trying to reinforce a particular interpretation, Feldman keeps the hermeneutics open. The "self" moves perennially "back and forth" through recurring, unresolved motives that, like the artforms themselves, reach "neither".

If we return to Lawrence Kramer's suggestion in Chapter 1 that "a poem and a composition may converge on a structural rhythm: that a shared pattern of unfolding can act as an interpretive framework for the explicit dimension of both works" (Kramer, 1984, 10), it becomes clear that the Beckettian music of both Feldman and Fields correspond to his thesis. A "shared pattern of unfolding" succinctly describes how both composers translate transmedial repetition into music: Fields allows a certain amount of improvisation within the structure, while Feldman meticulously scores every note. As Calvin S. Brown, Peter Kivy, Heinrich Schenker and Lawrence Kramer suggest, repetition is central to musical discourse and Beckett's texts certainly enable a special kind of convergence as a result. Repeating Beckett's repeats yields multi-layered music. In Beckett's repetitive texts, Fields discovers "a form that accommodates the mess", a structure from which to improvise.

As we saw in Chapter 5, Feldman also responded to contemporary painters such as Rothko, Guston and Rauschenberg. Beckett, too, had a keen eye for the visual arts, collecting works by Jack Yeats and Giacometti, for instance. Might semantic fluidity also translate into visual art? Further study might explore aspects of stasis and semantic fluidity in Rothko perhaps.

152 *Conclusions*

Certainly, in Gustavo Alberto Garcia Vaca's *neither*[2] (front cover) the "inner to outer shadow" of the text is clearly depicted, but in a very different manner to Feldman's approach. Lois Oppenheim's *The Painted Word: Samuel Beckett's Dialogue with Art* (2000) and edited collection *Samuel Beckett and the Arts: Music, Visual Arts, and Non-Print Media* (1999) offer insights into this visual impact of Beckett's work.

Fields' and Feldman's translations of Beckett's texts are far beyond tautologies. As we have seen, they employ the inherent repetition of the author's works in creative and imaginative ways. Theirs is a positive Deleuzian repetition. Beyond Beckett, of course, the dialogue between "original" and "copy" continues, having troubled philosophers and artists for millennia. For Plato, the imitation was always inherently inferior, whereas Aristotle saw such repetition in a more positive light, linking it to the most fundamental example: human reproduction. DNA tells us that we are all, for the most part at least, copies of our ancestors.[3] In this sense, evolution can be considered a kind of Deleuzian repetition. Biology repeats but with subtle improvements, alterations and differences occurring slowly over vast canvasses of time. Nietzsche built on the Greek idea of the Eternal Return, while Kierkegaard was greatly concerned with doubles, recognising early the impossibility of exact repetition. Benjamin taught us that the original is, like exact repetition, a kind of myth in itself. In many ways, our idea of the original is itself a reproduction. A painting is often a representation, an interpretative copy of what it depicts: a kind of reproduction. A film, even documentary film, is always the interpretation of its director; fundamentally its light is caught and copied by the lens. Erich Auerbach's seminal *Mimesis* ([1946] 2003) explores, with great insight, the representation of realism in literature in a manner that highlights the fact that such copying of the real world was not simply a nineteenth-century phenomenon like pictorialism, but instead goes back much further in time.

Consider the perennial and often irritating documentation of the tourist or concert-goer. The camera provides the means of copying the original for one's own memento – looking and hearing through the device is seemingly of more importance than doing so without it. Whether acting as memory aid, proof of "presence", or as means of undergoing a kind of Wordsworthian "emotions recollected in tranquillity" ([1800] 1971), it is clear that ubiquitous technology, the recording "equipment" (Heidegger, [1953] 1996, 15: 97) is now an extension of our being, a part of our involvement in the world.

Yet in contemporary society we still place the greatest weight on the "original". An original Picasso might sell for millions, and yet a high-quality print will be worth no more than a few pounds. Warhol and Hirst might factory-print multiple works, but these "originals" are still awarded higher economic value than a well-made "copy". When Warhol placed quotidian objects in the context of art galleries in an attempt to alter our perception of such objects, he was interrogating such assumptions concerning copies and repetition, as did Duchamp's ready-mades. A can of soup might be ubiquitous, but every

Conclusions 153

time we see it on canvas, it does something to the original itself. The original is altered by repetition.

In Borges' famous story about the fictional character Pierre Menard, the protagonist attempts to unlearn what history and culture 1602–1918 might have taught him, in order to go about the seemingly impossible task of composing the *Quixote* word for word with the "original". Borges writes:

> Pierre Menard did not want to compose *another* Quixote, which surely is easy enough – he wanted to compose *the* Quixote. Nor, surely, need one be obliged to note that his goal was never a mechanical transcription of the original; he had no intention of *copying* it. His admirable ambition was to produce a number of pages which coincided – word for word and line for line – with those of Miguel de Cervantes.
>
> (Borges, [1939] 1998b, 91)

In the end, Menard achieves his goal and indeed his Quixote outshines that of Cervantes. Though Harold Bloom informs us that Menard could never have avoided the "anxiety of influence" of the intervening years, the pages that he produces, although seemingly exact repetitions, are, in fact, positive Deleuzian clothed repeats. Furthermore, the original is altered and improved by such imitation, as deep study is focused on the original text (Benjamin). In this light, might musical translations of the kind we have explored also offer this new outlook on the "original"?

Tom Philips' *Humanent: A Treated Victorian Novel* (2016) finds new material latent in W. H. Mallock's novel *The Human Document* (1892), and this idea of finding new works within existing ones further calls into question the problem of authorship and "original".

Cortázar's *Hopcotch* (Spanish 1963, English [1966] 1987) was indebted to Mallarmé's early experiments while the "book in a box" concept pioneered by Marc Saportha's in *Composition No. 1* ([1962] 2011) and B. S. Johnson's *The Unfortunates* ([1969] 1999), incorporated loose pages, and thereby deconstructed traditional narrative sequences in a manner fitting the digital age – *Composition No. 1* has now been re-imagined as an app that randomly shuffles pages.

Burroughs' cut-ups, influencing Bowie, Cobain and Radiohead, to name a few, brought chance procedures to the mainstream, while internet hypertexts and contemporary video games are providing ways for the reader to self-construct narrative through interactive choices. The initial limitations of memory in the technology was one practical reason for loops and leitmotifs, but in modern gaming, developers are using repetition in explorative ways – take the interactive stems in games like *Red Dead Redemption* (2010), for instance, in which a vast array of loops in a single key interweave in conjunction with certain choices and actions in the gameplay. In a way, the player can become the composer or conductor of his or her own soundworld.

We must repeat to practice, to learn an instrument, a sports technique, a language, indeed to become proficient at any endeavour – 10,000 hours or not,

154   *Conclusions*

as Malcolm Gladwell (2008) would have it. Our lives are dominated by routine and ritual, from birth to death and after (Sir Thomas Browne's seminal text "Hydriotaphia: Urne Burial" ([1658 1968) comes to mind). T. S. Eliot discussed the important dialogue between the canon and originality in his famous essay "Tradition and the Individual Talent" ([1919] 2005), positing that in order for an artist to innovate and create something worthwhile, he or she must first engage with what has gone before. An artist does not reinvent the wheel, and if they did, there would be no audience there to understand it, no network, as the listener would have nothing to compare it with, and wouldn't have learned the aesthetic criteria at hand. With innovations, there is, for this reason, often a period of acclimatisation; consider the relative silence between J. S. Bach's death in 1750 and Mendelssohn's revival with the St Matthew Passion in 1829, which was the first major performance of the work outside Leipzig.

Repetition is, as Fink points out, around us everywhere in modern life. With 3D printing, perhaps soon we will have the facility to replicate and repeat physical objects in our homes as easily as they are presented on television. There are also the implications of repetition in viral video on YouTube: how does such vast repetition of experience affect how music is consumed in the modern world? And how do streaming sites like Spotify impact reception? If a piece of music is repeated *ad infinitum* on a playlist in an office, for instance, how does a listener's perception of said music alter as a result?

The repetitive krautrock of Neu!, Can and Faust did much for destigmatising repetition in popular culture, a music that links the ambient music of Brian Eno, 1990s rave culture, David Bowie's Berlin years, the minimalism of Glenn Branca and Rhys Chatham, and the avantrock experimentalism of Sonic Youth. Simon Reynolds' study of normalised anachronism and atemporality in contemporary pop music, *Retromania* (2011), highlights the prevalence of another kind of repetition, one that encompasses nostalgia and longing for past styles. If we go beyond the modernist baggage of the "new", how will repetition continue to shape modern music? Repetition was perhaps never more prominent in music than it is today; the stigma that it once had is certainly no more. No longer is it kept "secret" as Snead described; repetition is ubiquitous but also everything is up for grabs, an "infinite music" of possibility (Harper, 2011). We are now in a more Aristotelian period of music than a Platonic one.

Aristotle saw metaphors as didactic tools that, through contrasting separate artforms, enabled new insight and could thus "teach us something new" (Prieto, 2002a, 23). Going forward in Word and Music Studies, it is imperative that we keep this in mind. We must avoid the pedantry of trying to pin down metaphors for their supposed correctness, as many in the field have futilely done. Outdated methodologies must be abandoned and the focus must move forward towards deeper investigations. As we remember Webern's suggestion that repetition is itself a form of variation, we must not repeat the mistakes in the field and instead vary the methodology in new and exciting ways.

Notes

1 Glitch music highlights this failure through repetition in another way, by deliberately emphasising the scratches and bumps in samples of electronic music. By focusing on what would traditionally be hidden or removed, a fetishisation occurs wherein the glitches themselves become pleasant and are, in the end, like any other musical sound. Such a practice is reminiscent of similar aesthetics in noise music, as we saw in Chapter 2.
2 See chamanvision.com [accessed 7 August 2017].
3 Whether these are degraded or inferior copies is another question – evolution would seem to negate such an idea – though it is certainly the case in current cloning technology.

Bibliography

Abbate, Carolyn (1996) *Unsung Voices* (Princeton: Princeton University Press).

Abbott, H. Porter (2004) "How Beckett Fails, Once More with Music", *Contemporary Literature*, Vol. 45, No. 4, Winter, 713–722.

Abbott, Helen (2009) *Between Baudelaire and Mallarmé: Voice, Conversation and Music* (Farnham: Ashgate).

Adorno, Theodor W. (1973 [1949]) *Philosophie der neuen Musik* (New York: Seabury Press).

——— (2010 (1961]) "Notes on Beckett", Dirk Van Hulle and Shane Weller trans., *Journal of Beckett Studies*, Vol. 19, No. 2, 157–178.

Albright, Daniel (1999) "The Need for Comparison among the Arts", in *Samuel Beckett and the Arts*, ed. Lois Oppenheim (New York and London: Garland Publishing Inc.), xi–xviii.

——— (2000) *Untwisting the Serpent: Modernism in Music, Literature and Other Arts* (Chicago and London: University of Chicago Press).

——— (2003) *Beckett and Aesthetics* (Cambridge: Cambridge University Press).

Anon (n.d.), "Gilles Deleuze (1925–1995)", at www.iep.utm.edu/deleuze/ [accessed 14 August 2013].

Apollinaire, Guillaume (1991) *Oeuvres en prose completes* (Paris: Editions Gallimard).

Aristotle (1961 [*c*.335 BC]) *Poetics*, Francis Ferguson trans. (New York: Hill and Wang).

Attali, Jacques (1985) *Noise: The Political Economy of Music* (Minneapolis: University of Minnesota Press).

Auerbach, Erich (2003 [1946]) *Mimesis: The Representation of Reality in Western Thought* (Princeton: Princeton University Press).

Austen, Jane (2003 [1815]) *Emma* (Oxford: Oxford University Press).

Babbitt, Irving (1910) *The New Laokoon: An Essay on the Confusion of the Arts* (Boston, MA and New York: Houghton Mifflin Company).

Bailey, Derek (1980) *Improvisation: Its Nature and Practice in Music* (Ashbourne: Moorland Publishing, in association with Incus Records).

Ball, Philip (2010) *The Music Instinct: How Music Works and Why We Can't Do Without It* (London: Bodley Head).

Banfield, Ann (2003) "Beckett's Tattered Syntax", *Representations*, Vol. 84 No. 1, November, 6–29.

Baricelli, Jean-Pierre (1988 [1943]) *Melopoiesis: Approaches to the Study of Literature and Music* (New York: New York University Press).

Barthes, Roland (1977a [1964]) "Rhetoric of the Image", in *Image, Music, Text*, Stephen Heath ed. and trans. (New York: Hill and Wang), 32–51.

Bibliography 157

——— (1977b [1967]) "The Death of the Author", in *Image, Music, Text*, Stephen Heath trans. (London: Fontana), 142–148.

Baugh, Bruce (1993) "Prolegomena to Any Aesthetics of Rock Music", *Journal of Aesthetics and Art Criticism*, Vol. 51. No. 1, 23–29.

Beckett, Samuel (1963 [1945]) *Watt* (London: Calder).

——— (1999 [1931/1949]) *Proust and Three Dialogues with Georges Duthuit* (London: Calder).

——— (1980) *Company* (New York: Grove).

——— (1983a[1929])"Dante … Bruno. Vico … Joyce"(1929), in *Disjecta: Miscellaneous Writings and A Dramatic Fragment* (London: Calder), 19–34.

——— (1983b [1934]) "Recent Irish Poetry", in *Disjecta: Miscellaneous Writings and A Dramatic Fragment* (London: Calder), 70–76.

——— (1983c) *Worstward Ho* (London: Calder).

——— (1984) *Collected Poems* (London: Calder, repr. 1999).

——— (1992 [1932]) *Dream of Fair to Middling Women* (London: Calder).

——— (1993 [1934]) *More Pricks than Kicks* (London: Calder).

——— (1994) *Trilogy: Molloy (1951), Malone Dies (1951), The Unnamable (1953)* (London: Calder).

——— (1995) *The Complete Short Prose 1929–81*, S. E. Gontarski ed. (New York: Grove Press).

——— (1997 [1981]) *Ill Seen Ill Said* (London: Calder).

——— (2003 [1938]) *Murphy* (London: Calder).

——— (2006) *Complete Dramatic Works of Samuel Beckett* (London: Faber).

——— (2009) *The Letters of Samuel Beckett, Vol. 1, 1929–1940*, Martha Dow Fehsenfeld and Lois More Overbeck eds (Cambridge: Cambridge University Press).

——— (2011) *The Letters of Samuel Beckett, Vol. II, 1941–1956*, George Craig, Martha Dow Fehensfeld, Dan Gunn and Lois More Overbeck eds (Cambridge: Cambridge University Press).

Beckett, Samuel and Alan Schneider (1998) *Better Served: The Correspondence of Samuel Beckett and Alan Schneider*, Maurice Harmon ed. (Cambridge, MA: Harvard University Press.

Begbie, Jeremy (2000) *Theology, Music, and Time* (Cambridge: Cambridge University Press).

Benjamin, Walter (1973 [1936]) "The Work of Art in the Age of Mechanical Reproduction", in *Illuminations* (Glasgow: Fontana), 242–243.

Benson, Stephen (2005) "Beckett, Feldman, Joe and Bob: Speaking of Music in *Words and Music*", in *Essays on Music and the Spoken Word and on Surveying the Field*, Suzanne M. Lodato and David Francis Urrows eds (Amsterdam and New York: Rodopi), 165–180.

——— (2006) *Literary Music: Writing Music in Contemporary Fiction* (Aldershot: Ashgate).

——— (2012) "Beckett's Audiobooks", in *The Yearbook of English Studies Vol. 42, Literature of the 1950s and 1960s*, MHRA, 223–237.

Bergson, Henri (2002 [1946]) *The Creative Mind: An Introduction to Metaphysics* (New York: Citadel Press).

Berkeley, George (2008 [1710]) *A Treatise Concerning the Principles of Human Knowledge* (Rockville, MD: Arc Manor LLC).

Bernhart, Walter, Steven Paul Scher and Werner Wolf eds (1999) *Word and Music Studies: Defining the Field* (Amsterdam and Atlanta: Rodopi).

Best, David (1980) "The Objectivity of Artistic Appreciation", *British Journal of Aesthetics*, Vol. 20, 115–127.

158 *Bibliography*

Bloom, Harold (1997 [1973]) *The Anxiety of Influence: A Theory of Poetry* (Oxford: Oxford University Press).

Blum, Eberhard (2000) "Morton Feldman: Neither", review of Sebastian Claren's *Neither: Die Musik Morton Feldmans*, first published in *Positionen* (November), Chris Villars trans., available at www.cnvill.net/mfblumre.htm [accessed 14 July 2017].

Bohlman, Philip (1999) "Ontologies of Music", in *Rethinking Music*, Nicholas Cook and Mark Everist eds (Oxford: Oxford University Press), 17–34.

Borges, Jorge Luis (1998a [1944]) "The Library of Babel", in *Jorge Luis Borges: Collected Fictions*, Andrew Hurley trans. (London: Penguin Books), 112–118.

——— (1998b [1939]) "Pierre Menard, Author of the Quixote", in *Jorge Luis Borges: Collected Fictions*, Andrew Hurley trans. (London: Penguin Books), 88–95.

Bowen, Zack (1974) *Musical Allusions in the Works of James Joyce* (Albany: State University of New York Press).

Brater, Enoch (1975) "Dada, Surrealism and the Genesis of *Not I*", *Modern Drama*, Vol. 18, 49–59.

Breatnach, Mary (1996) *Boulez and Mallarmé: A Study in Poetic Influence* (Burlington, VT: Ashgate).

Brienza, Susan and Enoch Brater (1976) "Chance and Choice in Beckett's Lessness", *ELH*, Vol. 43, No. 2, Summer, 244–258.

Brown, Calvin S. (1948) *Music and Literature: A Comparison of the Arts* (Athens, GA: University of Georgia Press).

Brown, Susan (2007) "The Mystery of the Fuga per Canonem Solved", *Genetic Joyce Studies*, Issue 7, Spring, www.antwerpjamesjoycecenter.com/articles/GJS7/GJS7brown [accessed 21 July 2017].

Browne, Sir Thomas (1968 [1658]) "Hydriotaphia: Urne Burial", in *Selected Writings*, Sir Geoffrey Keynes ed. (London: Faber & Faber), 113–156.

Bryden, Mary (1998) "Beckett and the Sound of Silence", in *Samuel Beckett and Music*, Mary Bryden ed. (Oxford: Clarendon), 21–47.

——— and Margaret Topping eds, (2009) *Beckett's Proust/Deleuze's Proust* (Basingstoke: Palgrave Macmillan).

Budd, Malcolm (1985) *Music and the Emotions: The Philosophical Theories* (London: Routledge and Kegan Paul).

Butler, Christopher (1994) *Early Modernism: Literature, Music and Painting in Europe, 1900–1916* (Oxford: Clarendon Press).

Cage, John (1973) *Silence: Lectures and Writings* (Middletown, CT: Weslyan University Press).

Calder, John (2001) *The Philosophy of Samuel Beckett* (London: Calder).

Carter, Tim (2001) "Word Painting", in *The New Grove Dictionary of Music and Musicians* (2nd edn), Stanley Sadie ed. (London: Macmillan), Vol. 27, 563.

Carvalho, John M. (2010) "Repetition and Self-Realization in Jazz Improvisation", *The Journal of Aesthetics and Art Criticism*, Vol. 68, No. 3, Summer, 285–290.

Claren, Sebastian (2000) *Neither: Die Musik Morton Feldmans* (Hofheim: Wolke Verlag).

——— (2006) "A Feldman Chronology", Christine Shuttleworth trans., in *Morton Feldman Says: Selected Interviews and Lectures 1964–1987*, Chris Villars ed. (London: Hyphen Press), 255–275.

Bibliography 159

Coetzee, J. M. (1973) "Samuel Beckett's *Lessness*: An Exercise in Decomposition", in *Computers and the Humanities*, Vol. 7, No. 4, March, 195–198.

Cohn, Ruby (1973) *Back to Beckett* (Princeton: Princeton University Press).

—— (1980) *Just Play: Beckett's Theater* (Princeton: Princeton University Press).

—— (2001) *A Beckett Canon* (Ann Arbor: The University of Michigan Press).

Cone, Edward T. (1968) *Musical Form and Musical Performance* (New York: W. W. Norton & Co., Inc.).

Connor, Steven (2006) *Samuel Beckett: Repetition, Theory and Text* (Aurora, CO: The Davies Group Publishers).

Conrad, Klaus (1959) "Gestaltanalyse und Daseinsanalytik", *Nervenarzt*, Vol. 30, 405–410.

Cortázar, Julio (1987 [1966]) *Hopscotch*, Gregory Rabassa trans. (New York: Pantheon-Random House).

Dante, Alighieri (2008) *The Divine Comedy*, C. H. Sisson trans. (Oxford: Oxford University Press).

Davenport, Guy (1984) "The Symbol of the Archaic", in *The Geography of the Imagination* (London: Picador), 16–28.

Davies, Stephen (1999) "Rock versus Classical Music", *Journal of Aesthetics and Art Criticism*, Vol. 57, No. 2, 193–204.

Dayan, Peter (2006) *Music Writing Literature: From Sand via Debussy to Derrida* (Aldershot: Ashgate).

—— (2002) "On the Meaning of 'Musical' in Proust", in *Word and Music Studies, Essays in Honor of Steven Paul Scher on Cultural Identity and the Musical Stage*, S. M. Lodato, S. Aspden and W. Bernhart eds (Amsterdam and New York: Rodopi), 143–158.

Deleuze, Gilles (1994 [1968]) *Difference and Repetition* (New York: Columbia University Press).

DeLio, Thomas ed. (1996) *The Music of Morton Feldman* (Westport, CT and London: Greenwood Press).

Derrida, Jacques (1973) *Speech and Phenomena*, David B. Allison trans. (Evanston, IL: Northwestern University Press).

—— (1974) *Of Grammatology*, Gayatri Spivak trans. (Baltimore: The Johns Hopkins University Press).

—— (1978) *Writing and Difference*, Alan Bass trans. (Chicago: University of Chicago).

—— (1994) *Spectres of Marx* (1993) (New York: Routledge).

Donoghue, Denis (1986) *We Irish: Essays on Irish Literature and Society* (Berkeley: University of California Press).

Drew, Elizabeth and Mads Haahr (2002) "*Lessness*: Randomness, Consciousness and Meaning", at www.random.org/lessness/paper/ [accessed 7 August 2017].

Eco, Umberto (1989) "The Poetics of the Open Work", in *The Open Work*, Anna Cancogni trans. (Cambridge, MA: Harvard University Press), 1–23.

Eisenstein, Sergei (1977 [1949]) *Film Form: Essays in Film Form*, Jay Leyda ed. and trans. (New York: Harcourt Brace & Company).

Eliot, T. S. (2005 [1919]) "Tradition and the Individual Talent", in *Modernism: An Anthology*, Lawrence Rainey ed. (Oxford: Blackwell), 152–155.

Ellmann, Richard (1982 [1959]) *James Joyce* (Oxford: Oxford University Press).

Esslin, Martin (2004 [1962]) *The Theatre of the Absurd* (London: Eyre & Spottiswoode).

Feldman, Morton (1950) *Projection 1* (New York: C. F. Peters Corporation).

160   *Bibliography*

——— (1966) "Interview with Alan Beckett", in *International Times* (later renamed *IT*), No. 3 (14–27 November), at www.cnvill.net/mfbeckett.htm [accessed 13 September 2013].

——— (1970) *The Viola in My Life (3)* (Vienna, London, New York: Universal Edition).

———(2000a [1967]) "After Modernism", in *Give My Regards to Eight Street: Collected Writings of Morton Feldman*, B. H. Friedman ed. (Cambridge: Exact Change).

——— (2000b [1971–72]) "The Viola in My Life", in *Give My Regards to Eight Street: Collected Writings of Morton Feldman*, B. H. Friedman ed. (Cambridge: Exact Change).

———(2000c [1981]) "Crippled Symmetry", in *Give My Regards to Eight Street: Collected Writings of Morton Feldman*, B. H. Friedman ed. (Cambridge: Exact Change).

——— (1977) *Neither* (Vienna, London, New York: Universal Edition).

——— (1983) *String Quartet No. 2* (Vienna, London, New York: Universal Edition).

——— (1985) "Darmstadt Lecture", in *Essays*, Walter Zimmerman ed. (Kerpen: Beginner Press).

——— (1987) *Words and Music* (Vienna, London, New York: Universal Edition).

——— (2000) *Give My Regards to Eight Street: Collected Writings of Morton Feldman*, B. H. Friedman ed. (Cambridge: Exact Change).

Ferguson, Margaret W., Mary Jo Salter and Jon Stallworthy eds (1996) *The Norton Anthology of* Poetry (New York: W. W. Norton & Company Incorporated).

Fiennes, S., J. Wilson, M. Rosenbaum, K. Holly and S. Žižek (2012) *The Pervert's Guide to Ideology* (film).

Fink, Robert (2005) *Repeating Ourselves: American Minimal Music as Cultural Practice* (Berkeley: University of California Press).

Fletcher, John (1964) *The Novels of Samuel Beckett* (London: Chatto & Windus).

Foster, R. F. (2000) *The Oxford Illustrated History of Ireland* (Oxford: Oxford University Press).

Freud, Sigmund (1961) *Beyond the Pleasure Principle*, James Strachey trans. (New York: Norton).

Freud, S., Mclintock, D. and Haughton, H. (2003 [1919]) *The Uncanny* (New York: Penguin Books).

Friedman, Alan Warren ed. (2000 [1934]) *Beckett in Black and Red: The Translations for Nancy Cunard's Negro* (Lexington: The University Press of Kentucky).

Frith, Fred (2006) interviewed by Pedro Rebelo at the Sonic Arts Research Centre (SARC), Queen's University Belfast, 24 May, at www.youtube.com/watch?v=gnyunVs-aaU&feature=relmfu [accessed 14 August 2013].

Frost, Everett (1998) "The Note Man on the Word Man: Morton Feldman on Composing the Music for Samuel Beckett's *Words and Music* in *The Beckett Festival of* Radio *Plays*", in *Samuel Beckett and Music*, Mary Bryden ed. (Oxford: Clarendon), 47–57.

Frye, Northrop (1941–42) "Music in Poetry", in *University of Toronto Quarterly*, 11, 178.

Gendron, Sarah (2008) *Studies in Literary Criticism and Theory, Volume 19: Repetition, Difference, and Knowledge in the Work of Samuel Beckett, Jacques Derrida, and Gilles Deleuze* (New York: Peter Lang).

Genette, Gérard (1979) *Narrative Discourse, An Essay in Method*, Jane. E. Lewin trans. (Ithaca, NY: Cornell University Press).

Gladwell, Malcolm (2008) *Outliers: The Story of Success* (New York: Little, Brown & Co.).

Bibliography 161

Golan, Zev (2007) *God, Men and Nietzsche* (New York, Lincoln, Shanghai: iUniverse, Inc.).

Gorbman, Claudia (1987) *Unheard Melodies: Narrative Film Music* (London, IN: Indiana University Press/BFI).

Gracyk, T. A. (1993) "Romanticizing Rock Music", in *Journal of Aesthetic Education*, Vol. 27, 43–58.

Graham, Daniel W. (n.d.) "Heraclitus", in *The Stanford Encyclopaedia of Philosophy*, at http://plato.stanford.edu/archives/sum2011/entries/heraclitus [accessed 15 August 2013].

Greenaway, Peter (1983) *Four American Composers*, at www.ubu.com/film/greenaway.html [accessed 14 August 2013].

Greenberg, Clement (1940) "Towards a Newer Laocoon", *Partisan Review*, Vol. 7, No. 4, July–August, 296–310.

Gummere, Francis B. trans. (2008 [1910]) *Beowulf* (Rockville, MA: Wildside Press LLC).

Gussow, Mel (1981) "Beckett at 75 – An Appraisal", *New York Times*, 19 April, at www.nytimes.com/1981/04/19/theater/beckett-at-75-an-appraisal.html?pagewanted=all [accessed 6 August 2017].

Hanninen, Dora A. (2012) *A Theory of Music Analysis: On Segmentation and Associative Organization* (Rochester, NY: University of Rochester Press).

Harmon, Maurice ed. (2000) *No Author Better Served: The Correspondence of Samuel Beckett and Alan Schneider* (Cambridge, MA: Harvard University Press).

Harper, Adam (2011) *Infinite Music: Imagining the Next Millennium of Human Music Making* (Winchester, UK and Washington, USA: Zero Books).

Hasty, Christopher F. (1997) *Meter as Rhythm* (Oxford and New York: Oxford University Press).

Heaney, Seamus (1992) *The Makings of a Music: Reflections on the Poetry of Wordsworth and Yeats* (Liverpool: Liverpool Class Monthly).

Hegarty, Paul (2009) *Noise/Music: A History* (New York: Continuum).

Heidegger, Martin ([1996] 1953) *Being and Time: A Translation of Sein und Zeit*, Joan Stambaugh trans. (Albany: New York Press).

Hesmondhalgh, David (2006) "Digital Sampling and Cultural Inequality", *Social Legal Studies*, Vol. 15, No. 1, March, 53–75.

Higgins, Dick (1998) *Horizons: The Poetics and Theory of the Intermedia* (New York: Roof Books).

Hirata, Catherine Costello (2006) "How to Make a Difference", *Contemporary Music Review*, Vol. 25, No. 3, June, 211–226.

Hulse, Brian, (n.d.) "A Deleuzian Take on Repetition, Difference, and the 'Minimal' in Minimalism", available at www.operascore.com/files/Repetition_and_Minimalism.pdf [accessed 14 August 2013].

Huxley, Aldous (1978 [1928]) *Point Counter Point* (London: Granada).

Jakob-Hoff, Tristan (2008) "The Minotaur is Pretty but Incomprehensible", in *The Guardian* 21 April, at www.guardian.co.uk/music/musicblog/2008/apr/21/minotaurisprettybutincompr [accessed 27 September 2008].

Johnson, B. S. (1999 [1969]) *The Unfortunates* (London: Macmillan).

Joyce, James (1975 [1939]) *Finnegans Wake* (London: Faber).

——— (1996 [1914]) "The Dead", in *Dubliners*, (London: Penguin Classics).

——— (2000 [1922]) *Ulysses* (London: Penguin).

Kant, Immanuel (1998 [1781]) *Critique of Pure Reason* (Cambridge: Cambridge University Press).

162   *Bibliography*

Kassabian, Anahid (2001) *Hearing Film: Tracking Identifications in Contemporary Hollywood Film Music* (London: Routledge).

———— (2013) *Ubiquitous Listening: Affect, Attention, and Distributed Subjectivity* (Berkeley and Los Angeles: University of California Press).

Katz, Ruth (1992) *Contemplating Music: Essence*, Carl Dahlhaus ed. (London: Pendragon).

Keats, John (1817), letter of 22 December, at www.oxfordreference.com/view/10.1093/oi/authority.20110803100227203 [accessed 14 August 2013].

Kierkegaard, Søren (2009 [1843]) *Repetition and Philosophical Crumbs*, M. G. Piety trans. (Oxford: Oxford University Press).

Killeen, Terence (2004) *Ulysses Unbound* (Dublin: Worwell Ltd. in association with the National Library of Ireland).

Kim-Cohen, Seth (2011) "I Have Something to Say, But I'm Not Saying It", in *Tact 1*, Fall.

Kivy, Peter (1993) "The Fine Art of Repetition", in *The Fine Art of Repetition: Essays in the Philosophy of Music* (Cambridge: Cambridge University Press).

———— (2004) "Continuous Time and Interrupted Time: Two-Timing in the Temporal Arts", in *Musicae Scientiae*, Discussion Forum 3.

Knowlson, James (1996) *Damned to Fame: The Life of Samuel Beckett* (London: Bloomsbury).

Knowlson, James and John Pilling (1979), *Frescoes of the Skull: The Later Prose and Drama of Samuel Beckett* (London: John Calder,).

Kounios, John, Sonja A. Kotz and Phillip J. Holcomb (2000) "On the Locus of the Semantic Satiation Effect: Evidence from Event-related Brain Potentials", in *Memory & Cognition*, Vol. 28, No. 8, 1366–1377.

Kramer, Jonathan (1988) *The Time of Music: New Meanings, New Temporalities, New Listening Strategies* (New York: Schirmer Books).

Kramer, Lawrence (1984) *Music and Poetry: The Nineteenth Century and After* (Berkeley, Los Angeles, London: University of California Press).

Latartara, John (2011) "Laptop Composition at the Turn of the Millennium: Repetition and Noise in the Music of Oval, Merzbow, and Kid606", *Twentieth-Century Music*, Vol. 7, No. 1, 91–115.

Lauffer, David and Geneviève Mathon eds (2014) *Beckett et la musique* (Strasbourg: Presses universitaires de Strasbourg).

Laurence, Dan H. ed. (1960) *Bernard Shaw: How to Become a Music Critic* (London: Rupert Hart-Davis).

———— ed. (1981) *Shaw's Music: The Complete Criticism in Three Volumes* (London: Bodley Head).

Lawley, Paul (1984) "Beckett's Dramatic Counterpoint: A Reading of *Play*", *Journal of Beckett Studies IX*, 25–42.

Laws, Catherine (1996) *Music and Language in the Work of Samuel Beckett*. (D. Phil, University of York).

———— (1998) "Morton Feldman's *Neither*: A Musical Translation", in *Samuel Beckett and Music*, Mary Bryden ed. (Oxford: Clarendon Press), 57–87.

———— (2006) "Beckett and Contemporary Music", The Contemporary Music Centre Ireland, 9 April, at www.cmc.ie/articles/article1457.html [accessed 9 September 2013].

———— (2013) *Headaches Among the Overtones: Music in Beckett/Beckett in Music* (Amsterdam and New York: Rodopi).

Bibliography 163

Lessing, Gotthold (1984) *Laocoön: An Essay on the Limits of Painting and Poetry*, Edward Allen McCormick trans. (Baltimore, MA: Johns Hopkins University Press).

Libera, Antoni (1980) "Structure and Pattern in 'That Time'", *Journal of Beckett Studies*, No. 6, Autumn, 81–89.

―――― (1988) "Reading *That Time*" in *"Make Sense Who May": Essays on Samuel Beckett's Later Works*, R. J. Davis and L. St J. Butler eds (Gerrards Cross: Colin Smythe), 91–2.

Limb, Charles (2010) "Your Brain on Improv" TED talk, available at www.ted.com/talks/charles_limb_your_brain_on_improv.html [accessed 13 August 2013].

Lodato, Suzanne M. and David Francis Urrows eds (2005) *Essays on Music and the Spoken Word and on Surveying the Field* (Amsterdam and New York: Rodopi).

Lodge, David (1968) "Some Ping Understood", in *Encounter*, February, 85–89.

Lyotard, Jean-François (1997) "Music, Mutic", in *Postmodern Fables*, Georges Van Den Abbeele trans. (Minneapolis: University of Minnesota Press).

McClary, Susan (2004 [1998]) "Rap, Minimalism, and Structures of Time in Late Twentieth-Century Culture", in *Audio Culture: Readings in Modern Music*, Christoph Cox and Daniel Warner eds (New York and London: Continuum), 289–298.

McGrath, John (2012) "Musical Repetition in Samuel Beckett's *Ill Seen Ill Said*", in *Time and Space in Words and Music*, Mario Dunkel, Emily Petermann and Burkhard Sauerwald eds (Frankfurt am Main: Peter Lang, 31–42.

McLuhan, Marshall (1964) "The Medium Is the Message", in *Understanding Media: The Extensions of Man* (New York: Signet Books), 23–35.

Magee, Bryan (2000) *Wagner and Philosophy* (London: Allen Lane).

Maier, Franz Michael (2006) *Becketts Melodien: Die Musik und die Idee des Zusammenhangs bei Schopenhauer, Proust und Beckett* (Würzburg: Königshausen & Neumann).

―――― (2008) "The Idea of Melodic Connection in Samuel Beckett", *Journal of the American Musicological Society*, Vol. 61, No. 2 (Summer), 373–410.

Mallarmé, Stéphane (1897) *Un coup de dés jamais n'abolira le hazard* (Paris: Armand Colin).

Margulis, Elizabeth Hellmuth (2013) *On Repeat: How Music Plays the Mind* (New York: Oxford University Press).

Martin, Timothy (1991) *Joyce and Wagner* (Cambridge: Cambridge University Press).

Marx, Groucho (1959) *Groucho and Me* (New York: Bernard Geis).

Meisel, Martin (1963) *Shaw and the Nineteenth-Century Theater* (Princeton: Princeton University Press).

Mercier, Vivian, (1956) quoted in *The Irish Times*, 18 February, 6.

―――― (1977) *Beckett/Beckett* (New York: Oxford University Press).

Metzer, David (2006) "Modern Silence", *Journal of Musicology*, Vol. 23, 331–74.

Metzidakis, Stamos (1986) *Repetition and Semiotics: Interpreting Prose Poems* (Birmingham, AL: Summa Publications).

Meyer, Leonard B. (1994 [1967]) *Music, the Arts, and Ideas: Patterns and Predictions in Twentieth-Century Culture* (Chicago and London: University of Chicago Press).

Middleton, Richard (1983) "'Play It Again Sam': Some Notes on the Productivity of Repetition in Popular Music", in *Popular Music, Vol. 3, Producers and Markets* (Cambridge: Cambridge University Press).

―――― (1990) *Studying Popular Music* (Milton Keynes: Open University Press).

164 *Bibliography*

——— (1996) "Over and Over: Notes Towards A Politics of Repetition", at http://www2.hu-berlin.de/fpm/textpool/texte/middleton_notes-towards-a-politics-of-repetition.htm [accessed 14 August 2013].

Mithen, Steven (2006) *The Singing Neanderthals: The Origins of Music, Language, Mind and Body* (London: Phoenix).

Monk, Meredith (2013) "Life in Reverse", interview in *The Wire Magazine*, August, 40–47.

Montgomery, Scott L. (2010) *The Powers That Be: Global Energy for the Twenty-first Century and Beyond* (Chicago: University of Chicago Press).

Morash, Christopher (2002) *A History of Irish Theatre 1600–2000* (Cambridge: Cambridge University Press).

Morin, Emilie (2011) "Look Again: Indeterminacy and Contemporary British Drama", *NTQ*, Vol. 27, No. 1, February, 71–86.

Nattiez, Jean-Jacques (1989) *Proust as Musician* (Cambridge: Cambridge University Press).

Newark, Cormac (2011) *Opera in the Novel from Balzac to Proust* (Cambridge: Cambridge University Press).

Negus, Keith (1992) *Producing Pop: Culture and Conflict in the Popular Music Industry* (London, New York, Melbourne: Edward Arnold).

Nietzsche, Friedrich (1974 [1882]) *The Gay Science: With a Prelude in Rhymes and an Appendix of Songs*, Walter Kaufmann trans. (New York: Random House).

——— (2007 [1891]) *Thus Spake Zarathustra*, Thomas Common trans. (Stilwell: Digireads.com Publishing).

Nyman, Michael (1999 [1974]) *Experimental Music: Cage and Beyond* (Cambridge: Cambridge University Press).

Ockelford, Adam (2005) *Repetition in Music: Theoretical and Metatheoretical Perspectives* (Aldershot: Ashgate).

O'Hara, J. D. (1988) "Beckett's Schopenhauerian Reading of Proust: The Will as Whirled in Representation", in *Schopenhauer: New Essays in Honor of his 200th Birthday*, Eric von der Luft ed. (Lampeter: Edwin Mellen Press), 273–92.

Oppenheim, Lois ed. (1999) *Samuel Beckett and the Arts* (New York and London: Garland Publishing Inc.).

——— (2000) *The Painted Word: Samuel Beckett's Dialogue with Art* (Ann Arbor, MI: University of Michigan Press).

Overbeck, Lois (2011) "Audience of Self/Audience of Reader", *Modernism/Modernity*, Vol. 18, No. 4, November, 721–737.

Ozment, Kurt (2011) "Musical, Rhetorical, and Visual Material in the Work of Feldman", *CLCWeb Comparative Literature and Culture*, Vol. 13, No. 3, Article 17.

Paddison, Max (2004) "Aspects of Time in the Creation of Music II: Responses and New Departures", in *Musicae Scientiae* Discussion Forum 3, 111–124.

Parr, Adrian ed. (2005) *The Deleuze Dictionary* (Edinburgh: Edinburgh University Press).

Pater, Walter (1980 [1873]) "School of Giorgione", in *The Renaissance: Studies in Art and Poetry* (Berkeley and Los Angeles: University of California Press), 102–122.

Paton, Steven (2009) "Time-Lessness, Simultaneity and Successivity: Repetition in Beckett's Short Prose", *Language and Literature*, Vol. 18, No. 4, 357–366.

Perloff, Marjorie, (1981) *The Poetics of Indeterminacy* (Princeton: Princeton University Press).

Bibliography   165

——— (2003) "The Beckett/Feldman Radio Collaboration: Words and Music as Hörspiel", at http://marjorieperloff.com/stein-duchamp-picasso/beckett-feldman/ [accessed 13 August 2013].

Philips, Tom (2016) *A Humanent: A Treated Victorian Novel*, a reworking of W. H. Mallock's *The Human Document* (1892), Sixth and Final Edition (London: Thames & Hudson).

Pilling, John (1998) "Proust and Schopenhauer: Music and Shadows", in *Samuel Beckett and Music*, Mary Bryden ed. (Oxford: Clarendon Press), 173–181.

Plato (1968 [*c*.380 BC]) *The Rebublic*, Benjamin Jowett trans. (New York: Airmont Publishing Company).

Poe, Edgar Allan (1846) "The Philosophy of Composition", in *Graham's American Monthly Magazine of Literature and Art*, George R. Graham ed., Volume XXVIII (Philadelphia: George R. Graham & Co.), 116–118 and 163–167.

Polanyi, Michael (2009 [1967]), *The Tacit Dimension* (Chicago: University of Chicago Press).

Pope, Alexander (2004 [1743]) "The Dunciad", Book 1, in *Eighteenth-Century Poetry: An Annotated Anthology*, 2nd edn, David Fairer and Christine Gerrard eds (Oxford: Blackwell), 167–177.

Porter, Jeff (2010) "Samuel Beckett and the Radiophonic Body: Beckett and the BBC", *Modern Drama*, Vol. 53, No. 4, Winter, 431–446.

Potter, Keith (2002) *Four Musical Minimalists: La Monte Young, Terry Riley, Steve Reich, Philip Glass* (Cambridge: Cambridge University Press).

Prieto, Eric (2002a) *Listening In: Music, Mind, and the Modernist Narrative* (Lincoln, NE and London: University of Nebraska Press).

——— (2002b) "Metaphor and Methodology in Word and Music Studies", in *Essays in Honor of Steven Paul Scher*, Suzanne M. Lodato, Suzanne Aspden and Walter Bernhart eds (Amsterdam and Atlanta: Rodopi).

Proust, Marcel (2001 [1913]) *In Search of Lost Time*, Vol. 1, C. K. Scott Moncrieff and Terence Kilmartin trans. (London: Everyman).

Rabinowitz, Peter J. (1992) "Chord and Discourse: Listening Through the Written Word", in *Music and Text: Critical Enquires*, Steven Paul Scher ed. (Cambridge: Cambridge University Press), 38–56.

Rajewsky, Irina O. (2005) "Intermediality, Intertextuality, and Remediation: A Literary Perspective on Intermediality", *Intermédialités*, No. 6, Autumn, 43–65.

Reich, Steve (2002 [1968]) "Music as a Gradual Process", in *Writings on Music, 1965–2000*, Paul Hillier ed. (Oxford: Oxford University Press).

Reid, Alec (1968) *All I Can Manage, More Than I Could: An Approach to the Plays of Samuel Beckett* (Dublin: Dolmen Press).

Reynolds, Simon (2011) *Retromania: Pop Culture's Addiction to Its Own Past* (London: Faber and Faber).

Rose, Tricia (1994) *Black Noise: Rap Music and Black Culture in Contemporary America* (Hanover, NH: Wesleyan University Press).

Ross, Alex (2006) "American Sublime" in *The New Yorker*, 19 June, at www.newyorker.com/archive/2006/06/19/060619crat_atlarge [accessed 14 September 2013].

Russolo, Luigi (2001 [1913]) "The Art of Noises", in *Manifesto: A Century of Isms*, Mary Ann Caws ed. (Lincoln, NE: University of Nebraska Press), 205–211.

Saportha, Marc (2011 [1962]) *Composition No. 1* (London: Visual Editions).

Scher, Steven Paul (1972) "How Meaningful is 'Musical' in Literary Criticism?", *Yearbook of Comparative and General Literature*, Vol. 21, 52–56.

166 Bibliography

——— (1992) *Music and Text: Critical Enquires* (Cambridge: Cambridge University Press).

——— (1999) "Melopoetics Revisited: Reflections on Theorizing Word and Music Studies" in Walter Bernhart, Steven Paul Scher and Werner Wolf eds, *Word and Music Studies: Defining the Field* (Amsterdam and Atlanta: Rodopi).

——— (2004) *Essays on Literature and Music (1967–2004)*, Walter Bernhart and Werner Wolf eds (Amsterdam and New York: Rodopi).

Schopenhauer, Arthur (1969 [1818]) *The World as Will and Representation*, E. F. L. Payne trans., 2 vols (New York: Dover).

Segrè, Elisabeth Bregman (1977) "Style and Structure in Beckett's 'Ping': *That Something Itself*", *Journal of Modern Literature*, Vol. 6, No. 1, 127–47.

Sharp, Elliott (1997) interviewed by Joe Gore, "Where Order Meets Chaos", in *Guitar Player*, Vol. 3, No. 1, January, 10–11.

Sinclair, Ian (2015) *London Overground: A Day's Walk Around the Ginger Line* (London: Hamish Hamilton).

Skempton, Howard (1977) "Beckett as Librettist", in *Music and Musicians*, May, 5–6.

Small, Christopher (1987) *Music of the Common Tongue: Survival and Celebration in Afro-American Music* (London: John Calder).

Smith, L. C. and Klein, R. (1990) "Evidence for Semantic Satiation: Repeating a Category Slows Subsequent Semantic Processing", in *Journal of Experimental Psychology: Learning, Memory, & Cognition*, Vol. 16, 852–861.

Snead, James A. (1981) "On Repetition in Black Culture", in *Black American Literature Forum*, Vol. 15, No. 4, 146–154.

Sontag, Susan (1994 [1967]) "The Aesthetics of Silence", in *Styles of Radical Will* (London: Vintage), 3–34.

Spielmann, Yvonne (2001) "Intermedia in Electronic Images" in *Leonardo*, Vol. 34, No. 1 (February), 55-61.

——— (2008) *Video: The Reflexive Medium* (Cambridge, MA and London: The MIT Press).

Spitzer, Michael (2003) *Metaphor and Musical Thought* (Chicago: Chicago University Press).

Steiner, George (1985 [1961]) "The Retreat from the Word", in *Language and Silence: Essays 1958–1966* (London: Faber), 30–54.

Sudo, Phillip Toshio (1998 [1997]) *Zen Guitar* (London: Simon & Schuster).

Tagg, Philip (2012) *Music's Meanings: A Modern Musicology for Non-Musos* (New York and Huddersfield: Mass Media Music Scholar's Press).

Till, Nicholas and Sara-Jane Bailes eds (2014) *Beckett and Musicality* (Aldershot: Ashgate).

Toynbee, Jason (2000) *Making Popular Music: Musician, Aesthetics and the Manufacture of Popular Music* (London: Bloomsbury Academic).

Tubridy, Durval (2012) "Beckett, Feldman, Salcedo ... *Neither*", in *Beckett and Nothing*, Daniela Caselli ed. (Manchester: Manchester University Press), 143–159.

Warburton, Dan (n.d.) "A Working Terminology for Minimal Music", at www.paristransatlantic.com/magazine/archives/minimalism.html [accessed 14 August 2013].

Weagel, Deborah Fillerup (2010) *Words and Music: Camus, Beckett, Cage, Gould, American University Studies*, Vol. 38 (New York and Bern: Peter Lang).

Welsh, John P. (1996) "Projection 1 (1950)", in *The Music of Morton Feldman*, Thomas DeLio ed. (Westport, CT and London: Greenwood Press), 21–39.

White, Harry (1998) "'Something Is Taking Its Course': Dramatic Exactitude and the Paradigm of Serialism in Samuel Beckett", in *Samuel Beckett and Music*, Mary Bryden ed. (Oxford: Clarendon Press), 159–173.

———— (2008) *Music and the Irish Literary Imagination* (Oxford: Oxford University Press).

Wilde, Oscar (1997a [1891]) "The Critic as Artist", in *The Collected Works of Oscar Wilde* (London: Wordsworth), 965–1016.

———— (1997b [1891]) "The Decay of Lying", in *The Collected Works of Oscar Wilde* (London: Wordsworth), 919–945.

———— (1997c [1891]) *Dorian Gray*, in *The Collected Works of Oscar Wilde* (London: Wordsworth), 1–154.

Wimsatt, W. K. Jr., and Monroe C. Beardsley (1954) "The Intentional Fallacy", in *The Verbal Icon: Studies in the Meaning of Poetry* (Lexington: University of Kentucky Press).

Wittgenstein, Ludwig, (1971) *Tractatus Logico-Philosophicus* (Ithaca, NY: Cornell University Press).

———— (2009 [1953]) *Philosophical Investigations*, G. E. M. Anscombe, P. M. S. Hacker and Joachim Schulte trans. (Chichester: Wiley Blackwell).

Wolf, Werner (1999) *The Muzicalization of Fiction: A Study in the Theory and History of Intermediality* (Amsterdam and Atlanta: Rodopi).

———— (2005) "Language and/or Music as Man's 'Comfort'? Beckett's Metamedial Allegory *Words and Music*", in *Essays on Music and the Spoken Word and on Surveying the Field*, Suzanne M. Lodato and David Francis Urrows eds (Amsterdam and New York: Rodopi).

———— ed. (2009) *Metareference across Media: Theory and Case Studies*, with Katharina Bantleon and Jeff Collabs Thoss (Amsterdam and New York: Rodopi).

Wordsworth, William (1971 [1800]) "Preface to Lyrical Ballads", in *Critical Theory Since Plato*, Hazard Adams ed. (New York: Harcourt Brace Jovanovich), 437–446.

Worth, Katharine (1998) "Words for Music Perhaps", in *Samuel Beckett and Music*, Mary Bryden ed. (Oxford: Clarendon), 9–21.

Yeats, W. B. (1990) *Collected Poems* (London: Picador and Macmillan).

———— (2008) *The Collected Works of W. B. Yeats, Volume XIII: A Vision* (1925), Catherine E. Paul and Margaret Mills Harper eds (New York: Scribner).

Zukofsky, Louis (1978) "*A*" (Baltimore: Johns Hopkins University Press).

Zurbrugg, Nicholas (1987) "*Ill Seen Ill Said* and the Sense of an Ending", in *Beckett's Later Fiction and Drama: Texts for Company*, James Acheson and Kateryna Arthur eds (London: Macmillan), 145–159.

Websites

http://rhetoric.byu.edu/Figures/Groupings/of%20Repetition.htm [accessed 14 August 2013].

www.random.org/lessness [accessed 14 August 2013].

168 *Bibliography*

Discography

Beckett, Samuel, and Morton Feldman, *Words and Music*, with Omar Ebrahim and Stephen Lind (voices) and Ensemble Recherche, CD (Westdeutscher Rundfunk/Audvidas, 1996).

Feldman, Morton, *For Samuel Beckett* (1987), Ensemble Modern, Conducted by Arturo Tamayo, CD (Basel, Switzerland: Hat Hut, 2006).

———, *The 1986 Darmstadt Lecture*, and *Neither*, Günter Woog, camera and director, DVD (Vienna: Universal Edition, 2001).

———, *Neither*, Radio Sinfonie Orchester Frankfurt, conducted by Zoltan Pesko, Sarah Leonard soprano, CD (Basel, Switzerland: Hat Hut, 2011).

Fields, Scott and the Scott Fields Ensemble, *Beckett*, CD (Lisbon: Clean Feed, 2007).

———, *Samuel*, CD (New York: New World Records, 2009).

Index

Page numbers in *italic* refer to figures in the text.

Abbate, Carolyn 48–9, 72
Abbott, Helen 22, 47
"abrash" 93, 94
abstraction 23, 138, 149
absurdity 72, 84n4
Adams, John 95
Adorno, Theodor 18–19, 23, 36, 70, 71, 90, 128
African American/black music 36, 40, 51n7
Agamben, Giorgio 129
Albright, Daniel 6, 7, 19, 22, 55, 72, 84
aleatoric methods 4–5, 130–1, 153; Beckett 84, 98, 125, 126, 127, 128, 145
alliteration 2, 46
AMM group 132
anadiplosis, rhetorical device 77, 79, 102, 105
analogy, musical 24, 29, 31
anaphora 2, 47, 48, 81, 133, 150
animation films 18
apophenia 43
Aristotle 30, 35, 152, 154
art, avant-garde 9, 12
art, modern 88, 151–2
art, Renaissance 9
Art Ensemble of Chicago 131
art installations 33, 34
art music 15, 16–17, 33, 37, 41, 132; Ireland 53, 54
arts, visual 7–8, 19, 151
Association for the Advancement of Creative Musicians (AACM) 131, 132
Attali, Jacques 35
"attributive screens" 26, 27, 28, 71
Auerbach, Erich 152

Austen, Jane 13
authenticity 35, 44; *see also* originality
authorship 42, 153
avant-garde movement 9; Beckett 12, 54, 149; Feldman 88, 95

Babbitt, Irving 8, 32n3
Bach, J. S. 16–17, 118, 154
Bailey, Derek 43, 131
Baricelli, J. P. 30, 149
Baroque music 17
Barrett, Richard 86, 150
Barrett, William 96
Barry, Gerald 86–7
Barthes, Roland 20, 28, 37, 48, 58, 130
Bartok, Béla 37
Batman 12
Baudelaire, Charles 25, 143
BBC Third Programme 117
Beats group 2
Beckett, Gerald 55
Beckett, John 55, 87, 117
Beckett, Samuel, background 55–6
Beckett, Samuel, collaborations 86–8; and Feldman 4, 5n2, 86–123, 89, 90, 97–9; and Fields, Scott 5, 122, 132, 135, 137–42, 151; *Words and Music* 22, 56, 87, 88, 96, 117–23; *see also* *Neither* (Beckett and Feldman); *Not I* (Beckett)
Beckett, Samuel, influences 2, 59, 101; influence on music and composers 86, 132, 148, 150, 151; Irish literature and music 3, 4; *see also* Joyce, James, influence on Beckett; Schopenhauerian philosophy

170   *Index*

Beckett, Samuel, music and musicalisation 2, 6, 42, 53–65, 99, 151–2; Adorno on 70, 71; aleatoric methods 84, 98, 125, 126, 127, 128, 145; avant-garde movement 12, 54, 149; and Cage 5, 84, 86, 129–30; indeterminacy 86, 124, 125, 126–7, 130, 138; innovation 83, 117, 148; jazz 4–5, 122, 124, 132, 146; Modernism 60, 72, 149, 150; Romanticism 3, 68, 118, 148, 149, 150; *see also* improvisation

Beckett, Samuel, themes *see* silence; stasis; time; waiting

Beckett, Samuel, works: *...dead calm...* 150; *All That Fall* 9, 85n11, 87; "Best Negro Jazz Orchestra" 132; *Breath* 132; *Cascando* 87, 88; *Come and Go* 132; *Company* 77; *Dream of Fair to Middling Women* 58, 59; *Eh Joe* 132, 142; *Endgame* 96; *Film* 100; *Footfalls* 100; *Four Quartets* 149; *Ghost Trio* 56, 87, 132; *Happy Days* 96; *Krapp's Last Tape* 83, 87; *Molloy* 81, 83, 96, 124, 125, 149; *More Pricks and Kicks* 58; *Murphy* 4, 51, 58, 59–65, 83, 127; *Nacht und Träume* 56, 87; *Nohow On* 77; *Now and Then* 150; *Ping/Bing* 125; *Play* 57, 96, 125, 132, 149, 150; *Proust* 5n2, 14, 57, 69, 96, 99, 118; *Rockaby* 62–3, 132; *Stirrings Still* 150; *Texts for Nothing* 128; *That Time* 15, 74, 151; *Three Dialogues* 127; *Trilogy* 4, 59, 96; *Unnamable* 83, 86, 96, 129; "Walking Out" 58; *Watt* 15, 58–9, 86; "What Is the Word" 150; *What Where* 132, 150; "Whoroscope" notebook 58; *see also Ill Seen Ill Said* (Beckett); *Lessness* (Beckett); *Neither* (Beckett and Feldman); *Not I* (Beckett); *Waiting for Godot* (Beckett); *Worstward Ho* (Beckett)

Beckett, Samuel, writing methods and language: French language 12–13, 98, 126, 130; originality 61, 96–7, 152–3; pattern in literature 56, 59, 81, 101, 126–7, 142; *see also* binaries; human condition; *Lessness* (Beckett); Schopenhauerian philosophy; semantic fluidity

Beckett on Film production 137

Beethoven, Ludwig van: Piano Sonata in F minor 26; Piano Trio No. 1 56, 87;

Symphony No. 5 37; Symphony No. 7 37, 70, 128

Begbie, Jeremy 38–9, 50

Benjamin, Walter 96, 152

Benson, Stephen 22, 118, 130

Beowulf 10, 46

Bergson, Henri 50, 90

Berio, Luciano 86

Berkeley, George 35

Berlioz, Hector 18

Bernhart, Walter 22

Best, David 39

binaries 11–12, 57, 64, 130, 140, 149; self/unself binary 100–1, 107; *see also* "intelligible"/"inexplicable" binary

binary oppositional repetition 99, 127, 134–5, 151; *Ill Seen Ill Said* 73, 78, 79, 80; *Lessness* 125, 126, 129; *Neither* 100, 102; *Worstward Ho* 81, 82–3

Birtwistle, Harrison, *The Minotaur* 17

Bloom, Harold 38, 48, 153

Bond, James 12

boredom *see* redundancy, in music

Borges, Jorge Luis 153

"Boundaries" conference (RMA) 22

Bourne, Jason 12

Bowie, David 153, 154

Brahms, Johannes 38

Branca, Glenn 41, 154

Brater, Enoch 125, 126, 133

Braxton, Anthony 131

Breatnach, Mary 22, 47

Brienza, Susan 125, 126

Broch, Hermann, *Death of Virgil* 20

Brown, Calvin S. 21, 22–3, 29, 48–50, 151

Brown, Earle 88

Bruckner, Anton 11

Bryars, Gavin 132

Bryden, Mary 22, 55, 58

Budd, Malcolm 70–1

Buddhism 68, 129

Bukowski, Charles 142, 143

Burroughs, William 2, 153

Cage, John: *4'33"* 88, 128–9; and Beckett 5, 84, 86, 129–30; improvisation 44–5, 132; indeterminacy 86, 88, 130; modern music 41, 43–4, 88, 126, 130, 132, 143; silence 63, 88, 128–9

Calder, John 87

Index 171

Cale, John 41
Can, band 154
canons 37
Carvalho, John M. 146
Cervantes, Miguel de 153
Cézanne, Paul 90, 93
chance procedures *see* aleatoric methods
chansons, sixteenth century 18
characterisation 96, 102, 117, 138
Chatham, Rhys 52n14, 154
chiasmus 64, 134
Chopin, Frédéric 28
chords, inverted 92, 94
Christianity 36
circles 36
Claren, Sebastian 99–110
Cline, Nels 42
clocks 96
Cobain, Kurt 153
Coester, Edouard 87
Coetzee, J. M. 127
Cohn, Ruby 51, 61, 95, 96, 124, 125, 126
Coleman, Ornette 44, 131
collaborations, musical 86–8, 99–110,
    117–18, 122, 123; *see also* Feldman,
    Morton; Fields, Scott; *Neither*
    (Beckett and Feldman); *Words and
    Music* (Beckett and Feldman)
Colleen 42
Coltrane, John 41
commodification 35, 44
compositional process 50, 98–9, 126,
    130–1
computer software 126–7
Cone, Edward T. 24–5, 50
Connor, Stephen 83
Conrad, Tony 41
consciousness 11, 12, 18, 34, 35, 54, 145
contradiction 68, 73, 97, 118; *Lessness*
    126, 129; Schopenhauerian philosophy
    70–1, 149
contrafacta 17
contrapuntal texture 30, 50–1
copies 35, 70, 152–3, 155n3
Cortázar, Julio, *Hopscotch* 50, 153
cuckoos 17
Cunard, Nancy 132
cut-ups 2, 15, 153

da capo form 17, 57, 96, 125, 127, 149, 150
da Sousa Correa, Delia 22
Dadaism 126
Dahlhaus, Carl 38, 50

dance music 41
Dante Alighieri, *Purgatorio* 58
Dark Side of the Rainbow 43
Darmstadt lecture 93
Darwinism 35, 68
Davis, Miles 146
Davis, Thomas 3
Dayan, Peter 14, 22, 24, 28–9, 57
de-essentialization 31
De Quincey, Thomas 27
Debussy, Claude 143
Dedalus, Stephen 12, 13, 45, 53
Deleuzian repetition 3, 34–6, 42, 48, 72,
    92, 150; and difference 34, 36, 38–9,
    45; exact clothed repetition 35, 73–4,
    92–3, 153; Feldman 91, 92–3, 94, 151,
    152; Fields 145, 151, 152; *Neither* 102,
    111; *Words and Music* 117–18, 119
Dembski, Stephen 132
Derrida, Jacques 20, 28, 45, 98, 148
Descartes, René 61
development, and repetition 40–1
difference 10, 33, 34–5, 50; and
    Deleuzian repetition 34, 36, 38–9, 45;
    Feldman 93, 98
discursive repetition 40, 73, 99, 135, 150,
    151; *Ill Seen Ill Said* 74, 78, 80, 81;
    Neither 110, 111, 114
dissonance, cognitive 9, 31, 38, 138
Donizetti, Gaetano 18
Doppelgangers 34
Drew, Elizabeth and Haahr, Mads 126
drumming, African 15, 41
Duchamp, Marcel 152
duckrabbit, Wittgensteinian 39
Dujardin, Édouard 11
dynamics 43, 143–5

echoes 33, 47, 59, 105; *Ill Seen Ill Said*
    72, 74, 77
Edinburgh, University of 22
Egk, Werner 87
Einselreferenz 10
Einstein, Albert 68
Eisenstein, Sergei 9, 31, 38
Eliot, T. S. 20, 26, 30, 38, 54, 154
emotion 14, 41, 69, 70, 71, 118
Enlightenment 1, 6, 7, 10–11
Eno, Brian 45, 154
epistrophe 2, 59, 64, 74, 81, 133, 150
Esslin, Martin 84n4, 150
"eternal return" 34, 36, 152
evolution 35, 43, 68, 152, 155n3

172 *Index*

exact clothed repetition 62, 99, 111, 122, 135, 151; Deleuzian repetition 35, 73–4, 92–3, 153; Feldman 90, 94, 95; *Ill Seen Ill Said* 73–4, *75*, *76*, 79
Existentialism 97
experience 27, 34, 48, 50, 71–2, 89, 90–1
expression 11; in literature 70, 127, 129; in music 41, 53, 118, 145; self-expression 16, 69; *see also* meaning

failure 148, 150, 155n1; "failing better" 42, 45, 81, 84; of language 70, 79, 119
Faust, band 154
Feldman, Morton 86–123; Deleuzian repetition 90, 91, 92–3, 94, 95, 151, 152; difference 93, 98; graphic scores 88–9, 124; human condition 110, 146; improvisation 124, 132; indeterminacy 88, 89, 151; instrumentation 94, 104, 110–11, 114; interpretation 98, 123, 151; listening/hearing 91–2, 93; modern art 88, 95, 151–2; motifs 90, 92; opera 5n2, 88, 99–100; painting 18, 88, 89–90, 97, 110; pattern in music 88, 93–4, 102, 108, 121, 151; *Projection 1* 88–9, 93–4, 112; rhythm 104, 107, 113, 142–3; Romanticism 88, 117; semantic fluidity 86, 92, 99, 151; "shimmering" 93, 95, 96, 105, 108; silence 89, 90; stasis 4, 90, 92, 94, 95, 151; String Quartet No. 2 89–90, 92, 93–4, 123; time 4, 83, 89, 90–2, 95, 151; *see also Neither* (Beckett and Feldman); *Words and Music* (Beckett and Feldman)
Ferguson, Samuel 3
Ferneyhough, Brian 86, 118–19
Festival of Radio Plays 117
Fields, Scott 124; and Beckett 5, 122, 132, 135, 137–42, 151; Deleuzian repetition 145, 151, 152; improvisation 122, 151; interpretation 132, 137, 139; painting 132, 143; pattern in music 140, 142, 151; *see also Not I* (Beckett)
film 9–10, 11, 18, 137, 152; film music 9, 14, 17, 31, 38
Fink, Robert 33, 154
Finnissey, Michael, *Enough* 150
Flaubert, Gustave 77, 124, 150
Fletcher, John 58
folk music, traditional 53, 54
Fortner, Wolfgang 86
Foster, Roy 12
French language 13, 98, 126, 130
Frisell, Bill 42

Frith, Fred 43, 131
Frith, Simon 44
Frost, Everett 98, 100, 110, 117
Frye, Northrop 29
fugues 3, 24, 29, 37, 51, 53, 138

Galilei, Vincenzo 18
gamelan, Balinese 15, 41
Gendron, Sarah 35, 36, 77, 92, 98
Genette, Gérard 50, 92
Geworfenheit (Heidegger) 83
Giacometti, Antonio 86, 151
Ginsberg, Allen, "Howl" 47
Gladwell, Malcolm 154
Glass, Philip 40, 41, 86, 95
glitch music 155n1
Goehr, Lydia 54
Goethe, Johann Wolfgang von 18, 83, 95
Goffin, Robert 132
Gontarski, S. E. 77
Gorbman, Claudia 17
Gormley, Anthony 33, 34
Gould, Glenn 129
Greeks, Ancient 1, 6, 7–8, 10, 36, 152
Greenberg, Clement 8–9, 31
Grove's *Dictionary of Music and Musicians* 53
Guston, Philip 90, 97, 151

Hanninen, Dora A. 143
Hassan, Ihab 129
Heaney, Seamus 16, 46
hearing *see* listening/hearing
Hegarty, Paul 42, 43, 44, 83
Hegel, Georg Wilhelm Friedrich 34
Heisenberg principle 68
Hendrix, Jimi, "Machine Gun" 18
Henebry, Richard 54
Henze, Hans Werner 149
Heraclitus 33
Hess, Hermann, *The Glass Bead Game* 20
Higgins, Dick 9
Hindu philosophy 36
Historically Informed Performance (HIP) 49
Hollinger, Heinze 86
Homer 10
homonyms 73, 77
human condition 83, 84, 99, 126, 130, 148; Feldman 110, 146; *Human Condition* (Magritte) 67
Humanism 18
Husserl, Edmund 34
Huxley, Aldous 2, 11, 26

identity 34, 35

Ill Seen Ill Said (Beckett) 4, 51, 72–81, 133; binary oppositional repetition 73, 78, 79, 80; discursive repetition 74, 78, 80, 81; echoes 72, 74, 77; exact clothed repetition 73–4, *75, 76,* 79; improvisation 77, 81; motifs 72–3, 77, 78; musematic repetition 73–8, 79, 81

images: Beckett's 90, 96, 125, 134; intermediality 18, 19, 31, 39, 47

improvisation 45, 124–46; Beckett 77, 81, 122, 130–2; Cage 44–5, 132; Feldman 91, 124, 132; Fields 5, 122, 132, 151; jazz 5, 131, 142, 145–6; noise music 43, 44; *see also Not I* (Beckett)

indeterminacy 124, 126–33; Beckett 86, 124, 125, 126–7, 130, 138; Cage 86, 88, 130; Feldman 88, 89, 151

innovation 11, 22, 31, 36, 41–2, 124, 154; Beckett 83, 117, 148

Institute of Musical Research (IMR) 22

instrumental music 18, 24, 58, 87, 117, 132, 138

instrumentation 38, 148; Feldman 94, 104, 110–11, 114

"intelligible"/"inexplicable" binary: Beckett 53, 57, 69–70, 83, 85n10; *Murphy* 5, 51; *Not I* 133, 137; Schopenhauerian philosophy 53, 66, 72, 85n10

intention 8, 45, 58, 131

intermediality 6, 7, 8–10, 20, 22, 27, 33–51; intermedial images 18, 19, 31, 39, 47; Lessing 18–19, 20, 24, 91, 119; and poetry 8, 16, 19–20, 24–6, 29; Prieto, Eric 11, 12, 24, 29–32; *see also* Feldman, Morton; Fields, Scott; *Lessness* (Beckett); music and literature; music in literature; *Neither* (Beckett and Feldman); *Not I* (Beckett); painting; *Words and Music* (Beckett and Feldman)

International Association for Word and Music Studies (WMA) 21–2, 29

International Summer Courses for New Music, 33rd 93

interpretation 14, 26, 39, 48, 67, 152; Feldman 98, 123, 151; Fields 132, 137, 139; in literature 17, 18, 39, 110; in music 18, 27, 43, 98, 123, 124; *Not I* 137, 139

Irish culture 1, 3, 4, 6

Ives, Charles 123

Jameson, Frederic 35

Jaws, film 17, 38

jazz 41, 45, 49, 131–2; avantjazz 5, 124; Beckett 4–5, 122, 124, 132, 146; free 44, 131, 132; improvisation 5, 131, 142, 145–6

Johnson, B. S., *The Unfortunates* 153

Jordan, Neil 137

jouissance 37, 146

Joyce, James: *Finnegans Wake* 3, 50, 53, 68; language/writing style 13, 77, 124, 129, 150; Modernism 12, 60, 96; "The Dead" 13, 14, 53; *Work in Progress* 68, 129; *see also Ulysses* (Joyce)

Joyce, James, influence on Beckett 38, 59, 73, 80, 150; and music 53, 68, 129; *Ulysses* 77, 111

Joyce, James, and music 50–1, 53, 54, 68, 129; fugue 3, 24, 29, 51, 53, 138

Judaism 36

K2, *Molekular Terrorism* 43

Kant, Immanuel 34, 66–7, 101

Katz, Ruth 38

Keats, John 11, 16, 28, 32n18, 130

Kierkegaard, Søren 34, 36, 48, 152

Kim, Earl 86, 150

Kivy, Peter 8, 15–16, 39, 43, 50, 93, 151

Klee, Paul 19

Kline, Franz 88

knowing/unknowing 130

knowledge, prior 27

Knowlson, James 55, 56, 59, 72, 97, 100

Kötting, Andrew 127

Kramer, Jonathan 90–2, 95, 102, 105

Kramer, Lawrence 21, 24–5, 151

Kuonios, John, Kotz, Sonja A. and Holcomb, Philip J. 51

Kurtág, György 86, 150

Lachenmann, Helmut 149

Lang, Art 101

language: English 13, 46, 130, 134; failure of 70, 79, 119; French 13, 98, 126, 130; Joyce 13, 77, 124, 129, 150; music and literature 1–2, 6, 13, 20, 72; "unword" 12, 13, 77, 150; *see also* binaries; *Ill Seen Ill Said* (Beckett); semantic fluidity; *Words and Music* (Beckett and Feldman)

Laocoön 7, 8–9

Latartara, John 35, 43

Lauffer, David and Mathon, Geneviève 55

174 *Index*

Lawley, Paul 149
Laws, Catherine 22, 55, 70, 149; on
  Feldman 89, 90, 98, 105, 118
Leibniz, Gottfried 69
leitmotifs 38, 62, 73, 150, 153
Lessing, Gotthold: classification 3, 6,
  7–8, 10, 38, 53, 91; intermediality
  18–19, 20, 24, 91, 119; *Nacheinander*
  and *Nebeneinander* 8, 19, 32n2, 53
Lessness (Beckett) 4–5, 125–7, 128,
  129–30, 145, 150
Limb, Charles 145
liminality 97–8, 148
listening/hearing 13–14, 15–16, 23, 25,
  50, 59, 68; Feldman 91–2, 93; and
  repetition 17, 34, 38–9, 43
Liszt, Franz 18, 25
literature 1; expression in 70, 127, 129;
  interpretation in 17, 18, 39, 110;
  literature in music 24, 138, 151;
  repetition in 2, 20, 46–7, 48–9; rhythm
  10, 24–5, 26, 41, 47–8, 62; *see also*
  music and literature
Literature and Music Research Group,
  Open University 22
loop music 41–3, 83, 153
Low, band 42
Lyotard, Jean-François 6

McClary, Susan 8
McCormack, John 53
MacGreevy, Thomas 55–6
madrigals 18
Magee, Bryan 66
Magritte, René, *The Human Condition* 67
Mahler, Gustav 11, 17
Maier, Franz Michael 9, 55
Mallarmé, Stéphane 20, 47, 98, 153
Mallock, W. H. 153
Mamet, David 142
Mangan, James Clarence 3
Mann, Thomas 20
Margulis, Elizabeth Hellmuth 38
Martyn, John 145
Marx, Groucho 30
Matisse, Henri 94
May, Matthew 127
meaning: musical 25, 31, 57, 84, 151;
  and repetition 45, 121; and semantic
  fluidity 99, 148–9; *see also* expression
medieval times 6
"melopoetics" 21, 26, 29–30
memory 23, 34, 35, 46, 131, 153
Mercier, Vivian 55, 57

Merzbow 42, 43, 44
metaphor, musical 4, 29–30, 57, 58–65
metronomes 56, 137
Metzer, David 128
Metzidakis, Stamos 48
Meyer, Leonard B. 38, 50
Middleton, Richard 40, 42, 73
Mihalovici, Marcel 87
mimesis 19, 121, 150, 152
minimalism 33, 40–1, 95, 154
mirrors 12, 31, 64
mistakes, jazz 45
Mithen, Steven 49
mobility, of music 24, 29
Modernism 36, 50, 54, 150; Beckett 60,
  72, 149, 150; Joyce 12, 60, 96; music
  and literature 2, 6, 11–12, 19–20, 27,
  53, 54; music in literature 60, 72, 149;
  repetition 2, 41, 154; Schopenhauerian
  philosophy 12, 20
Moerman, Ernst, "Louis
  Armstrong" 132
Monk, Meredith 90
Monteverdi, Claudio 17, 32n12
Moore, Julianne 137–8, *139*
Moore, Thomas, *Irish Melodies* 3, 13
Morin, Emilie 130
Mothersbaugh, Mark 17
motifs 33, 35, 37, 38, 62; Feldman 90, 92;
  Ill Seen Ill Said 72–3, 77, 78; *Neither*
  (V1) 102, 107, 108, 115–16; *Neither*
  (V2) 105, 106–7, 108, 111, 112, 114;
  Neither (V3) 110, 111, 113, 114
Mozart, Wolfgang Amadeus, *The Magic
  Flute* 17
musematic repetition 40, 79, 99, 102,
  118, 151; *Ill Seen Ill Said* 73–8, 79, 81;
  Not I 133, 134
music: as an art form 1; interpretation
  18, 27, 43, 98, 123, 124; meaning 25,
  31, 57, 84, 151; mobility 24, 29; and
  repetition 151; and silence 151
music, absolute 18, 19, 84n2
music, antiphonal 37, 51n7
music, diegetic 13–14
music, experimental 40–5, 95, 128,
  130, 132
music, modern 54, 154; Beckett's
  influence on 86, 132, 148, 150, 151;
  Cage, John 41, 43–4, 88, 126, 130,
  132, 143; and technology 41–2, 83,
  85n11, 153, 154; *see also* Feldman,
  Morton; Fields, Scott; improvisation;
  repetition; silence

Index 175

music, programme 11, 18, 24, 28
music, pure 68, 84n2, 87, 99
music, sensual 59
music, tonal 37
music, vertical 90–1, 92
music and literature 1–2, 4, 6–32, 53–65,
    148, 151; language 1–2, 6, 13, 20,
    72; Modernism 2, 6, 11–12, 19–20,
    27, 53, 54; and poetry 8, 16, 19–20,
    24–6, 29; *see also* Feldman, Morton;
    Fields, Scott; intermediality; *Lessness*
    (Beckett); literature; *Neither* (Beckett
    and Feldman); *Not I* (Beckett); *Words
    and Music* (Beckett and Feldman)
"Music and Literature" panel (RMA) 22
music in literature 138, 151; *da capo*
    form 17, 57, 96, 125, 127, 149, 150;
    and Modernism 53, 54, 60, 72;
    musicalisation 2, 4, 10, 11, 26–7;
    repetition 15, 61–3
musicality/"musical" 1–2, 10, 15, 23–4,
    27, 28, 29; Beckett 5, 56, 57; *see also*
    music in literature

Nacheinander and *Nebeneinander* 8, 19,
    32n2, 53
narrators, multiple 26
nationalism, cultural 54
Nattiez, Jean-Jacques 14, 22
"negative capability" 28, 32n18, 130
Negus, Keith 42
Neither (Beckett and Feldman)
    5n2, 88, 96, 99–117, 122; binary
    oppositional repetition 100, 102;
    Deleuzian repetition 102, 111;
    discursive repetition 110, 111, 114;
    instrumentation 104, 110–11, 114;
    pattern in music 102, 108; rhythm 104,
    107, 113; Schopenhauerian philosophy
    101, 110; semantic fluidity 105, 107,
    114, 116–18; "shimmering" 105, 108;
    stasis 102, 111; *see also* motifs
Neu!, band 154
Nietzsche, Friedrich 34, 36, 152
Nobel Prize for Literature 128
noise, atmospheric 126
noise music 42–4, 83
nostalgia 154
Not I (Beckett) 56, 98, 124, 132, 133–46;
    and Fields, Scott 135, 137–42;
    improvisation 137, 139, 140–2, 145–6;
    "intelligible"/"inexplicable" binary
    133, 137; interpretation 137, 139;
    musematic repetition 133, 134; rhythm

137, 139; screams 134, 135, 143; self
    145, 146; semantic fluidity 137, 139,
    143; silence 133, 134–5, 137, 142, 143
noumenon and *phenomenon* 66–7, 69
Noveller 42
novels 13, 26–7, 50, 58, 83
number games 124
Nyman, Michael 40, 86, 95, 124

O'Hara, J. D. 57
Ockelford, Adam 38
Oliveros, Pauline 132
One Flew over the Cuckoo's Nest
    (Kesey) 61
onomatopoeia 17
opera 3, 17, 20, 48, 57, 117; Beckett and
    Feldman 5n2, 88, 99; *see also Neither*
    (Beckett and Feldman)
Oppenheim, Lois 55, 152
oppositional repetition *see* binary
    oppositional repetition
oral tradition 10
originality 37, 38, 61, 96–7, 152–3, 154;
    see also authenticity
ostrich tuning 41, 52n14
Ovid 53

Paddison, Max 50, 90
painting 8–9, 19, 32n2, 67–8, 152;
    Feldman 18, 88, 89–90, 97, 110; Fields
    132, 143; word painting 17, 18, 77,
    110, 132, 143
Palestrina, Giovanni Pierluigi da 17
palindromes 105
Parker, Evan 131
Parker, Jeff 132
paronomasia 64
Parr, Adrian 35, 45, 145
Partch, Harry 42
Pass, Joe 45
"passive synthesis" 34
Pater, Walter 1, 11, 18, 57, 129
pattern in literature 56, 59, 81, 101,
    126–7, 142
pattern in music 15–16, 25, 39, 43;
    Feldman 88, 93–4, 102, 108, 121, 151;
    Fields 140, 142, 151
Pavement 42
Perloff, Marjorie 117
Philip Glass Ensemble 41
Philips, John J. H. 86
Philips, Tom 153
photography 11
Picasso, Pablo, *Guernica* 12, 19–20, 149

176   *Index*

pictorialism 18
Pinget, Robert 11
Pinter, Harold 142
Plato 11, 33, 35, 68, 150, 152, 154
Poe, Edgar Allen, "The Raven" 46–7
poetry: and music 8, 16, 19–20, 24–6, 29; and repetition 10, 46; rhythm 10, 24–5, 26, 47–8
Polanyi, Michael 25
Pollock, Jackson 88, 110
Pope, Alexander, *Dunciad* 46
postmodernism 8, 37, 68, 70, 149
poststructuralism 8, 20
Potter, Keith 40, 41
Pound, Ezra 19, 20, 54
practice, repetition for 153–4
Prado, Maryjo 56
Prévost, Eddie 132
Prieto, Eric 22, 83; on Beckett 54–5, 59, 71; intermediality 11, 12, 24, 29–32
printing, 3D 154
process music 23, 40, 91, 95
Proust, Marcel 2, 14, 20, 48; *see also* Beckett, Samuel, works
pseudomorphosis 19
psychoanalysis: Freudian 11, 34, 35, 133; Lacanian 146
purpose/purposeless 130

questions, unanswered 72, 99, 110

Rabinowitz, Peter 26, 27, 71
Radiohead 153
Rajewsky, Irina O. 10
randomness/chance 45, 125, 126, 129, 153
ratios, of repetition 74, 81, 82, 119
Rauschenberg, Robert 88, 93, 151
realism 11–12, 126, 129–30, 152
reality 18, 66, 67–8, 69, 70
recording technology 41–4, 85n11, 152; loop music 41–3, 83, 153
Red Dead Redemption, game 153
redundancy, in music 50, 89
Reed, Lou, "The Ostrich" 41
refrains 2, 46–7, 111
Reich, Steve 37, 40, 41, 91
Reid, Alec 4, 20
religion 16–17
Renaissance 9, 17, 18
repeats, cutting of 15–16
repetition: intermediality 33–51, 148; listening/hearing 17, 34, 38–9, 43; in literature 2, 20, 46–7, 48–9; meaning

45, 121; Modernism 2, 41, 154; in music 2, 37–40, 48–51, 86, 143, 151; music in literature 15, 61–3; poetry 10, 46; ratios 74, 81, 82, 119; technology 153, 154; *see also* binary oppositional repetition; Deleuzian repetition; discursive repetition; musematic repetition; pattern in literature; pattern in music
repetition, didactic 39, 43, 121
repetition, transmedial 2–5, 15, 23, 33, 124, 148, 151
reproduction, human 152
reproduction, mass 35
rests, musical 64, 70
Reynolds, Roger 86
Reynolds, Simon 154
rhetorical devices 48, 64, 77, 119, 134
rhyme 10, 46–7, 143
rhythm: drumming 15, 41; Feldman 104, 107, 113, 142–3; in literature 41, 62; *Not I* 137, 139; poetry 10, 24–5, 26, 47–8
riffs 40, 90, 111
Riley, Terry 40, 41, 52n12, 91
rock music 40, 41, 44, 132
rocking 61, 62, 63
Rolland, Romain 20
Roller, Scott 132, 139
Romanticism 1, 2, 11, 13, 16, 57; Beckett 3, 68, 71, 118, 148, 149, 150; Feldman 88, 117; Schopenhauer 68, 71, 129
Rose, Tricia 36
Rothko, Mark 88, 89–90, 93, 110, 151
routine 130, 154
Rowe, Keith 132
Royal Musical Association (RMA) 22
rugs, Turkish 93–4, 95, 117
Russolo, Luigi 42
Rzewski, Frederic 91, 146

sameness 8, 34, 38–9, 50, 93, 129
Sand, George 28
Saportha, Marc, *Composition No. 1* 153
Saussure, Ferdinand de 20, 45
Schenker, Heinrich 15, 18, 37, 151
Scher, Steven Paul 22, 23–4, 27, 29–30, 138, 151
Schneider, Alan 137
Schopenhauerian philosophy 1, 11, 12, 18; Beckett 2, 53–4, 57, 66–73, 87, 99; contradiction 70–1, 149; "intelligible"/ "inexplicable" 53, 66, 72, 85n10; Modernism 12, 20; *Murphy* 4, 59;

Neither 101, 110; reality 66, 67–8, 69, 70; Romanticism 68, 71, 129; semantic fluidity 72, 86, 148
Schubert, Franz 18, 56, 58, 87, 150
scores, graphic 88–9, 124
Scott Fields Ensemble 132, *133*, 139, 142
screams 7, 134, 135, 143
sculpture 7, 8, 33, 91
Searle, Humphrey 117
self 145, 146, 151; self/unself binary 100–1, 107
semantic fluidity 2–3, 4, 5; Beckett 15, 58, 66–84, 99, 124, 127, 148–50; Feldman 86, 92, 99, 151; and meaning 99, 148–9; *Neither* 105, 107, 114, 116–17; *Not I* 137, 139, 143; Schopenhauerian philosophy 72, 86, 148; *Words and Music* 119, 122
semantic satiation/saturation 3, 51
serialism 40, 41, 52n12, 95
shadow 88, 97, 100, *101*, 102, 104, 111
Shakespeare, William 21, 39, 47, 49
Sharp, Elliott 131, 132
Shaw, George Bernard 3, 20, 48, 53, 65n1, 72, 119
Shelley, Percy Bysshe 9
"shimmering" 93, 95, 96, 105, 108
Shoegaze music 145
silence: Beckett 5, 63–4, 70, 87, 127–9, 148; Cage 63, 88, 128–9; Feldman 89, 90; in music 86, 128, 151; *Neither* 101, 112, 113; *Not I* 133, 134–5, 137, 142, 143
Sinclair, Iain 127
Skempton, Howard 89, 99, 102
Small, Christopher 36
Smith, Barbara Herrnstein 25
Smog 42
Snead, James A. 36, 154
sonata form 15, 37, 49, 96
Sonic Youth 154
spatialisation 19, 23
Spielmann, Yvonne 9–10
spirals 36, 37
Spotify 154
stage directions 58, 83, 133, 140
stasis 4; Feldman 90, 92, 94, 95, 151; *Neither* 102, 111, 116–17
Stein, Gertrude 2
Stein, Leonard 52n12
Steiner, George 20, 82
Sterne, Laurence, *Tristram Shandy* 27
Stockhausen, Karlheinz 132
Strauss, Richard 8

Stravinsky, Igor 19, 23, 128
structuralism 20, 58
structure, deep 25, 26, 31, 34
surprise 31, 43
Swift, Jonathan 80
Symbolism 1, 2, 6, 11, 28, 71; refrains 2, 47
Synge, J. M. 3, 53

Tagg, Philip 34
Tandy, Jessica 137
Taylor, Cecil 131
technology, musical 41–2, 83, 85n11, 153, 154
theatre 50, 83–4, 130, 137
Theatre of Eternal Music 41
themes 20, 47, 73, 84, 99, 100, 150; *That Time* 15, 32n10; *see also* silence; stasis; time
Thomas, Dylan, "Do not go gentle into that good night" 47
Thuringus, Joachim 17–18
Tilbury, John 86
Till, Nicholas and Bailes, Sara-Jane 55
time 8, 24, 32n2, 35, 38, 48, 50; Beckett 83, 89, 95–7, 125, 126, 150; Feldman 83, 89, 90–2, 95, 151; images 90, 96
time, extended 4, 95
time, vertical 91, 95, 105, 111
tone 38, 149
Tonmalerei 18
Toynbee, Jason 42
transformation 2, 9, 24, 35, 37, 101, 150
translation 4, 18, 86, 90, 98–9, 102
transmediality 10; transmedial repetition 2–5, 15, 23, 33, 124, 148, 151
transposition 10, 102, 143
trios 37
Tubridy, Derval 98

Ulysses (Joyce) 12, 50, 60, 96; fugue 3, 24, 29, 51, 53, 138; influence on Beckett 77, 111
understanding 23, 48, 130; understanding/non-understanding 39, 57, 97, 111

Vaca, Gustavo Alberto Garcia 152
value 31, 42–3, 49
Van Hulle, Dirk 128
variation 23, 89, 94, 95, 154
Velvet Underground 41
vertical music composition 90–1, 92
Vicentino, Nicola 18

Index

Virgil 7–8
Vivaldi, Antonio, *Nulla in Mundo pax sincera* (RV 630) 17

Wagner, Richard 1, 11, 13–14, 38, 71; *Gesamtkunstwerk* 6, 8, 32n3; and Shaw, George Bernard 53, 65n1
waiting 4, 151
Waiting for Godot (Beckett) 87, 109, 125, 128, 151; *da capo* form 57, 96, 150
Warburton, Dan 40
Warhol, Andy 41, 152
Webern, Anton 40–1, 60, 88, 95, 128, 154
Welsh, John P. 88–9
Western music 15, 36, 37
White, Harry 3, 22, 54, 60, 150, 151
Whitelaw, Billie 137–8
Wiener, Norbert 93
Wilde, Oscar 12, 13–14, 39, 129–30
Williams, John 17
Wimsatt, W. K. Jr. and Beardsley, Monroe C. 58
Wittgenstein, Ludwig 20, 28, 39
Wolf, Werner 2, 22, 26–7, 33, 119
Wolff, Christian 88, 95

Wolpe, Stefan 95
Wong, Dustin 42
Word and Music Association Forum (WMAF) 22
Word and Music Studies 1, 3, 21–32, 33, 154; *see also* music and literature; music in literature
word painting 17, 18, 77, 110, 132, 143, 152
Words and Music (Beckett and Feldman) 22, 56, 87, 88, 96, 117–23
Wordsworth, William 26, 152
Worstward Ho (Beckett) 36, 42, 77, 81–2, 83, 150
Worth, Katharine 117

Yeats, Jack 151
Yeats, W. B. 3, 16, 46, 53, 59, 80
Young, La Monte 40, 41, 95, 132

Zimmerman, Walter 92
Žižek, Slavoj 27
Zorn, John 132
Zukofsky, Louis 20
zygonic theory 38